REVIEWS FOR *READY FOR TAKEOFF*

Would you like to understand what it is like to serve a 20-year career as an officer and aviator in the United States Air Force? David Dale describes that accurately in this book, *Ready For Takeoff*. Every military career is unique, but David captures the excitement, the challenges, the highs of victory, the lows of disappointment, and the satisfaction of serving his country in the wide variety of assignments which a career officer can be expected to complete. He, his wife Karin, and their children, comprised the quintessential Air Force family, facing all the highs and lows of military life together and supporting others on the same path. They are just a single example of thousands of military families who have served, and serve today, throughout the world. David's book will be of interest not only to those who are just looking for a really good read, but also to young men and women contemplating service to their country as Air Force officers and airmen. David tells it like it is!

Dennis Dolle
Colonel, USAF, Retired

Ready For Takeoff is the engaging story of Air Force pilot David Dale, a lifelong aviator who soloed at age 16 and got his pilot's license one week before starting college. His remarkable adventures directly intersect with important points in our recent history, including the Cold War, Gulf War, Somalia, Rwanda, 9/11, and the wars in Iraq and Afghanistan, among other pivotal events. Often expressed with a sense of humor, he describes the life of a career Air Force pilot, officer, and crewmember in a very engaging and personable way. Skillfully told from the perspective of a family man with faith, integrity, and pride in what he represents, this book is for all military, aviation, and history enthusiasts who want to gain a deeper appreciation of each of those areas. Enjoy.

Bruce Hurd
Colonel, USAF, Retired
Author of Amazon #1 Bestseller
Aim Point: An Air Force Pilot's Lessons for Navigating Life

This remarkable memoir of Dave's life and career reminds me again that a man makes his plans, but it's the Lord who directs his steps. And in the end, God's direction far exceeded Dave's initial hopes and expectations. That's especially true for one blessed with a supportive wife to encourage him along their path. What an exceptional path that has been! It's been a distinct joy and privilege for me to have served with Dave both in the KC-10 and at Southwest Airlines.

W.J. "Dub" Splawn
Lieutenant Colonel, USAF, Retired
Captain, Southwest Airlines, Retired

Ready for Takeoff puts you in the cockpit with vivid descriptions, taking you through training, testing, and actual missions for multiple Air Force aircraft. David gives us a unique view of world events from his "work space" 40,000 feet in the sky. This book shares military success, yes, but also relatable tales of failure that extend beyond military life. It is through these disappointments that we see the grit and determination to reach one's goals and when that doesn't work, the flexibility to forge a new path. Ribbons of family, friends, love, and leadership wind their way through these captivating stories.

Lucy Pendleton
Purple Pen Copy Editor

I thoroughly enjoyed reading of David's incredible pathway through the labyrinth of military life as an Air Force pilot! The diversity of adventures and experiences along with his bits of wisdom are truly inspiring. I just wish the book was available before I started my own career -- it would have saved me a lot of angst. Very well written and a great read.

Carl Meade
Colonel, USAF, Retired
Former NASA Astronaut, STS 38, 50, and 64

Ready For Takeoff

Stories From an Air Force Pilot

David Dale

Ready For Takeoff

Copyright © 2022 David Dale

ISBN: 979-8-9868336-0-6 (Hardcover)
ISBN: 979-8-9868336-1-3 (Paperback)
ISBN: 979-8-9868336-2-0 (eBook)

Library of Congress Control Number: 2022918409

Cover design by Cherie Fox at www.cheriefox.com
C-37 front cover photo by Paul Bowen
KDC-10 and F-16 back cover photo by Henk Van Dijk, RNLAF

Printed in the United States of America

David Dale
Spicewood, Texas 78669
ReadyForTakeoff310@gmail.com
Facebook: David S. Dale

To my wife, Karin,
    who has made me a better person every day since April 1984.

To my children, Daniel and Shelby,
    we are so proud of the wonderful adults you are.

To Mom,
    thank you for your boundless love and encouragement.

To my late Dad,
    thank you for being a gracious provider to our whole family.

To my siblings, Jack, Lucy, and Hannah,
    you make me so happy whenever we are together.

To my late stepmom, Karen,
    I wish you were here to take a purple pen to my manuscript.

To my late stepdad, Ralph,
    for being the right man at the right time of my teenage life.

To Mr. Richard Lovell,
    for teaching me to fly.

TABLE OF CONTENTS

Acknowledgments. xi

Preface. xiii

Prologue: Attention Step xv

Chapter 1:   Walking Through Downtown in a Speedo. 1

Chapter 2:   Aspirations 15

Chapter 3:   Swing and a Miss. 21

Chapter 4:   Hang'n Out in Austin 25

Chapter 5:   The Happy Pessimist. 32

Chapter 6:   Helo or Nav?. 36

Chapter 7:   Karin Smith 39

Chapter 8:   "What's 16 Minus 16?" .45

Chapter 9:   Running Around in the BUFF 52

Chapter 10: Barksdale B-52 Hijinks .58

Chapter 11: A Crappy Flight 68

Chapter 12: Blue Ribbon Crew. 70

Chapter 13: Wild Blue Yonder 74

Chapter 14: Then the Wheels Fell Off 82

Chapter 15: Where'd He Go? 85

Chapter 16: A Monumental Event 89

Chapter 17: Becoming A Gucci Boy. 96

Chapter 18: Operation Deny Christmas. 102

Chapter 19: Go Navy! For Two Days 106

Chapter 20: SOS 112

Chapter 21: Desert Shield. 115

Chapter 22: Mogadishu, Part I 129

Chapter 23: Desert Storm 133

Chapter 24: Barksdale is That Way, I Reckon 144

Chapter 25: Covering All of My Bases .147

Chapter 26: Testimony 154

Chapter 27: Southern Watch, The No-Fly Zone 160

Chapter 28: Death of a Friend 166

Chapter 29: The Mission Continues 168

Chapter 30: Mogadishu, Part II 174

Chapter 31: 1993 Airlift Rodeo 178

Chapter 32: Mogadishu, Part III 183

Chapter 33: Going Dutch 189

Chapter 34: Moving Across the Pond 198

Chapter 35: Small Country, Small World 203

Chapter 36: Cultural Differences 209

Chapter 37: Refueling Around the Perfect Storm 212

Chapter 38: "Have You Ever Been Scared?" 216

Chapter 39: Major Dale, Are You Ready? 219

Chapter 40: Emergency Air Refueling Over the Adriatic 228

Chapter 41: Flying A Desk 233

Chapter 42: Air Force Appreciation Tour 242

Chapter 43: First ATP Checkride 248

Chapter 44: Andrews AFB Gulfstream Training 251

Chapter 45: Moscow and the Holy Land in Five Days 255

Chapter 46: Sydney 2000 Olympics 262

Chapter 47: Don't Get Cocky 273

Chapter 48: Timing is Everything 278

Chapter 49: Creating A Squadron 281

Chapter 50: First Trip to Bogota, Colombia 287

Chapter 51: 9/11 290

Chapter 52: Coin Toss 296

Chapter 53: Bishkek, Kyrgyzstan 297

Chapter 54: Providing Five-Star Service to the Four-Stars 300

Chapter 55: "Thanks for Keeping Me Safe." 304

Chapter 56: Highs and Lows 308

Chapter 57: Coming Full Circle 312

Appendix 1: Thanks Mom AND Dad .317

Appendix 2: "The Loss of Our Friend, Ken Reed" 321

Appendix 3: 310 AS/DO Memo to All Aircrew Personnel 322

Appendix 4: Change of Command and Retirement Speech 324

Appendix 5: Letter Before My Wedding from Mr. Lovell 327

Appendix 6: Military Ranks 328

Appendix 7: B-52G Fact Sheet 330

Appendix 8: KC-10 Fact Sheet 331

Appendix 9: C-37A Fact Sheet 332

About the Author 333

ACKNOWLEDGMENTS

I began writing this memoir using my paper logbooks for dates and details of various flights and missions. But a logbook only contains one line of brief information for each flight and these flights took place many decades ago. One of the most fulfilling experiences of writing this book has been reconnecting with so many friends from my past – high school, college, and every Air Force assignment. Karin and I had 11 assignments and 16 addresses in 20 years and I cannot thank her enough for her support then and now. She lived most of this memoir as well.

With so many moves and meeting so many people from 1978 to 2004, please forgive any inaccuracies found in this memoir. The mistakes are mine and not intentional, but are the recollections from many years ago. As a funny quote goes, "I only have two brain cells left and I'm using one of those for breathing."

I sent various chapters out to friends far and wide for their review and comment, and I thank all who have helped shaped this project. In particular, I'd like to thank Karin, Mom, my siblings – Jack, Lucy, and Hannah, and Carolyn McClelland for proof-reading this manuscript for clarity. I thank my editor and mentor Bruce Hurd (USAF Colonel, retired) for his probing questions that drew out more information. From my aviation past, I thank Larry Leonard, Michael Rafferty, Stacey Samuels Bie, Dub Splawn, Kreg Lukens, Dave Denman, Joe Gallucci, Jose Martinez, Kevin Oatley, Keith Peloquin, and Lee "Ice" Icenhour.

PREFACE

I have been a pilot since I was 16 years old, taking my first flight at Weiser Air Park in northwest Houston, in June 1978. In 1984, I began a 20-year flying career for the United States Air Force. Since retiring in July of 2004, I have been an airline pilot with Southwest Airlines. A lot of people ask what we do up in the cockpit during flight. They assume we are as busy flying the plane as you would be driving your car down the highway. The truth is, we usually only hand-fly the first and last three minutes of a flight, typically below 2,000 to 5,000 feet. The rest of the time is spent programming and managing the autopilot to do most of the smooth flying, so we spend a lot of time talking. We share stories of our family, our past, our flying in the military, or our backgrounds in civilian aviation. I am fortunate to have done a little bit of everything in aviation, from getting my private license in small Piper Cherokees, flying a hang-glider over Central Texas, navigating a B-52 bomber, and then flying the Air Force's heavy KC-10 air refueling tankers, and the elegant Gulfstream G-IIIs and G-Vs. One week after my military retirement I began flying Boeing 737s for Southwest. My varied background has allowed me to share stories with a diverse group of fellow aviators, from deployments with military pilots, cargo flights with freight pilots, to carrying VIPs on executive jets with corporate pilots.

I was not a combat pilot; I didn't drop bombs on the Iraqi Republican Guard or dogfight over the Middle East. I did, however, fly during numerous historic world events, from the Cold War to the invasion of Panama, Operation Desert Storm over Iraq, the Bosnian War in the mid-1990s, and the events during and after September 11, 2001.

This book is not meant to be an autobiography or a history of the United States Air Force. It is an aviation memoir of my intersections with history. As I wrote this, my college friend and accomplished writer, Corey King, told me that if I'm going to write about myself then I need to be willing to "walk through downtown naked." As a former swimmer, let's just say I'm willing to walk through downtown in a Speedo. These are my often-told flying stories from 1978 to 2004. The flight plan has been filed. You are ready for takeoff.

PROLOGUE
ATTENTION STEP

JUNE 2004, MacDILL AFB, TAMPA, FLORIDA

U.S. Air Force C-37A at MacDill AFB (Photo by Robin Parrish)

On a muggy Monday morning as I stood in the hallway just outside my office, my phone rang. Hustling around my desk, I grabbed it.

"310th Airlift Squadron, Lieutenant Colonel Dale."

"Dave, this is Colonel Zepf at CVAM. Do you have a STU-III in your squadron?"

"Yes, sir, we do," I answered, still standing over my phone.

"Okay, please call me right back."

Colonel Mike Zepf was the division chief of CVAM (pronounced "See-Vam") at the Pentagon. "CVAM" was the office designation for the Special Air Missions division at Air Force headquarters in Washington D.C. That office scheduled the highest-ranking civilian and military Distinguished Visitor travel on military aircraft, also known as "DV Airlift." They were the scheduling agency for both Andrews Air Force Base (AFB), Maryland, supporting the Pentagon and Washington-based DVs, and also for my squadron at MacDill

AFB, just outside Tampa. Our STU-III telephone was used only for encrypted classified conversations, so Colonel Zepf's request meant that the topic had to be extremely sensitive.

I wasn't concerned about this call when I answered because I was very familiar with Colonel Zepf. He and I had been friends for fifteen years, since our days flying the KC-10 air refueling tanker at Barksdale AFB, Louisiana. We not only flew together, we also played intramural softball on the KC-10 team when he was a major and I was a captain.

Since July 2002, I had been the squadron commander of the 310th Airlift Squadron (310 AS) at MacDill AFB. Our squadron of 65 men and women flew three brand new C-37As, the military version of the Gulfstream V executive jet. We provided VIP-level service to the seven four-star general and admiral combatant commanders based within the United States. Our squadron motto, which I coined a year earlier when the squadron opened, put it more succinctly: "We provide Five-Star Service to the Four-Stars."

Our squadron took up the entire upper left side of a huge 1950's hangar along the flightline of the Florida air force base. At the opposite end of our long, skinny squadron from my office lay the Sensitive Compartmented Information Facility (SCIF), a locked room containing the STU-III telephone and files of classified information. I rarely spoke to Colonel Zepf directly, so walking down the 100-foot-long hallway to the SCIF, I wondered if we had a seriously ticked-off four-star general following one of our squadron's recent trips.

I quickly called Colonel Zepf back.

"Dave, what I'm about to tell you … only you, me, and five people in the White House know about."

As an opening statement in a presentation, that's called the "attention step" and he had mine now.

"I need your squadron to plan a classified mission to Amman, Jordan, for two weeks from now. It will probably take two crews. I can't tell you much more, but work the details directly through me." As we said in the military, I now had my marching orders.

I knew it would be a real challenge keeping everything a secret. Because of the highly sensitive nature of this mission, we would need two five-person crews plus mission planners to get the ball rolling on putting this mission together. We had to get this done without letting the news slip outside of our squadron. Our online flight scheduling program could be seen by other units and was color coded for training missions, operational missions, and aircraft that may require downtime for maintenance. We needed to handle this carefully, so that we didn't raise interest outside of the squadron.

After the call, I walked back down the long hallway to the Squadron Operations Center (SOC) desk, the hub of all activity in the middle of our squadron. There, I briefed a handful of squadron members who would be involved in planning and carrying out this mission. Talking with Lieutenant Colonel Keith Kreeger, my Director of Operations (DO), we decided to block out a week-long "off-station training mission" for one of our three C-37s. It would last from Friday, June 24 to Friday, July 2 and appeared as a long blue line on the scheduling program created by our pilot, Major "Arnie" Palmer. It wouldn't raise any suspicions because these off-station training missions often were used to qualify a group of new crewmembers in our special airlift mission.

As planning continued, we faced a couple of questions. Who were we carrying? At this point, Saddam Hussein had been captured and was still confined in Iraq. Perhaps we were bringing him to the United States to face justice? This was definitely a high- priority mission, being monitored directly from the Pentagon and White House.

We also realized that although the C-37 could fly 11 hours before stopping for fuel, in order to get in and out of Jordan quickly, we needed to "pony-express" the airplane and have a fuel stop and crew swap at some point during the mission. As the plan unfolded, the first crew, piloted by Lieutenant Colonel Kevin Oatley and my eventual replacement, Lieutenant Colonel Monty Perry, would depart a day early and overnight at U.S. Naval Air Station Sigonella on the island of Sicily. They would then depart for Amman, Jordan the next morning, quickly pick up the unknown passenger, then depart for the westward flight home.

Our five-person C-37 crew, consisting of two pilots, a flight engineer, communications system operator, and flight attendant could work a 16-hour day, but the trip from Sicily to Jordan to the U.S. would exceed that time. This meant a second crew and a fuel stop on their way home was required. Our planners suggested Kevin's crew stop for fuel at Lajes Air Base, a USAF/Portuguese airfield in the Azores Islands off the coast of Portugal in the Atlantic. The first crew would be met by Lieutenant Colonel Pete Martin and Lieutenant Colonel Dean Metz, who would take over the mission with a second full crew for the trans-Atlantic flight to Washington, D.C.

To ensure a quick gas-and-go at Lajes Air Base, I knew that Major Rob Crone, working in the Lajes command post, could be of great help. Rob had previously been an Andrews AFB Gulfstream evaluator pilot when I was based there, and Colonel Zepf knew him well. I hoped to brief Rob over a STU-III telephone on the mission and the need for a quick refueling and crew swap. He would fully understand the need for secrecy, and this would help keep the mission under wraps.

A bit selfishly, I thought this mission came at a critical point in my life. After 20 years in the Air Force, I was set to retire on July 27. I even had my final family vacation planned for the last week of late June as this classified mission. I wondered how this mission might affect my family's plans. I also wondered when I'd be allowed to tell my boss, Colonel Brian Kelly at MacDill's 6th Operations Group and his boss, Brigadier General Snyder, at the 6th Air Mobility Wing headquarters about this secret mission.

As I updated Col Zepf on the planning progress, he readily agreed that I could brief Major Crone in the Azores on our quick-stop fuel requirement for the return leg. He also said I could tell my chain of command about the mission the day before I left for vacation. Finally, he dispelled any notion that our crews were bringing Saddam Hussein to the United States when he said to make sure the flight attendant had a selection of beer and liquor for the return flight home. Well, that was certainly different.

The mission details all fell into place. The crews obtained their required visas and diplomatic clearances, the food and beverages were procured, and Rob assured me that Lajes Air Base would be ready for the crew swap on the trans-Atlantic flight home. On my day before starting vacation, I stopped by the operations group to see Colonel Kelly to make sure my leave form was processed.

"Sir, do you have a minute?"

"Come in, Dave. What have you got?"

"I need to tell you about that mission that is blocked out next week as an off-station-trainer. It's not really training . . . It's a classified mission to Amman, Jordan."

"And you're just now telling me about this?"

I could tell he wondered why a lieutenant colonel was keeping a secret from a colonel.

"I couldn't before. It came down directly from Colonel Zepf at CVAM to our squadron."

"Who is the passenger?"

"We don't know. But they have to get in and out of Jordan quickly, and back to the States."

On June 28, 2004, just days ahead of the June 30 deadline, Paul Bremer, the Presidential Envoy to Iraq, formally transferred sovereignty of Iraqi territory to the Iraqi Interim Government. The U.S. and Iraqi governments wanted to accomplish this before the deadline to prevent any civil unrest during the transfer of power. Intelligence reports suggested that terrorists were coming into Baghdad from the west and the south, to conduct car bombings and other attacks on June 30. Additionally, reports indicated on June 26 that the insurgents planned to capture a city--perhaps Ramadi or Baquba--on June 30 to wound the new government before it could take power. I later discovered these details after reading Ambassador Bremer's memoir, *My Year in Iraq*.

Bremer, wearing a business suit and desert brown combat boots, departed Iraq for Jordan on June 28, and he boarded our 310th Airlift

Squadron C-37 for his flight back to Washington D.C., complete with cocktails. The entire mission, including the quick turn and crew change at Lajes Air Base, all went off as smooth as glass. I could not have been prouder of our flight crews and squadron personnel as they provided five-star service to the President's envoy.

Thankfully, my vacation and retirement from the Air Force also happened just as planned. Ten years later, while visiting the George W. Bush Presidential Library, I came across a notecard written by National Security Advisor Dr. Condoleezza Rice to President George W. Bush on June 28, 2004. Her message stated: "Mr. President, Iraq is sovereign. Letter was passed from Bremer at 10:26 a.m., Iraq time. – Condi"

The President's handwritten reply in red felt-tip marker read, "Let Freedom Reign!"

Beaming with pride, I snapped a photo of the index card to share with the 310 AS alumni.

Chapter 1

WALKING THROUGH DOWNTOWN IN A SPEEDO

Mom and Me

My mother, Judy, rocked me, her six-month old son, Davy, as she and my dad watched President John F. Kennedy inform the nation of the grave danger we faced from the Soviets. Their missiles were now pointing at us from Cuba, 90 miles south of Florida. On that October, 1962 evening, my mom and dad feared for the safety of their young family: my 6-year-old brother "Jacky," later known as Jack, and cute little 3-year-old Lucy. Two years after this frightening showdown passed, Hannah Elizabeth arrived to complete our All-American family.

I was born April 2, 1962, in the Hunter's Creek area on the west side of the growing metropolis of Houston, Texas. We lived in a single-story ranch-style house, the second one on the right side of

Cape Cod Lane, a cul-de-sac with only eight houses. Cape Cod Lane was one of many dead-end streets sprouting off Pifer Road, named for the family farm that originally settled there 100 years earlier. The term dead-end street is not derogatory. Every street in our neighborhood, including Pifer Road, had a large yellow diamond-shaped sign announcing Dead End. We lived on a dead-end street off a dead-end street ... but we were going places. I didn't know or use the word "cul-de-sac" until I was in my twenties.

My parents met because of football. My dad, David Sr., was raised in a large two-story "almost mansion" in central Houston. His house lay just off River Oaks Blvd, an eight-block street capped by the River Oaks Country Club at one end and Lamar High School at the other.

His father, Warren Dale, Sr., was a successful lawyer with the renowned Vinson and Elkins law firm. My dad was a "happy surprise," arriving in 1933, thirteen years after his brother and sister. He was expected to go to boarding school on the east coast, but as a young teenager he rebelled. Dad ran away from the Connecticut school as a young teenager and took a train back to Texas. His parents accepted his decision and enrolled him at Kincaid, the local private preparatory school. There, my dad excelled at track and football, but there was only one problem. Kincaid School only played 7-man football, but my dad wanted to play "real" football.

Football was life for my father and in the late-1940s he would go to nearby Lamar public high school and kick his football on their field. One Sunday afternoon, another young man was there, six years older, who was practicing his kicking as well. The 22-year-old man's name was George Blanda. Dad spent that Sunday afternoon shagging footballs for the future Houston Oiler quarterback, kicker, and Hall of Fame NFL player. By 1950, at 17 years old, Dad convinced his parents to let him attend Lamar High School and join the real football team as their tailback. That was where he met Judy Sanders.

My beautiful mom was the daughter of a proud railroad man, Jack Sanders, Sr. He was born in the tiny town of Crossett, Arkansas, in the state's southeastern pocket. My mother's mom, Joecile Garrison Sanders, was a grade-school teacher and talented piano player, born in Abilene, Texas. Her birth name was Lucile, named after her mom. Her dad was Joe Garrison and over time she began going by a combination of both names: Joecile. My grandmother eventually changed her name legally to Joecile, which my grandfather lovingly called her.

In 1922, at the age of 14, Jack Sanders began working for the Missouri Pacific (MoPac) Railroad. Standing by the railroad tracks far from the terminal, he handed out the lane assignments to the incoming freight train operators using a large hoop made of bamboo. My grandparents married during the Great Depression and started their family.

Papa moved his family all throughout the Midwest, never saying no to a MoPac job. Even without a college degree, he progressed up the office hierarchy, eventually retiring as Vice President of MoPac freight. By the late 1940s, the Sanders family, which included Mom's little brother, Jack, Jr., moved to Houston. Mom enrolled at Lamar High School and fell in love with a slim, 6-foot-tall tailback with thick, wavy rust-colored hair and sparkling blue eyes.

Our dad was athletic, playful, and apparently very smart, too. In the early 1950s he became a third generation Texas Longhorn. Following his maternal grandfather, Ebenezer Dohoney (UT Class of 1896) and both of his parents (Class of 1918), Dad enrolled at The University of Texas at Austin. Within just three years he completed his bachelor's degree in an accelerated program. In another three years Dad, like his father, earned his law degree from the prestigious University of Texas law school. He married Mom while still in law school and their first son, (another Jack!) arrived two years later.

I spent the 1960s in a loving, happy family, free to roam around our suburban neighborhood. My best bud, Larry Leonard, was born six months after me and just around the circle at the end of our street. We spent afternoons learning to ride our bikes without training wheels as our moms gave us a push while chatting by our mailbox.

Our idyllic life was rocked when mental illness took hold of my dad by 1969. Dad was diagnosed as manic depressive (Bipolar 2) in the late 1960s and sought treatment in Topeka, Kansas. A person with Bipolar 2 experiences major depressive episodes, rather than shorter cycles. I was too young to understand what was going on, but I soon learned that we'd be moving to Topeka in 1970, after I completed second grade.

Our life resumed up north, with Dad receiving the excellent treatment he needed. We joined the Westminster Presbyterian Church, just across the street from Boswell Junior High. Dad then began teaching Oil and Gas law classes at Washburn University, not far from our two-story "Little White House" on High Avenue.

Life was very different in Topeka. Not bad, just different. We had been born and raised in a very white area of Houston, where almost every suburban housewife had a maid who rode in weekly on a bus from Houston's east side. I now attended Kansas public schools with more African American kids than I had ever seen before.

The good thing about being an 8-year-old kid was that I didn't care about skin tone. I had many great friends throughout grade school, scouting, and junior high who were black, and thought nothing of it. In 7th grade I had a crush on Shelley Douglas, a beautiful African American girl with straight black shoulder-length hair and a huge smile. She often wore pretty embroidered denim shirts. We flirted but never kissed.

Like many families in the 1970s, our family fell victim to divorce. From my young perspective, I don't remember my parents arguing. I believe my parents simply fell out of love from the strain of Dad's condition and trying to raise four children, the third one (me) being hyperactive.

I was in 6th grade (11 years old) and remember sitting on our red living room sofa and being told by my parents that they were separating. I didn't think it was a big deal at that moment and wasn't upset because Dad was just moving five blocks down the street into an apartment. I thought this was a temporary arrangement.

While still in grade school that year (junior high in Kansas was 7th to 9th grade) I talked to my classmate, Kirk Porteous, the only child with divorced parents that I knew.

"What's it like having your parents divorced?" I asked.

"Sometimes it sucks when my dad can't be around," he answered as we walked home from school. Some days he went to his mom's, other days to his dad's house.

By 1974 my brother, Jack, graduated from Topeka High School and Mom continued to raise Lucy, Hannah, and me on High Avenue. To me, Lucy was the extrovert of the family –beautiful, athletic, and self-assured. From junior high through high school, she and her best friend, Diane Deeter, were on the cheerleader squad. Hannah and I enjoyed hours of playing outdoors with neighborhood kids on both sides of our house. Around that time, Dad and I bought matching running shoes, and I would run to his apartment, and we then jogged around the college campus.

At the time, Dad was battling mid-life sedentary weight issues and I was trying to outgrow the skinny, asthmatic kid I had been. When I was 15, Dad told me something that became my life fitness goal. I weighed just over 120 pounds and Dad, with his basketball-size belly, weighed over 200. One day he pointed out, "Just remember, Davy. When I was your age, I looked just like you, too."

I vowed that day to never have a pot belly. I'm sure my dad taught me some life lessons growing up, but that's the only one that I really remember to this day. He didn't dispense advice but mainly was a storyteller of what happened in his youth.

Later that same year, Mom, Lucy, Hannah, and I gathered again in the living room and were told that Mom and Dad would not be getting back together. This time I sobbed on my mom's shoulder as the news sank in. As sad as this was, it helped knowing that Dad was still just a few blocks away in his apartment.

Looking back on my life now as an adult, I can see that I suffered from low self-esteem and a lack of confidence –growing up I was never impressed with my looks or abilities. Our family was pretty active and tried to stay physically fit. From YMCA activities through junior high teams, I tried but didn't succeed at the popular sports: basketball, football, and wrestling, the last of which my parents suggested as a way to toughen me up.

There's no doubt I was a Momma's Boy. With little guidance from my dad, my loving mom set her expectations. All of us kids had to learn piano before picking another instrument (trombone for both Jack and me). In high school, we had to take a year of Latin before choosing a language. I chose poorly. I rebelled against the Hispanic community surrounding me and chose French. My siblings all chose Spanish, which turned out to be a much more useful language later in life, as I now fly throughout the Caribbean and Central America. Mom gave me a classical upbringing and I freely admit that because of her, I enjoy singing and love watching plays or musicals.

As for wrestling, the practices were good, but it was hard to toughen up when my matches lasted only about fifteen seconds. I never had the killer instinct, but I did learn some cool moves.

My neighbors on High Avenue were three boys, Aaron, Brett, and Craig Zlatnik. Their mom thought that out: A, B, C, to Z. All of them wrestled in school and rough-housed with each other at home, which I often joined. I mainly hung out with Craig, who was Hannah's age, two years younger than me. This was probably because he was less of a threat since I was older.

Brett was one year older than me and became an inspiration, though I never told him so. He was a back-to-back state champion wrestler with muscular arms. Brett, deaf in one ear since birth, earned almost straight A's, and was the first-chair trumpet player in the junior and high school band. And he could kick your ass if you made fun of him for being in the band. I never attained his greatness, but he showed me what was possible.

Tennis was our family sport, and by 9th grade I earned the #1 spot on our Boswell Junior High tennis team, thanks to private lessons, my strong double-handed Bjorn Borg backhand and my Tasmanian Devil serve. I had a very powerful serve for a 14-year-old but didn't always know where it was going. In later years, fellow aviators would call this "All thrust, no vector." My matches usually consisted of a mix of double faults and aces. I lived and died by my serve. I was quick and agile on a tennis court over the short distances but never fast enough for basketball and football.

I also took up swimming while in junior high. Hannah and I swam in a summer league and at the Topeka YMCA throughout the school year. This was great for my growing body and for overcoming childhood asthma. My best event was the 100-yard backstroke, but my performance was lackluster.

Throughout our seven years in Kansas, we visited Houston almost every year. I'd get to see my two good friends, Larry Leonard, and Michael Rafferty. Michael lived next door from Larry and diagonally across from me. Like Craig, he also was two years younger, but his older sister, Libby, was my age. I knew from these Texas visits that most of my friends swam on the Dad's Club YMCA team and that Larry was quite good.

Academically, I was a solid B student who hated to read. Unless it was mandatory reading, I rarely read anything for fun. After 9th grade, my interest in aviation led me to read a biography about Charles Lindbergh. I was captivated by how he taught himself to fly an old Jenny biplane years before piloting his plane solo over the Atlantic. Watching Jimmy Stewart in *The Spirit of Saint Louis* inspired me to become a pilot. Dad even told me that his mom was at the 1927 New York City ticker tape parade honoring Lindbergh after he returned from Paris.

I enjoyed creative writing at school and was pretty good at math. I specifically remember the day in 8th grade Algebra when the light-bulb came on. Suddenly, the equations made sense and my hand shot up excitedly time and time again in Miss Andrews' class. I can still picture her smiling face and I'm sure it made her feel good, too, seeing one of her students "get it."

By 1977, Lucy had graduated from Topeka High, and I graduated from Boswell Junior High. Mom married a very nice family man named Ralph Slavens, whom she met at our Presbyterian church. Ralph was the right man at the right time in my teenage life. Although my dad was a kind provider, he was non-confrontational and would never broach a touchy subject.

I never heard "the talk" from Dad, or how to interact with girls. As a result, I think I learned how I wanted to parent by what was missing in my life. To this day I enjoy bear hugs with both of my grown kids. When our son was in grade school and junior high, I spoke with him about how to treat and talk to others. "Ask questions and let a girl tell you about themselves, rather than you talking about yourself," I advised.

Ralph filled that fatherly void and was the "dad" that took me hunting once on a Kansas prairie. We were hunting doves and pheasants, but I shot a rabbit, which my mom graciously cooked. Ralph was a barrel-chested man with a hearty baritone laugh. He was an accountant for hospitals by day but could be a pool shark in the evening. He let out his big laugh and admitted, "I had a misspent youth."

Hannah, Ralph, and Mom at Lucy's wedding.

We shot a lot of pool, and I became pretty good, too. Ralph smoked cigarettes and a pipe of whisky-flavored tobacco. I never took up smoking (my first and only cigarette burned my throat) but I never minded the smell, either.

Ralph suffered from heart disease throughout his life, and retired to Tonganoxie, Kansas, just west of Kansas City. After his brief marriage to my mom ended in divorce, he married a wonderful lady named Betty. Ralph died of a sudden heart attack in 2019 in his backyard. His oldest son, Sean, called to give me the news and I cried hard later that night for the man that got me through my teenage years. Sean used my quote, "He was the right man at the right time of my teenage life" in his eulogy for Ralph.

By 1977, Mom decided it was time for her, Hannah, and me to move back to Houston. Lucy enrolled in Abilene Christian University, where she continued her cheerleading and studied to be a teacher. Our brother, Jack, had a full-time job in Topeka and a serious girl-friend, Carol Wolf. Academically, Jack personified perseverance. He didn't head to college after high school, but in his late 30s he earned his bachelor's degree at night school. Once the study bug kicked in, he applied for and was accepted to Washburn Law School, where our dad had taught 20 years earlier. In a bit of serendipity, some of my brother's professors were my dad's students. Jack earned his law degree in his early 40s, never giving up on his dreams.

Dad, Hannah, me, Lucy, Jack, and Carol in 1979.

Before moving to Texas, our dad, much to his credit, took Hannah and me on a very memorable two-week adventure throughout the American Northwest and Canada. This was an epic road trip for this 15-year-old kid. Departing Topeka on June 26, with my Lindbergh biography in hand, we set out in Dad's 1974 brown, four-door Chevrolet Chevelle. With a small, blue dome tent and three sleeping bags packed in the trunk, we arrived at our camping sites outside Sioux Falls and Rapid City, South Dakota.

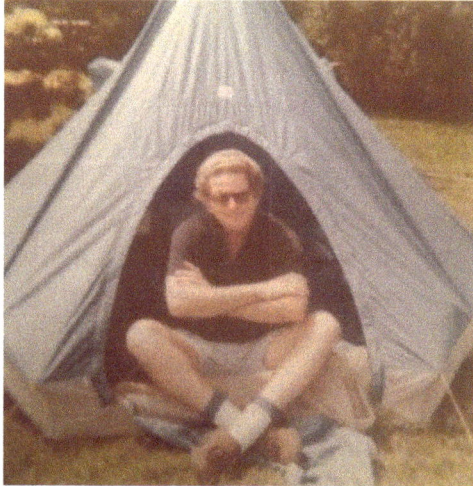

Dad in the Dakotas, outside of our tent in June 1977.

The first night Hannah woke up worried about a bear in the camp, only to realize the snorting animal was our dad snoring loudly. Using Dad's large telephoto camera, I took amazingly close-up photos of the presidents carved into Mount Rushmore. From South Dakota, we headed north to Montana, where we walked around the Battle of Little Big Horn and surveyed the ground and gravity of Custer's Last Stand. While listening continuously to our cool dad's 8-track tape of Fleetwood Mac's new *Rumors* album, the "brown bomber" Chevy crossed into Canada.

We arrived in Calgary on June 30 in time for the huge Calgary Stampede annual rodeo, which we could see and hear from our hotel room. On a freezing cold first day of July, Hannah and I found ourselves swimming in the steamy, heated pool of the Lake Louise luxury hotel, as large snowflakes drifted down around our heads. I knew then that if and when I ever got married, I'd bring my future wife here to this romantic site. That visit is still on my list.

Boarding a train, we headed west on a two-day scenic ride to Vancouver, traveling in an observation glass-top train car to soak in the Canadian landscape and herds of elk. Hannah and I gobbled down juicy cheeseburgers for lunch and dinner both days. Dad raised his eyebrow and shook his head "no" when we tried to order them for breakfast, too.

Our tour continued south in a Hertz rental car through Washington state, where we all stepped into the frigid waters of the Pacific. Dad only went in ankle-deep, but I dove under, and got a brain-freeze headache I'll never forget. Hannah and I patriotically celebrated July Fourth by striking matchsticks near a fire pit as our fireworks. By July 7, we reached our eventual destination of Crater Lake, Oregon. Standing on the shoreline, we soaked in the breath-taking beauty of the shimmering, cold mountain lake.

From our turn-around point, we reversed course, retrieved Dad's Chevy in Calgary and pointed it back toward Kansas. Although many hours were spent together on this epic road trip, no meaningful conversations stick out in my memory. But the three of us were certainly happy being together. By July 13, the best trip of my teenage years came to a close and we were back in Topeka, packing up our goods for the move south.

After seven years of renting out our Houston home, Mom, Hannah, and I moved back into #7 Cape Cod Lane and I prepared to enter 10th grade at Memorial High School. I knew I'd play trombone in the concert band, but it was time to decide on a sport. I chose swimming over my promising tennis abilities because of my friendship with Larry Leonard. Looking back, I think this speaks volumes. I had a great fear of rejection. I wanted to belong and didn't want to launch out on my own and join a tennis team where I didn't know anybody. To this day, my high school friends have no idea how good I was at tennis. Neither swimming nor tennis were "cool" sports, but who wants to be alone playing an uncool sport?

Instead, I attached myself to Larry's hip and continued my teenage years as a mediocre swimmer. I succeeded in qualifying for the Texas State Regionals swim meet in my 100-yard backstroke event before calling it quits. It's obvious to me now that I chose to live in Larry's shadow.

Like Brett Zlatnik in Kansas, Larry was smart, excelling in the equivalent of Advanced Placement (AP) courses today, and learning computer programming through his Explorer Scout post. He was a strong swimmer and his freestyle relay team won the state title during our 1979 junior year. In my mind, Larry was everything I wasn't: cool, confident, and he had a girlfriend. I couldn't even talk to girls for fear of rejection. I was fortunate to go to two proms because both girls made it clear they'd say yes if I asked them.

By 1978, my dad had also returned to Houston, teaching law at the University of Houston (known locally as U of H), where he met my stepmom, Karen Lewis. Karen, also a UT graduate, was an English professor at U of H and a force of nature. She smoked constantly, had a husky voice, large framed glasses, and an ego as big as her home state of Texas. In her mind she was never wrong. She was opinionated but I loved her, especially for loving my dad.

Karen encouraged my writing and that was one thing we could talk about. I wrote a paper about aviation safety, detailing all the steps a pilot goes through in preparing to fly a small airplane. She entered my paper in a Houston-area writing contest, and although I really don't remember the results of the contest, I liked that she was impressed with my writing.

Karen had a very bright young daughter, Alison, who was 12 years younger than I was. Eventually, my dad adopted Alison and his face lit up whenever they were together. I truly did not resent that at all. I was happy to see him act like a dad. Perhaps he just didn't know how to relate to his sons. As a testament to my loving family, my mom and dad remained close throughout their life, and we often got together for the holidays. I remember a 1978 Thanksgiving gathering in particular where my mom held Karen's 4-year-old daughter on her lap. In 2006, as a pilot for Southwest Airlines, I wrote an article for our local paper, entitled "Thanks, Mom AND Dad" (found in Appendix 1) which illustrates the relationships within our loving but unusual family.

Dad and Karen in 1997

Karen passed away unexpectedly in mid-January 2020, at the outset of the Covid pandemic. She was hospitalized just days after a family Christmas party and the doctors were perplexed at her fatigue and low oxygen levels. They thought she either had the flu or a mild heart-attack, but fortunately, Karen had given up smoking many years earlier. Like my father, she did not want an autopsy or a funeral. We will never know the cause of her death, but it saddens me greatly that she wasn't here to tear up this manuscript with her vicious purple pen.

My dad, even with his mental illness, was never violent or threatening. He would have a lot of "great ideas" during a manic episode, and then become very withdrawn for many months when depression took over. Fortunately, he was stable and enjoyed his life at the end, watching sports in his assisted living facility and attending family gatherings. Dad passed away suddenly in his bed on a cold afternoon in February 2014. Whatever took him happened so fast that he didn't press his Medical Alert emergency button that he wore on a lanyard.

My mom continues to thrive in Denver, Colorado. She exudes the motto, "Live, Love, Laugh." Mom has always demonstrated a love of life, enjoying socializing with everyone and playing her favorite games of Canasta and Scrabble. She has been such an interactive grandmother for all her growing family. Mom is a brave example of being a survivor, persevering through life after breast cancer and facing Parkinson's Disease head-on. She has been a loving example for all her children, grandchildren, and great-grandchildren.

Like me, my little sister, Hannah, also struggled with low self-confidence. Hannah is the kindest, most caring member of our family. She is non-competitive to a fault but has a heart of gold. And what does every girl want? A horse. So, our Great Provider Dad bought 14-year-old Hannah an Appaloosa horse named Poco. The horse actually should've been named BOGO, because my dad unknowingly bought a pregnant horse! By the following Mother's Day, Poco delivered Bonnie, a beautiful brown filly.

Hannah's horses were stabled in Katy, Texas, 30 minutes west of us. Hannah had the responsibility of feeding, cleaning, and caring for not one, but two horses. Her self-confidence soared! I watched my shy little sister take control of her full-grown mare and train a cute filly. This was equine therapy at its finest. I needed something like that.

My therapy would come from airplanes. At age 16, I joined the Aviation Explorer post, attending meetings at Ellington Air Force Base on Houston's southwest side. I rose through the ranks to become the leader of the post by my senior year. I began my flying lessons at Weiser Airpark in northwest Houston and learned to solo a small plane. Flying would help me cut the cord and come out from behind Larry's shadow. I could become my own man.

What does not kill you, makes you stronger.

CHAPTER 2

ASPIRATIONS

July 24, 1978. Age 16. The day I soloed at Weiser Airpark.
Hosed down and had my "tail feathers" cut by Mr. Andrews.
(Photo by Larry Leonard)

Mr. Andrews, my flight instructor, turned to me and asked, "So, you think you're ready to solo in front of your friends?" After my half-hour flight lesson of three takeoffs and landings, with my childhood friends Larry and Michael watching from alongside the grassy airstrip, I was surprised by his question. I had no idea this might be "the day" I would solo at Weiser Airpark outside of Houston. It was all a blur. I don't remember what I answered, but I think I just smiled and nodded. Up to this point I had seven hours of flight instruction and had performed a grand total of 42 takeoffs and landings.

Mr. Andrews climbed out of the right seat of the Piper Cherokee, and I taxied to the end of the runway for what would be my 15-minute solo flight, performing three touch and go landings with Michael and Larry snapping away with a yellow Kodak disposable camera.

My main memory of the flight is that when I looked left and then right, ensuring the path was clear before making a turn, there was nobody sitting to my right in the cockpit. I was alone. Even as nervous as I was, I was also very excited. This was where I wanted to be.

Like a lot of teenagers growing up, I enjoyed going to airshows. At one point in the 1970s, both the Air Force Thunderbirds and the Navy Blue Angels flew the F-4 Phantom as they put on airshows throughout the country. As they performed beautiful diamond formation rolls and loops, trailing the ever-present tail of white smoke, or crossed show center cockpit-to-cockpit I thought, "*That is one bad-ass airplane.*"

Air Force flying was in my family. My uncle, Jack Sanders, was an Air Force fighter pilot, flying the F-100 Super Sabre during the Vietnam War. He then flew the A-7 Corsair II, and finally transitioned to the new A-10 Thunderbolt II tank-killer. He was an A-10 squadron commander, the pinnacle of a fighter pilot's career, before helping to set up a new squadron of A-10s at Eielson AFB, Alaska, during the Cold War (no pun intended). He closed out his 30-year career as a colonel and Vice Commander of First Air Force, in Tactical Air Command at Langley AFB, Virginia, during Desert Storm in the 1990s.

In 1979, Uncle Jack was a lieutenant colonel A-10 squadron commander at Davis-Monthan AFB, outside of Tucson, Arizona. That spring, I was 17 years old and went to visit my Uncle Jack, Aunt Elaine, and two cousins, Christy and Tina. During that trip, I got to tour the base control tower and from a bird's eye-view watched the fighters take off and land. One of the highlights of my visit was when Uncle Jack arranged for me to fly the A-7 simulator. I pretended to be a real fighter pilot as I simulated low-altitude strafing attacks.

I came home from that trip determined to be a fighter pilot. I had already started flying lessons a year earlier in June of 1978 at the grass runway of Weiser Airpark. I signed up for the Piper Flight School and gave the instructor $700, which he would draw from after each lesson. In hindsight, it worked to Mr. Andrews' advantage for me to solo quickly because the quicker I soloed the more money he kept.

Weiser Air Park had two WWII-era AT-6 Texan trainers on the grass field. Larry and Michael enjoyed airplanes as much as I did, so I invited them along for my seventh lesson. And that's when I soloed. After landing for the third and final time, I climbed out of the Piper Archer and took part in the ritual of having my shirttail (my tail feathers) cut off. The only problem was that I was wearing Lucy's favorite surfer T-shirt, a cool red shirt with an ocean wave on the front. Oops.

My name, the time and date of the flight, July 24, 1978, were written in black Marks-A-Lot on the cut-off portion of the red T-shirt and tacked to the wall of the flight school. I have no memory of what happened next. I guess my brain was so focused on the momentous solo flight. Larry and Mike tell me that Mr. Andrews then offered for them to join us on one more flight. The four of us, Mr. Andrews included, took off once again around the pattern with me at the controls.

The rest of my private flying license lessons took place at LaPorte Municipal Airport in Pasadena, Texas, located near the oil refineries along the ship channel east of Houston. We called this area Stinkadena, due to the foul smell of oil, referred to in Texas as the smell of money. I worked as a busboy and cook at The Mason Jar Restaurant near my house on the west side of Houston to pay for my flying lessons. In addition, I joined the Aviation Explorers division of Scouting, a coed branch of Boy Scouts that focused on one main area. My neighbor, Libby Rafferty, was in High Adventure Scouting, going on campouts and rafting trips, and Larry was in Computer Science, using an IBM mainframe to learn about computing in the late 1970s.

My flight instructor during Aviation Explorers was Mr. Richard Lovell. He was the owner of a beautiful 1973 Piper 180 horsepower Challenger, a white four-seater with a black and gray stripe down the side. Mr. Lovell was in the Navy during the Korean War, but not as a pilot, and he didn't deploy overseas. He laughed about earning the National Defense Service Medal for never going anywhere. He was a short, tough old man; a Navy boxing champ with a permanently crooked nose to prove it. Day in and day out, he dipped Copenhagen and swallowed it. During flying lessons over the Texas Gulf Coast as he gave me instructions, he'd suddenly let out a burp, filling the cockpit with the smell of Copenhagen. To this day my Pavlovian response is to equate the smell of dipping tobacco with a Piper four-seater.

Preflighting Mr. Lovell's plane

I owe Mr. Lovell a lot. He was demanding, telling me to "fight for centerline" when landing in a crosswind. As tough as he was, he was also very kind. Mr. Lovell donated his instructor time for free, as a way of giving back to the Scouting program. My flight lessons from 1978 to 1980 started at $22 an hour and eventually rose to $25 an hour. This, at a time of high inflation, when Certificates of Deposits earned 13% and I was making around $3 an hour at the restaurant.

The hour-long lessons, flown near the Houston ship channel, consisted of airwork – flying 360-degree turns, keeping my wingtip pointed at a blue, lollipop-shaped water tower below while adjusting for the wind changes, or a series of S-turns flown over a railroad track. These exercises taught me to take the varying winds into account.

Stalling the airplane, which occurs when the plane is in a climbing attitude but no longer has the power to fly, is a pilot's nightmare –even in practice. To build my confidence, Mr. Lovell demonstrated his Piper's ability to handle a stall. Reducing the throttle to idle, pulling the yoke back to his chest, this Copenhagen-dipping instructor proceeded to illustrate the magical gift of his aircraft. As I watched the airspeed bleed off, the stall warning light and buzzer distracting my attention, I noticed Mr. Lovell's hands suddenly release the straining yoke of the shuddering airplane. My heart and stomach raced each other for my throat as the plane transferred from 30 degrees nose high into a steep dive. "Shit!" I exclaimed as I looked down on the offshore drilling rig growing larger in front of the propeller. Without touching the controls, the airspeed rose, and the trusty Cherokee slowly pitched up and down, finally settling at the original level-flight attitude. This breathtaking demonstration of aerodynamic stability allowed me to confidently rehearse stall recoveries on my own.

Due to Mr. Lovell's instruction, encouragement, and generosity, I was ready for my Private Pilot's license checkride (flight evaluation) on Aug 20, 1980. I spent that afternoon with a renowned FAA-designated evaluator, Maybelle Fletcher, a fixture in the Houston aviation community. She and her husband operated Fletcher Aviation at Hobby Airport, south of downtown Houston.

This nerve-racking day began when I flew solo from quiet, tiny LaPorte Airport into the busy Hobby Airport. An 18-year-old kid in a small, single-engine propeller airplane had to fly into a big-city airport, sequenced between Learjets and brightly colored Braniff Airline 727s.

With that behind me, I then underwent an oral ground evaluation, as Maybelle quizzed me about aviation rules and navigation principles. Finally, we flew a one-hour flight to an outlying airport for three touch and go landings. With my checkride complete, I was now a licensed private pilot at the age of 18, just one week from starting college and the Air Force Reserve Officer Training Corps (ROTC) program at the University of Texas at Austin.

It had been an exciting day, but I still needed to fly back to LaPorte. It was 4:00 in the afternoon by the time I was debriefed and congratulated by Mrs. Fletcher. I sat in my small plane near the end of the Hobby runway, waiting for my turn to take off. But this was "rush-hour" and streams of Learjets and airliners continued to land.

Private Pilot Certificate, awarded August 20, 1980

Just before being cleared for takeoff, the Piper's engine began to sputter. The small plane had a left and right fuel tank, one in each wing, with a fuel selector by my left knee. Since most of my flying lessons lasted just one hour, switching fuel tanks was rarely required. Today, however, the engine had already been running for almost three hours, and the left fuel tank was almost dry.

Distracted by the excitement of passing my checkride, and impatiently watching the landing jets, I forgot to switch fuel tanks. I quickly threw the selector to the right wing tank and the engine continued running. Fortunately for me, I had not been cleared for takeoff a minute sooner or the engine would have quit during takeoff. That would have been a very short aviation career.

CHAPTER 3

SWING AND A MISS

Cadet Dale, University of Texas AFROTC

I remember the sensation of my first military haircut as a freshman beginning my ROTC training. I hadn't felt the wind on my ears since grade school. I kept rubbing the exposed tops of my ears and the back of my clean-shaven neck as I walked back to the Castilian dormitory from the barber shop on Austin's Guadalupe Street. Between joining the 50,000 students at the University of Texas and beginning my Air Force training, very little was the same as my life in Houston. My new haircut made me look and feel different as I transitioned from scruffy teenager to sharp cadet.

There are three avenues to becoming a military officer. First is by attending a military academy, such as the United States Air Force Academy in Colorado Springs. Second is to graduate from college and then attend three months of Officer Training School (OTS), where the graduates are known as "90-Day Wonders." Finally, the majority of officers are trained through university ROTC programs, where cadets attend classes twice a week and march or "drill" one day each week. I had hoped to attend the Air Force Academy but didn't think my 990 SAT score was high enough. The decision was made for me when as a 17-year-old kid I dug the application out of a box in my room and discovered that I had missed the deadline by two weeks. So, I became a fourth-generation Longhorn, following my great-grandfather, both of my dad's parents, and my dad.

Seventy-five Air Force cadets started as freshmen at UT in August 1980, but not everyone wanted to fly. Many cadets looked forward to non-flying career fields: engineering, missile operations, security forces, nursing, or the new Space Command. At this moment, the Space Shuttle program was preparing for its first launch in April 1981. I had high aspirations of either being a NASA astronaut or an Air Force fighter pilot and member of the Thunderbird Flight Demonstration Team, so I enrolled in Aerospace Engineering to improve my chances of becoming a test pilot.

Those of us hoping for a pilot slot went to Bergstrom Air Force Base (AFB) on the southeast side of Austin for our first military flight physical. This was a few years after the post-Vietnam military drawdown, and in the last few months of the Carter administration. Because of severe defense budget cuts, there were not many pilot slots available.

My eye-test results were disappointing; I had 20/20 vision in my right eye, but 20/25 in my left eye. There were far more pilot candidates than pilot slots, so no waivers were granted for poor vision. Swing and a miss.

Although disappointed, I never considered dropping out of ROTC to pursue a civilian aviation career. This was a setback to my aviation plan but after my first semester, the ROTC staff offered me a navigator candidate slot with a full scholarship, which I accepted. Although the scholarship certainly helped and was considered an honor, it felt like a consolation prize.

I was mostly a B-grade student and couldn't envision myself busting my butt for five years to earn an engineering degree just to be a navigator in the back of some aircraft. After my first semester, I changed majors to Computer Science for one year, and then switched to Business Management. That way I could graduate in four years and get on with my Air Force career. The Air Force didn't place any stipulations on what my degree was in, so I hoped to graduate from college as quickly as possible.

Thanks to my sophomore college roommate, I improved my eye-test score during college. Doug Griffith, whose dad was an Army ophthalmologist, told me that I only needed to correctly identify five of the eight characters on the vision test to receive credit for that line. If I could distinguish (or guess correctly) between Cs and Os or Xs, Ks, and Rs on the eye test, I would be able to demonstrate 20/20 vision after all. Squinting into the eye test viewer like a wanderer lost in the desert, I demonstrated 20/20 vision during my sophomore annual physical. Luckily, this was just prior to attending summer ROTC Field Training at McConnell AFB outside of Wichita, Kansas. With fingers crossed, I headed off to the Land of Oz, hoping for a pilot slot.

There was great incentive to do well during this intense four-week "officer boot camp" training program. Field Training was the center-piece of the entire four-year program and the top graduate in each flight of 20 cadets could either receive a coveted pilot slot or a full scholarship for their final two years. I was already on scholarship as a navigator candidate, but the ROTC program would not combine a pilot slot with a scholarship. If I was the top graduate in my flight, I would happily trade in my navigator scholarship for a pilot slot.

A few days before the end of Field Training, our section of cadets took an orientation flight on a KC-135 (similar to a Boeing 707) air refueling tanker. I was talking to a fellow cadet and friend, Ivan. He had been on the Michigan State gymnastics team and an alternate on the 1980 Olympic gymnastics team. Those games in the USSR were boycotted by the U.S. after the Soviets invaded Afghanistan in 1979. Now, Ivan needed a scholarship to continue his college degree. As we talked in the cabin of the noisy gray tanker, our flight commander, an active-duty Air Force captain, joined the two of us.

"It's good to see you two talking, but it doesn't make my job any easier."

"Why is that, sir?" I asked.

"I have you two neck and neck for my nomination for Top Cadet."

Well, that was a problem. I could earn the pilot slot I dreamed of or Ivan could win a badly needed scholarship. My dad had already assured me that college would continue for me with or without my scholarship. I had mixed feelings about this situation--I wanted the best for Ivan--but I really wanted that pilot slot. This is not the part where I graciously backed down and allowed Ivan to win the Top Cadet award. In the end, Ivan won the award fair and square on his own merit. Swing and a miss.

One year later, during the flight physical of my junior year, I again demonstrated 20/20 vision in both eyes. The Reagan-era military build-up was beginning, but not quickly enough for me. In the spring of 1983, I presented my new pilot-qualified physical to the Air Force ROTC detachment technical sergeant in charge of the administration section. Unfortunately, I was disappointed again.

"That's great," he said, "But all of the pilot slots for your fiscal year have been awarded."

Another swing and a miss. Feeling deflated, I had to make the best of this situation for the time being. The Air Force allowed 50 active-duty navigators to attend pilot training each year. I'd have to postpone the goal of my ambition until I was on active duty.

CHAPTER 4

HANG'N OUT IN AUSTIN

Hang gliding with Texas vultures. An accidental double exposure shot.
(My favorite photo, by Michael Rafferty)

By the summer of 1983, I had finished my junior year of ROTC, and our old neighborhood gang was reunited again. Larry and I roomed together our college freshman year at the Castilian dorm, which was where I met my future wife, Karin. Before starting our senior year in 1983, Larry Leonard and I moved into the same Austin apartment complex, each in a one-room efficiency, and Michael was in his sophomore year at UT.

Driving through the west Austin hill country one late summer day, Michael and I spied a hang-glider for sale in a front yard. We were both aviation enthusiasts and inspired to take up hang-gliding after watching James Bond in the opening scene of *Live and Let Die*. Although we didn't buy that particular glider, the owner put us in touch with the Austin hang-glider club in north Austin. The club was run by two Steves; Steve Burns and Steve Stackable, a 1975 U.S. Motocross National Champion. "Stack" was the ultimate cool dude. This wavy-haired motorcycle champion had raced in the Houston Astrodome in the 1970's and was now married to a Playboy playmate.

Michael and I entered Austin Air Sports' small wooden shop in north Austin and asked about hang-gliding lessons. Through Steve Burns' connections, we found a great deal. Michael and I split the $800 cost of a 1980 Spirit Electra Flyer hang-glider. Our glider featured an innovative crossbar, making the large, 200-square-foot glider pretty nimble and maneuverable. It had multi-colored earth-tone panels with brown in the center, then orange, tan, yellow, and red panels extending out to the purple wingtips. The entire disassembled glider was relatively easy to transport, fitting into an 18-foot blue canvas bag, about two feet in diameter.

Launching a hang-glider required a hill to run down, and that meant we needed a four-wheel drive vehicle. I bought my brother's green 1978 Subaru Brat, a tiny two-seat pick-up truck with a four-speed manual transmission and a four-foot truck bed, covered by a white plastic camper shell. Once loaded, our "glider-in-a-bag" extended two feet in front and behind the tiny 14-foot truck, but we were in business.

Learning to fly a hang-glider required a mastery of taking off and landing first and foremost, much like learning to fly any airplane. We only needed a small hill, and for that, Austin Air Sports used the football field sunken in a shallow bowl at Murchison Middle School. Our beginner's lessons reminded me of Charlie Brown skiing down his pitcher's mound. The flights lasted only seconds, but they suited our needs.

Our Spirit glider came complete with training wheels mounted on the control bar. I stepped into the blue harness that ran from shoulders to crotch like an old-fashioned men's swimming suit. Our knee-hanger harness had two thick six-foot ropes shrouded in material. The material was stitched into the harness at my shoulder blades and attached by wide Velcro straps just below my knees. This simple style of harness kept our legs and feet free to run down the launch ramp. The two thick ropes, held together with a large coupling (a carabiner) then hooked to the glider frame above and behind my shoulders.

Once safely buckled in and with my white half-shell motorcycle helmet in place, I hoisted the triangular control frame assembly onto my shoulders. My arms were draped around the down-tubes of the triangle and my wingtips extended out seventeen feet in each direction. I ran a few steps down the small hill and the large wing became airborne within seconds. For the initial training, my only goal was to fly straight ahead into the football field and belly-land. This allowed the wheels to touch and I coasted to a stop. After a flight shorter than Orville Wright's 12-second flight, I stood up and unhooked the carabiner. Holding onto the pointed nose of the kite, I pushed it up the hill for another go.

Larry joined Michael and me, and we each practiced numerous takeoffs before learning the art of flaring the large kite for a normal landing. As the glider approached the landing zone, I pushed gently forward on the control bar, raising the nose but not enough to climb back into the air. This allowed for a feet first landing, like a duck landing on water. If I pushed too aggressively on the control bar, I risked climbing ten feet up in the air, stalling the wing, and crashing to the ground. Hang-glider pilots have broken their legs from this sort of botched landing.

After a few weeks of Charlie Brown Pitcher's Mound practice, we were ready for a real hang-glider flight. The nearest location in flat Texas was a 400-foot hill on Packsaddle Mountain, an hour and a half west of Austin between Marble Falls and Llano. Michael and I strapped our bagged glider to the top of the Brat and set off for the Hill Country behind our instructors, Stack and Steve.

The little four-cylinder truck bounced its way along a two-mile dirt county road off Highway 71, finally turning off at the base of an outcropping of an oblong hill. Two hills merged into one, raised at both ends with the right side higher than the left, giving it the appearance of a horse's packsaddle. Our launch point was the southern, higher hill, and the Brat tackled the rutty dirt trail up to the 400-foot summit.

With the kite fully assembled and my harness and motorcycle helmet donned, I carried the kite on my shoulders to the wooden launch platform, which was painted like a gigantic Texas flag in red, white, and blue. Stack said the first few rides would just be sled-rides, a simple flight with only mild S-turns, from the launch platform to the cow pasture directly below. Given the increased speed of this flight versus the small football stadium hill, I was instructed to just make a belly-landing on the training wheels until I gained more experience.

Michael Rafferty preparing for his first launch from Packsaddle Mountain, with Steve "Stack" Stackable and Larry Leonard

Balancing the kite on my shoulders, I jogged down the ten-foot ramp and was airborne after just three steps. The wind whistled in my ears as the craggy hillside fell away below. Ahead lay a vast pasture used for grazing cattle, which made for an easy landing zone. My inaugural flight lasted perhaps a minute, and I glided toward the dry, brown, summer grass for a soft landing.

Now came the tedious part. During my short flight, Michael drove the Brat down the bumpy road and into the pasture, and together we partially disassembled the kite, folding the wings together along the central spar and taking apart the aluminum triangle. Hoisting our kite back onto our trusty little pack mule, we drove back up the hill for another flight. Lather, Rinse, Repeat. Early on, Michael and I would each take three short flights, then turn the kite over to the other person for their turn to practice. It became a very long day for just a bit of flying, but the experience was exhilarating.

After a few more sled rides, I began to get a feel for handling of our Spirit glider from takeoff to landing. I started to add gentle turns to the flights, cruising back and forth along the hillside in what is called ridge-lift, created from the southerly wind flowing toward Packsaddle Mountain. As long as the breeze blew and I stayed in a thermal or ridge-lift, the glider stayed airborne indefinitely. There were just two things limiting our flight time: Michael was waiting for his turn, and while gliding I was in a front-leaning-rest push-up position, which became very tiresome.

Typically, our flights lasted about twenty minutes and this was plenty of time to take in the rustic sights of the Texas Hill Country. Like a hawk scanning the land below, I could see the Colorado River to the north and east. The river was divided by dams to form Lake Buchanan, Lake LBJ and Lake Travis. To the south, I saw Highway 71 snaking its way west toward Llano, and miles and miles of cedar and scrub oak-covered hills. Gliding was very peaceful, with only the soft hiss of the wind in my ears and the creaking and clinking of the aluminum glider frame.

On occasion, our desire to fly like a bird was enhanced when we were shadowed by a pair of turkey vultures that launched from the surrounding trees to follow our kite. As the pilot, I was rarely aware that I was leading a formation of birds. With the large black birds following just aft of my wingtips, I couldn't see them, but they made for some excellent photographs.

Communing with nature occurred not only during flight but also during the evening landings. Our landing zone was the preferred dining spot of the roaming herd of cattle. Around 5:00 p.m., as the sun began to set and we were getting our last flights in, about thirty black cows began grazing right in our landing zone. Just as aircraft used to buzz sheep or cattle, I too, took part in that ritual.

After cruising in the hillside ridge-lift for a half hour, I flew away from the hill and out of the lifting wind currents to begin a shallow descent to the brown grassy field below. I gained enough speed to allow for a "go-around" if things didn't look right prior to landing. I whistled over the uninterested bovines just five feet above their backs. It was pure fun in the Texas sun. Once clear of the munching moos, I pushed forward on the control bar, raising the nose slightly. I then circled back to a clear grassy spot for a flare and touched my feet to the ground and shouldered the kite. I loved the calm, thrilling experience of hang-gliding.

Unfortunately, my flights didn't always go as planned. One evening, the winds started to pick up as our day came to an end. Wanting to get in just one more flight, I suited up for a last run. I ran down the launch and became airborne just as a gust of wind hit my left wing and blew me immediately toward the radio tower guy wires about 50 yards to the right of our launch ramp. I immediately shifted my position to the left corner of the control bar and threw it up and to my right, trying to counter the wind with a hard left turn. Fortunately, my right wingtip missed the guy wires by a few feet and I cruised away from the tower and into the hillside updraft.

My second incident involved a revolutionary way to launch hang-gliders by towing them up behind a powered ultralight. Just as airplanes tow sailplanes in soaring, a French company pioneered a tether system for their power gliders to tow us up from a pasture. Part of their three-ring release assembly included a weak link designed to snap if too many G's were pulled by the trailing glider. This way the powered leader would not drag a flailing kite, pulling them both back to the ground. Larry and Michael each took a turn, running with the kite for a few feet as the power glider gained speed and towed them safely to altitude for a smooth flight.

I suited up in the harness and helmet and gave the towing tricycle glider a thumbs up that I was ready. As he increased the thrust of his small propeller, I walked, then jogged as he gained speed. Just like launching from our hillside ramp, I was airborne quickly, but the cool sensation this time was that I was only a few feet above the grass. I enjoyed the low-altitude cruise at grass-top level as the power glider gained speed and altitude. We flew up to 200 feet and he began a gentle turn to the left. I must have been looking down or off to my right at the hill country scenery, because I didn't notice his turn and started mine too late and didn't aggressively get back into position behind him. Within a few seconds my kite was straining the tow rope and the weak link snapped as designed.

I now needed to make a quick landing back at the cleared field behind me. It's a situation I had been trained for in flying small planes, just like an engine failure after takeoff. Needing to immediately turn back to the landing zone, I continued my wide left-hand turn and saw trees and a power line between me and the pasture. Without the ability to add power, I could only hope my descent rate would clear the obstacles as the trees and powerline loomed closer. Luckily, my feet cleared the powerline and I successfully landed in the field. So much for that adventure. I was pretty shaken up by that episode, knowing that I had caused it by getting out of position. While Michael would go on to enjoy years of hang-gliding and soaring in a sailplane, I decided I would stick to powered flight. Give me an engine any day.

CHAPTER 5

THE HAPPY PESSIMIST

David Briscoe, Stacey Samuels Bie, and me, the Happy Pessimist.

With a parachute weighing heavily on my back, I eased my way to the doorway, where the side door of the high-wing Cessna had been removed. Reaching out with both hands, I grabbed the wing strut, a smooth piece of metal running at a 45-degree angle from the fuselage to the lower skin of the airplane. I then stretched my right foot out to touch the footrest alongside the right main landing gear. With both hands gripping the wing strut, my right foot held my weight on the small 6 by 12-inch metal plate and my left leg dangled in the 120-mile-per-hour wind. I was now standing outside of an airplane! Like a wing-walker in the barnstorming shows of the 1920s, I was now riding along outside a small plane similar to those I had piloted since 1978.

Not scared in the least, I took in the Texas countryside and a small wooden white house below. I wish I could have remained a barn-stormer longer, but the instructor must have thought I froze up because he yelled, "Go! Go! Go!" He was rightfully concerned I would drift out of the landing zone. Releasing the wing strut, I fell away from the airplane, arching my back and looking up, as the plane grew smaller.

Some military aviation emergencies involve parachutes, so why not go skydiving? That's what my college friend, Stacey Samuels Bie, and I did in October 1983, the fall of my senior year. On a beautiful Halloween weekend, we set out for Skydive Austin, east of the city near the town of Manor. Long before the really cool looking steerable rectangular airfoils used by skydivers today, our parachutes were the green Army surplus dome chutes used by Army Airborne units.

Stacey, her friend Briscoe, and I sat through a short ground school, where they showed us how to strap into our parachute harnesses. Our instructors then hung us in our harnesses from a metal frame, simulating the motions of the parachute descent and landing. We practiced turns by pulling on one set of risers above our shoulders and then the other set, turning or spinning to the left and right. Turning enabled us to land into the wind.

We also practiced the proper way to land, which the instructor called the Banana Technique, touching down with both feet together, then immediately rolling onto our right or left calf, thigh, hip, and butt to absorb the impact. Briscoe remarked that he didn't want to mess up the banana landing shape and land flat, with his innards exploding from his "banana skin."

Ours wasn't a tandem jump like people experience today, where they jump with an instructor connected to them. We were doing a static-line, solo jump. A ripcord deploying our chute was attached by a 25-foot-long lead to the airplane. As we each fell away from the aircraft the static line released our parachute once we were a safe distance from the airplane. The Army refers to this jump method as Dope on a Rope.

With our ground school successfully completed, the three of us headed out to the flightline, parachutes weighing heavily on our backs, and waited for our turn to board the high-wing Cessna. In an amazing small world coincidence, my future girlfriend and wife, Karin, sat on the curb waiting to watch her then-boyfriend skydive. I recognized Karin from our days in the dormitory and around campus. I said "Hello," and she replied, "Hi there," as Stacey, Briscoe, and I prepared to board the plane.

The white Cessna took off with the three rookie skydivers and one instructor onboard. We climbed into the blue October sky, gaining altitude as we circled up over the intended landing zone. One of the landmarks pointed out below was a white clapboard house used as the house of ill repute in the Burt Reynolds and Dolly Parton movie, *The Best Little Whorehouse in Texas*. It was filmed during my sophomore year, and in an ironic twist, University of Texas students around campus were extras. They portrayed the Texas A&M Aggie cadets in khaki uniforms and knee-high brown leather boots, frequenting the infamous Chicken Ranch near LaGrange, Texas.

Our pilot finally gave the indication that we were over the zone and it was time to "Skydive Austin." There really wasn't much to this type of skydiving. Just let go of the wing strut and let gravity do the rest. As expected, the 25-foot line stretched to its limit and released my main parachute. Had this not gone as planned, we had been trained to pull the cord on the smaller back-up chute on our chest, pound the side of it hard to get the pouch to open, then throw the auxiliary parachute out and away from us to inflate.

Fortunately, there was no need for any such dramatics, and within a few seconds I was dangling beneath a green silk half-circle. Many people would never consider sky-diving, afraid that the parachute might fail to open. Trained for that circumstance, I wasn't concerned at all. Now, with my full weight under the chute, I had a different uncomfortable thought.

"*What if the leg strap buckles at my crotch fail?*"

I knew if that happened, I would fall out from the bottom of the parachute. That would suck. It would be all over but the shouting.

Aviators are trained to always think about what can go wrong next. It leads us to have a rather pessimistic view of things but keeps us ready to react with the correct procedure. I've come to realize that I am a Happy Pessimist. While I have a positive view on life and I deeply appreciate and love my family and friends, I think quite a lot about things that can go wrong.

Perhaps this hasn't served me well for investment opportunities or entrepreneurial prospects, but I've always kept my guard up in various situations. I once delayed a laminated flooring project because I knew that just one degree of error would compound into a botched job. My exasperated wife finally yelled, "Just start it!" We did and it turned out fine. Regardless of those "what can go wrong next" thoughts, I'm not full of dread and gloom. Instead, day in and day out I'm a happy, smiling person.

Drifting peacefully toward the field below me, I happily descended under this huge green silk canopy. I pulled the left riser to get a view of sights to my left, then pulled the right riser to scan the opposite brown, flat Texas horizon. My entire parachute experience lasted perhaps three or four minutes and did not include the free-fall experience I would enjoy from 14,000 feet with my kids and their friend when I turned 50. This jump took place from 5,000 feet and I descended under my chute toward the autumn pastureland. Near the end of the descent, I turned to land into the wind, as instructed. With the ground rushing up, I assumed the landing position, eyes on the horizon (I might have cheated and looked down), feet together and knees slightly bent. My touchdown felt fine as I rolled along my right leg and onto my back, then watched the green silk drift softly to the ground.

I immediately released the parachute harness buckles at my shoulders to avoid being dragged by the chute, should a gust of wind decide my ride wasn't quite over. I stood, uninjured from my satisfactory banana landing. I gathered the Army parachute in my arms and walked over to join Stacey and Briscoe in a celebratory high five. We were all smiling from ear to ear. With the huge orange sun setting in the west, there was no chance to skydive again that day. I'm glad we jumped at the opportunity when we did.

CHAPTER 6
HELO OR NAV?

In April 1984, one month before commissioning, my ROTC Detachment Commander at the University of Texas, Colonel Smulczenski, called me into his office.

"Dave, we've just received word that there are helicopter pilot slots available if you want one."

"*Oh wow*," I thought. I definitely had mixed feelings about this news. After four years of trying, here was my chance to get my Air Force pilot wings--but in a helicopter. I wasn't excited enough to accept it on the spot, nor was I going to turn it down right then and there. I certainly didn't expect this news so close to graduation. Col Smulczenski said he could give me a few days to think about it.

At that time, the only Air Force pilot on the ROTC staff was Captain Gary Smith, who had recently piloted the KC-135 tanker in the Strategic Air Command (SAC). I asked him his thoughts on the advantages or disadvantages of this new opportunity. In his mind, the primary purpose of Huey helicopter pilots, the only Air Force helicopter operations he was familiar with, was to ferry the SAC nuclear missile crews out to the underground silos scattered throughout the central United States.

The Air Force's primary helicopter, the UH-1 Huey, flew at 125 miles per hour and I was already doing that with a Cessna 172 flying at the Bergstrom AFB Aero Club. The conventional wisdom at the time was, once a helicopter pilot, always a helicopter pilot. There might be an opportunity for a cross-flow tour to a fixed-wing airplane unit, but that wasn't guaranteed. And even if selected, I was told I would eventually have to return to a helicopter unit. At no point was I told about, nor did I think about, Special Operations helicopter units and their exciting, secret missions. I knew I wanted to follow in my Uncle Jack's footsteps and fly a combat aircraft, not a support aircraft, like an airlift transport, or an air refueling tanker.

I was in a real quandary. For four years I fought to get a pilot slot, and now one was offered, but it was for helicopter training, which I had never even considered. In my mind, the Air Force flew jets and C-130 propeller-driven transports. I fully expected to fly much faster than 125 mph. Did I want pilot wings so badly that I was willing to fly a "whop-whop" whirly-bird for the next twenty years? Or did I want to be a jet navigator and then hope to be selected for pilot training and upgrading to a cockpit window seat?

I was a pretty gung-ho, physically fit cadet. During this final spring semester of college, I was the Cadet Corps Commander, overseeing the detachment of 150 Air Force cadets. I often exercised with my sophomore college roommate, Doug Griffith, who attended the Marine Corps' Officer Candidate School in the summers at Camp LeJeune, North Carolina. We encouraged each other through 60 sit-ups, 30 pull-ups, and a 3-mile run along Austin's Town Lake. I scored high enough on the Marine Corps' Personal Fitness Test (PFT) to be approached by a clipboard-toting Marine recruiter to switch services. But I was content to pursue an Air Force career, fully intending to fly in a combat fighter unit.

Another factor I had not considered, nor was I told about by Captain Smith, was that pilots typically had stronger career opportunities in the Air Force than navigators. He was probably aware of this fact, but didn't want to portray navigators as second-class citizens. Leadership positions in flying units almost always went to pilots. A navigator wanting to lead usually had to cross-train to become the commander of a non-flying unit, such as a maintenance or security forces squadron. I would witness this as my career progressed, but it didn't enter my decision-making process back then. A 22-year-old soon-to-be second lieutenant couldn't think about what life would be like as a 40-year-old lieutenant colonel.

In later years I also found out that helicopter pilots could indeed become fixed-wing airplane pilots and remain so for the rest of their careers. I eventually crossed paths with numerous Air Force and airline pilots who began their careers flying helicopters. In the end, I told Colonel Smulczenski that I would rather be a combat aircraft navigator than a low-and-slow helicopter pilot. One of my ROTC classmates took the helicopter pilot slot and sure enough, ended up ferrying missile crews in his UH-1 Huey out to the nuclear missile silos around Wichita, Kansas.

On May 19, 1984, I was commissioned a second lieutenant and prepared to head out to Mather AFB, near Sacramento, California to become a navigator.

UNIVERSITY OF TEXAS AT AUSTIN
ROTC Commissioning
May 18, 1984

My commissioning ceremony as an Air Force officer

CHAPTER 7

KARIN SMITH

Karin Smith
Gamma Phi Beta sorority photo
University of Texas at Austin

A ir Force Undergraduate Navigator Training (UNT) was a nine-month course, consisting of academics and flights in both the T-37 "Tweet" (a side-by-side jet trainer carrying an instructor pilot and a student navigator) and the T-43 (a Boeing 737, carrying twelve student navigators and three instructors). To successfully complete the program, we needed to master multiple methods of navigation. The first method was dead-reckoning, tracking our position on a map by using a stopwatch and compass headings to find landmarks and turn points. We also learned radar navigation, interpreting the terrain from the images we saw on a ground mapping radar. Finally, we became proficient in celestial navigation, using the same trigonometry methods and a sextant like the ancient mariners used to "shoot the stars" and plot the plane's location over the earth.

Each block of training included a written test, and I was satisfied to receive a 93 on my first Air Force exam. My fiancée, Karin, always much smarter than I, asked why I didn't make a 100? "You're only studying one subject, after all."

Her gentle nudge reminded me of a well-known story of a wealthy CEO husband and his wife as they were pulling into a gas station. The lady recognized the greasy auto mechanic as a former high school boyfriend and pointed him out to her husband.

"Just think," said her cocky husband. "If you had married him, you would be an auto mechanic's wife."

"No, honey," she replied. "If I married him, HE would be a wealthy CEO."

I'd say that story fits our marriage.

I was lucky enough to begin dating Karin Smith in what I refer to as "Just-in-time Dating" – four weeks before our college graduation. We originally met our freshman year while living in the coed Castilian Dorm across the street from the college campus. Karin, like myself, is six feet tall, so she is hard to miss and easy to look at. I worked in the dormitory cafeteria and served her as she passed through the food line. We now tell people, "We lived together our freshman year."

Some couples have cute pet names for each other. Mine, apparently, was "There." Karin was a Little Sister to the Navy ROTC unit in a service organization called Anchorettes. The Air Force had a similar organization called Angel Flight, and many of my ROTC classmates met their future spouse this way. As six-foot tall Karin Smith walked through the ROTC building and I would say, "Hi Karin." Not knowing my name, she would simply reply, "Hi there." None of my Air Force friends ever caught on to this joke between us, otherwise, "There" might have become my Air Force callsign. Can you imagine: Maverick, Goose, Iceman, and … "There"?

We officially met at the Silver Dollar Dance Hall in north Austin where two long tables were filled with twenty ROTC cadets, Anchorettes, and Angels. Karin sat at the far end with a married Marine Corps friend of hers. He told her she should dance with me, so she came over and asked me to dance.

I answered, "No, not to this song."

This was not me playing hard-to-get. Not being a strong country dancer and not knowing the song that the band was playing, I thought the last thing I wanted to do was step on the toes of the girl I'd been admiring since our freshman year. From grade school through college, I was terribly shy around girls. I didn't have the self-esteem to put myself out there and risk being turned down. Instead, I just admired Karin whenever she walked by, never imagining that I'd be talking to her that night.

After being told "no," Karin sat down and asked what I was drinking. Now I became sheepish. This was the final Nickel Beer Night before The Silver Dollar closed down for good on Saturday. They served nickel beers and 50-cent pitchers of Budweiser on Thursdays … and I was drinking water. "*How NOT to make a good impression!*" was all I could think. But I had a good reason. I didn't want or plan to be there that night.

I had been going to The Silver Dollar for the past four years (not every Thursday, but close). I had just finished a college triathlon (1000-yard swim, 30-mile bike ride, and 6-mile run) the previous Saturday and was in the best shape of my life. When my friend, Wade, called to say everyone was heading out to The Dollar one last time, I said I was burned out on the place. Wade didn't relent and told me that our mutual friend, Alex, was not planning to drink that night, so I could "just come along and not drink with Alex." Alex and I downed numerous pitchers of water and I finally met Karin.

She and I did dance that night; it was the first time I ever looked directly across into the eyes of my dance partner. I was entranced and will never forget that first dance. Luckily for me, Karin needed a date for her final sorority spring dance in April 1984, and she picked me. Our whirlwind romance continued through college graduation four weeks later and on into the summer.

GAMMA PHI BETA
The Almost Summer Casual
April 14, 1984

My original report date for navigator training was October 1984, so I worked a construction job during the months after graduation. I was helping to build an apartment complex in south Austin while I roomed with my ROTC classmate, newly commissioned Second Lieutenant Jim Thomas. Meanwhile, Karin moved into a South Austin apartment and began using her finance degree as a bookkeeper for Pok-E-Joe's, a local Austin barbeque restaurant.

Jim and I were slated to attend Nav School together in the fall and planned to share an apartment in Sacramento. One evening in July, I received an unexpected phone call from the Air Force Personnel Center in San Antonio. They told me a slot had opened up in the August navigator training class and asked if I wanted to report for training two months early. I didn't hesitate for a second.

"You bet!" I replied, without even consulting Karin.

I knew I wanted to marry Karin, but now my timeline was accelerated. I had not even met her parents but I soon found out she came from a family of very tall people. In late July, we headed down to her hometown of Corpus Christi where I met her 6-foot, 6-inch father,

Jerry; 6-foot, 7-inch brother, Clark; and 5-foot, 10-inch mother, Barbara. At least at 6-foot tall, I wasn't the shortest in this family.

Later that first afternoon, Jerry and I sipped Miller Lite in their pool while Karin and Barbara went shopping. Jerry had enlisted in the Air Force during the Korean War because, as he put it, he would've been the tallest person in Korea and the Army "didn't make foxholes deep enough." Instead, Jerry attended the Defense Language Institute, near Monterey, California and served as a Russian Linguist in northern Japan, eavesdropping on the submarine pens in Vladivostok.

After his enlistment, Jerry became a store manager of various Woolco locations, moving his family around the country. Jerry served as an assistant store manager in California, Arizona, and Ohio, before being promoted to general manager of his own north Houston Woolco. This imposing gentle giant then had the task of turning around a poorly performing Woolco in Corpus Christi. The family settled there in 1974 where Karin would go on to graduate from high school in 1980.

Lounging in the pool, he asked me what a second lieutenant made in the Air Force these days. I told him, "About $17,000 a year."

He smiled and said, "Oh, that's pretty good!"

My $700 paycheck every two weeks far exceeded the $400 per month he made as an enlisted man thirty years earlier.

Once I worked up my courage (thank you, Miller Lite), I told Jerry that after completing navigator training next summer I would like to marry his daughter. I was totally going off the script at this point. Karin and I knew we wanted to get married but during the drive down to Corpus from Austin I wondered if I really should ask for his permission on this first meeting. But here I was, full of beer, sunshine, and courage, asking Jerry for his permission. Leaning up against the side of his pool, he said, "It's okay with me, but you better ask her."

A few minutes later Karin and her mom, whom I had hardly met, walked in the gate by the pool. Jerry announced, "Barbara, you better go get dressed. We are going out to dinner."

"Why?"

"David wants to marry our daughter."

I am certain Barbara was floored. She must have been thinking, *"Who is this 22-year-old kid sitting in my swimming pool? I don't know the slightest thing about him."*

A few days later, on a 105-degree July day, I drove Karin up to Mount Bonnell, in her 1979 Monte Carlo. I had recently purchased my brand new 1984 Monte Carlo Super Sport, but it was delivered without freon, so the air conditioner didn't work on that blistering hot day. As we overlooked Lake Austin I officially proposed. Karin said "Yes."

With sweat dripping down my face, I replied, "Good. Let's get back to the car!" and we drove to the Austin Hyatt Regency for a rooftop dinner celebration.

I left for Sacramento a week later, then flew home during my Christmas break from training on December 22. One week later, we were wed in Corpus Christi on December 29. We only dated four months before my departure for Air Force training and have been married ever since.

Karin's family on our wedding day.

CHAPTER 8

"WHAT'S 16 MINUS 16?"

2nd Lt Dale, student navigator at a T-43 Navigator Station

"Why didn't you make a 100? You're only studying one subject."

I had just scored a 93 on my first test in navigator training and Karin had a point. I wasn't trying to balance four or five college courses on various topics. Thanks to her push, I made 100 on the remaining academic tests in both Navigator and, later, Pilot Training.

The first navigation evaluation is visual low-level navigation in the T-37 Tweet, a twin-engine jet trainer known for producing more noise than thrust. The instructor pilot sat in the left seat, with a full panel of aviation instruments in front of him or her. The student navigator sat in the right seat and still had a control stick, but fewer instruments and no expectation to fly the jet. Students flew several training rides to learn how to navigate visually, using "timing and heading" to navigate to a target. This meant the student told the pilot to fly a heading for a prescribed number of minutes, identify a landmark, then turn to a new heading to complete a low-level route across the Sierra Nevada mountains east of Sacramento.

For my low-level evaluation, the target was a radio tower atop a Sierra Mountain. This might sound like it would be easy, but flying at 500 to 1000 feet above the ground limits forward visibility, so all that can be seen are easily identifiable landmarks: lakes, roads, or railroad tracks in the immediate vicinity. The low-level route was plotted on a colored map and the black line zig-zagged across the mountains toward the target. Flying a zig-zag pattern would avoid detection if this were a real combat sortie over enemy territory.

I knew one important landmark was the second of two small mountain lakes. My stopwatch was running as we clipped along at four miles per minute just 500 feet above the treetops. At the pre-scribed time, I looked out of the cockpit and saw a lake.

"*Okay, where is the second lake?*" I thought. "*Or was THAT the second lake?*" Hmm.

I glanced at the map and looked back outside a few more times. The pilot calmly asked me the all-important question.

"What do you want me to do?"

I was nervous, bewildered, and unable to hit a Pause button. I decided I had to trust my timing and told him to turn to the new heading. He threw the little jet into a hard right turn, rolled out, then turned his dark-visored helmet toward me. Concealing what must have been a smile under his oxygen mask, he keyed the interphone and said, "They drained that other lake years ago."

A few minutes later, after several more turns we rolled out on the final leg to the target. Peering ahead, I saw the red and white radio tower poking above the horizon on the wooded hilltop ahead of us.

"Nice job," he commented.

The radar navigation portion of training consisted of interpreting the green and black round radarscope to pick out terrain features and use them as turn-points enroute to a destination or target. Radar emissions bounce off anything solid, whether it's the buildings of a city or the rain in a thundercloud. The radarscope displayed the distance and rough shape of an object, including how solid it is.

The scopes we used were not the modern-day green, yellow, and red colored weather radar depictions. Ours just showed various shades of green and black. A favorite trick of the instructors during the simulator training sessions was to place a thunderstorm near a large city to see which one the student would avoid. We had to keep clear of thunderstorms by twenty nautical miles to avoid potential hail damage. During one simulator session in a room full of twenty students facing their scopes, the instructor slapped the student next to me on the shoulder, sarcastically chiding, "Congratulations. You just successfully deviated around St. Louis."

I successfully completed the radar navigation portion of training and moved on to the hardest phase, Celestial Navigation. After each navigation phase, those who did not pass the evaluation were washed back to the training class behind us. Students needed to pass each phase of the course. If they failed a portion after their second attempt, they washed out of training completely. After that, it was up to the Air Force to either retrain the officer in another career field or dismiss them entirely from the service. "The needs of the Air Force" was a common mantra that we heard. It was never a certainty that a student would pass a test or evaluation and move forward to the next phase.

A navigator training class started every two weeks at Mather AFB, so it was easy to wash back for many reasons. Catch a cold and miss three training flights? Wash back. Sprain your ankle playing volleyball? Wash back. Fail a checkride? Wash back. I knew if I stayed on track, I would graduate in April, but I told Karin, "I have no idea when I'll graduate. I've seen guys wash back at the drop of a hat."

For this reason, our original spring or summer wedding in 1985 was moved up to the Christmas break of 1984. I learned that only one thing is certain in Air Training Command, and that is the school shuts down between Christmas and New Year's Day. By the time we started Celestial Navigation we had lost one-third of our original classmates. Many would go on to graduate, but not with their original class.

I enjoyed math ever since junior high algebra and had taken trigonometry in high school. I was the smart-aleck kid who asked, "Mrs. Benedict, when am I EVER going to use this?"

Well, I found out. Remember tangent, sine, and cosine? They are all used in celestial navigation. A line of position (LOP) from three different celestial objects (stars, planets, or the moon) will plot a small triangle, identifying a location over the earth. Or, in daylight, a LOP from the Sun or Moon can be crossed with a radio signal from a known beacon and the geographic position is at that intersection. Sounds simple, right? It was all math and I really enjoyed it. During a later visit to Houston, I stopped by Mrs. Benedict's math class to tell her, "I found out where you use trig!"

After many weeks of theory, each student was loaned a sextant to take home for practice. Many of us second lieutenants lived in apartments in the Rancho Cordova area. I was now newly married, and thought what better way to entertain my new bride than to bring home a sextant to look at the moon and stars? From the monkey bars of the playground equipment in our apartment complex we hung the 10-pound metal sextants and looked skyward. It may all sound very nerdy and geeky, but my wife will always remember our evenings "shooting the stars."

The airborne training consisted of three flights in a T-43, a 1970's era Boeing 737 with the skinny engines. It was the same model that Southwest Airlines was famous for flying in the days of flight attendants in hot pants and go-go boots. The T-43 cabin had three sections (A, B, and C), each containing four navigation stations, one sextant porthole in the ceiling, and one instructor navigator to monitor his four students. In total, there were 12 student navigators and three instructors, plus the two pilots up front.

During a training flight, each student was responsible for navigating one segment of the flight. Even when it was not my leg, I had to keep up with the airplane's position so that when my turn came, I was ready to give the pilots a heading to fly. Things quickly turned interesting if a weak student navigator was in charge. If the student made a math or position error, they would believe the plane was way off course and direct a large heading change to the pilot ("Pilot, come 30 degrees right!"). Now we all had to continue to plot this errant course so that when our turn came, we could direct the pilot back on course.

To prepare to take a celestial shot of a star, navigators completed a pre-computation (called a precomp) worksheet so that we knew what area of the sky to look for our intended star. One navigator from Section A, B, and C stood on a stool, looking out the sextant port in the ceiling above their section. During the initial training flights all three were supposed to shoot the same star. The best rule of thumb was to hope that we all faced the same directions once we stood on a stool. Math errors could easily lead to some students facing 180 degrees from the intended stars. Sometimes "one of these navs didn't look like the others," to paraphrase the old *Sesame Street* song.

I cruised through both daytime and nighttime celestial navigation with 100s on all of the training rides and was #3 in my class of 30. Being in the Top 10% virtually assured me of my first choice of aircraft on Assignment Night, coming up in two weeks. This night was the moment we found out what airplane and to which Air Force base we would be assigned. An officer's entire life changed that night: it was a thrilling and nerve-wracking event.

I eagerly submitted my Dream Sheet of what I hoped to fly. On the top of my sheet were the F-111, FB-111, F-4, and RF-4, in that order. Behind them all, in a distant fifth was the B-52 bomber. I knew I wanted a combat aircraft and those five choices fit the bill. The F-111 and F-4 fighter aircraft all had two sets of flight controls, so even the navigator had a "stick." But in the F-111 and FB-111 the navigator sat beside the pilot, not behind him, like in the F-4 and RF-4. All I had to do was ace my daytime and nighttime celestial navigation evaluations and I knew a fighter assignment was mine.

The daytime celestial checkride (flight evaluation) consisted of three position fixes taken throughout the four-hour midday flight. Each position fix had to be within 5 miles of our actual position. Up to this point, all of my previous fixes on the training rides had been spot on. I ran my precomputations, completed the fixes and plotted the aircraft position on the navigation chart. To me, everything seemed to be going just great. At the end of the flight, each student rolled up his navigation chart and handed it to one of the three evaluators monitoring the flight. The charts would be graded overnight and the results debriefed in the next class. I slept well that night.

The next morning, we took our seats in the classroom and because I sat on the back row, the evaluators entered the room behind me. As they came into class, I was suddenly whacked upside the right side of my head by a rolled-up navigation chart. It was my instructor who looked at me and asked, "What's 16 minus 16?"

"Zero," I answered. *What a weird question for him to ask*, I thought.

"Well, yesterday you thought it was 10," he said shaking his head. Instantly, I knew that was not good. A critical math error meant my position fix was ten miles off and out of tolerance. But I also knew that one of the three fixes could be out of tolerance and I would still pass the checkride, but with a Good, instead of an Excellent rating.

I soon found out there was another problem. My checkride came at an unfortunate time. My second position fix was a Line of Position from the Sun, crossed with a radial from a VOR (VHF omnidirectional range) beacon in Wyoming. VOR stations are navigational beacons that give aircraft directional guidance. For one reason or another, I discovered that my second fix also fell outside of the 5-mile tolerance.

The next day, that particular VOR was posted as temporarily out of service. I can only assume that the radial reading I took during my checkride that day was not an accurate bearing. With two of my three fixes out of tolerance I failed the checkride with only two weeks before assignment night. Because of my near-perfect performance prior to that, and my successful completion of the nighttime celestial checkride, I was still projected to graduate on time. My class standing, however, fell from Top 10% to Top Third of the class. Not simply checking my math proved to be a pivotal moment in my life. That was my first episode of "Don't get cocky, Lieutenant Dale."

I was still hopeful I could get a fighter. After all, F-111s and F-4s don't have sextants or use celestial navigation, and I did well on the low-level and radar navigation evaluations. My flight commander, Captain Dahlgren, agreed. In the days leading up to Assignment Night, students in my class met with our flight commander and were given an assessment of our training performance and his thoughts on what aircraft we would receive. According to Captain Dahlgren and the other instructors, they thought I would receive an F-111, which really made me very relieved and excited.

One the other hand, the last flight in the T-43 was a low-level near the Grand Canyon, bouncing along in the stubby wing aircraft at 1,000 feet above the canyon rim. Nine of the twelve student navigators threw up on that turbulent flight. I was one of the three that did not. It looked like I could handle low-level flying in a large aircraft. Uh, oh. Although the aircraft assignments were made by the Air Force Personnel Center in San Antonio and not by the local Mather AFB training staff, I didn't like the way this was shaping up.

On Assignment Night, as I drove through the Mather AFB Main Gate, I told Karin, "I think I'm going to get a B-52. I have it too high up on my list." The Dream Sheet had room for 30 choices and many students put the old bomber at #30 and would have listed it even lower if they could have.

When my turn came, I was called up on stage and turned to face the crowd of classmates, spouses, and the navigator training staff. Captain Dahlgren said a few kind words about my performance and then announced, "Congratulations. You've been assigned to the 62nd Bomb Squadron at Barksdale AFB, Shreveport, Louisiana."

At that moment a picture of a B-52 flashed on the screen behind me.

I turned to face Captain Dahlgren and shook his outstretched hand. As we locked eyes I thought, *"That sure doesn't sound like the F-111 you thought I was going to get."* I'm certain he felt bad about getting my hopes up. Although I was prepared to receive a B-52 assignment, I was disappointed when it came true. All that Karin and I could think in this moment of confusion was, *"Where is Shreveport, Louisiana?"*

CHAPTER 9
RUNNING AROUND IN THE BUFF

B-52G taking off

B-52 training for navigators was a seven-month course at Castle AFB outside of Merced, in California's Central Valley. Navigators received an all-expense paid move to the California valley, to learn about the new Offensive Avionics System, or OAS. B-52 copilots arrived a month later to begin learning the aircraft's systems: hydraulics, electrics, pneumatics, and fuel systems.

These B-52G-models were built between 1958 and 1961 and were just coming out of a major bombing system upgrade. Leaving the key-punch card computer era behind, the B-52 now had a new bombing computer that received its data via metal cartridges rather than cards. It also got a new radar and inertial navigation system (INS) guiding it to a target.

The 1964 film dark comedy, *Dr. Strangelove,* was a good depiction of the inside of a B-52. The famous actor James Earl Jones portrayed was the radar navigator, known as the bombardier in World War II. He sat downstairs in the bomber to the left of the navigator, which is where I sat. In the bomber crew hierarchy, all navigators started in the right navigator seat. Then after two years, we typically upgraded to the left seat to become the radar navigator, just like a copilot starts in the right seat and upgrades to aircraft commander in the left seat. Strangely enough, I remembered our high school civics class watching *Dr. Strangelove* during my senior year in 1980. Now, five years later, I was training to be a B-52 crewmember.

Leading up to our first actual training mission, we watched several training films of B-52 incidents or accidents. Although their purpose was to instill a safety mindset or demonstrate the importance of teamwork in overcoming a bad situation, these definitely were not confidence boosters. One accident caught on grainy black and white film captured a B-52 crash-landing, then breaking apart as it slid off the runway into the grass. The cockpit portion snapped off to the side of the runway and the entire crew scrambled out before the bomber burst into flames. In the love/hate relationship we all had with our B-52s, we referred to the old bomber as the BUFF, which stood for Big, Ugly, Fat "Fellow" -- except the last word wasn't "fellow."

At that time, the B-52 had a six-man crew. The pilot team consisted of two pilots with the aircraft commander (AC) in the left seat and the copilot (CP) in the right. There was also an electronic warfare officer (EWO) and an enlisted gunner who sat facing aft, behind the pilots. The radar navigator and navigator sat on a lower level, under the pilots, but facing forward. In 1992, following the collapse of the Soviet Union, the gunner position was removed from the crew. By the mid-90s, women joined the combat crew force.

Training missions typically lasted seven to nine hours so that the crew was ready for the rigors of actual long-range bombing missions. The missions consisted of a rendezvous with a KC-135 or KC-10 tanker for mid-air refueling, followed by simulated high-altitude bomb drops and Air-Launched Cruise Missile (ALCM) releases.

The intense portion came next, as we descended into a low-level route over the Midwest, flying at about 400 to 1,000 feet above the ground, depending upon the cloud cover and weather.

When the time came for my first takeoff in the BUFF, I was pretty nervous. Before departing for an eight-hour training mission I stood for several minutes in the bathroom of Base Operations, not throwing up, but nervously trying to pee. Once onboard, there would only be a stand-pipe to use as a urinal, which often proved difficult on a bumpy flight.

With the training videos of mishaps lodged in my head, I wondered that night as the plane lumbered toward the runway if it was the exception or the rule that our flight would end successfully. Once off the ground and underway, I was too busy doing my job to think about anything bad happening.

We spent the next several hours flying around the western U.S., refueling behind a KC-135 tanker over Arizona, then descending into a low-level route over southern Colorado and New Mexico. We spent the next hour flying at the height of a modern-day cellular tower. The mission concluded with 45 minutes of practice landings (called touch and go's) for both of the pilots sitting directly above us.

My radar navigator during this training was a middle-aged major just returning to the B-52 following his air staff tour. As we taxied back into our parking spot at the end of that first flight, he couldn't contain himself any longer and threw up in his ever-present barf bag. Throughout all of my years of flying, getting airsick was one fate I never experienced.

The navigator is in charge of ensuring the aircraft stays on course and on time. He or she is responsible for overall crew pacing from preflight through arrival back home. Performing that job instilled a sense of timing that has stuck with me for the rest of my life. I hate running late and have difficulty being around folks with poor time-management skills. I fidget irritably in a group setting when a person rambles along with a story even though the meeting was supposed to end in five minutes. That lack of timing awareness grates on my nerves. Time's up! Move along!

Our low-level routes were flown over the farmlands of Kansas, Nebraska, the Dakotas, Colorado, and the deserts of Nevada and New Mexico. Each route had three bombing targets separated approximately twenty minutes apart along the twisting, turning route, over rolling pastures and around small towns. In an era before GPS was available, navigators used two-prong compass dividers to plot the aircraft's coordinates on paper charts. My job was to keep the plane within four miles of the route centerline.

Up at cruise altitude we still wore our flight helmets but allowed the oxygen mask to hang from one side. It was more comfortable that way and it typically wasn't important for us to talk instantly to the rest of the crew. If we needed to communicate, we'd raise the mask to our face and speak into the embedded microphone. At low altitude, however, each crewmember cinched the oxygen mask containing the mic tightly to our faces so we could continuously talk while working with both hands. If anything went wrong at this low altitude, we were immediately ready to eject.

Important safety note: The downstairs navigator ejection seats ejected downward. The minimum altitude for ejection was listed as 150 feet in our operating manual. This allowed for our ejection seats to blast out of the bottom of the aircraft. The navigators would then be propelled from their seats, and the parachutes opened just seconds before impact. We called that "one swing in the chute." At that low altitude, navigators knew we would probably still be traveling close to 100 mph when we hit the ground. Good luck.

The dangers we faced with low-level flying weren't just theoretical. I've known two bomber crews that crashed during low-level training missions. One involved a B-1 bomber that hit the rugged mountains at night in south Texas near the Mexico border. The radar navigator, Captain Scott Genal, had been a B-52 navigator friend of mine at Barksdale AFB before transferring to the brand-new B-1. All of the crewmembers died on impact.

The second crash involved a B-52 from a northern base that clipped the top of a pencil-thin peak in Arizona while descending into a low-level training route. The damage from the glancing blow was bad enough that the pilot knew the plane was unrecoverable. He pulled up quickly after striking the peak and began to roll the big bomber, commanding, "Bail out! Bail out! Bail out!" Everyone with an ejection seat immediately grabbed the yellow ejection handle between their legs and punched out. Because of the aircraft rolling sideways, all six crew members had an equal-opportunity to escape as both the upstairs and downstairs ejection seats blasted out of the now sideways bomber.

The navigator on that flight was a living testament for Nomex flame-retardant flightsuits worn by military crews. He descended in his parachute as the bomber exploded and he drifted through the aircraft's fireball. Miraculously, his only burn marks were on his wrists and the back of his neck, his only exposed areas. Although six people survived the crash, there were two other instructors on board, one pilot and one navigator, who did not. Instructors were not afforded an ejection seat and occupied a metal box seat. Neither instructor was able to escape through the holes left from the now-departed ejection seats, probably due to the centrifugal force of the rolling airplane. Sadly, they both died in the crash.

The B-52 low-level missions were exhilarating, requiring intense concentration from all six crewmembers for almost an hour and a half. Each of the three bombing runs started by arriving at the Initial Point (IP) on time. The IP was the last navigation point before we reached the target and the beginning of the bombing run. From there, the radar navigator provided steering data to the pilot's display upstairs. As long as the pilot kept the two lines centered and flew the speeds we requested, the bomber arrived at the release point on time. The pre-release checklist was succinctly choreographed, with each step called out by me and replied to over interphone by the appropriate crewmember.

Although the B-52 (with a 185-foot wingspan) flew low to evade simulated enemy radar, the bomb release altitude was a bit higher. Seconds before the release the pilots began a short, abrupt climb. This allowed the bombs to be pitched or lobbed toward the target. Finally, the radar nav would announce, "Bombs away," indicating the weapon had been released. During training missions, the only thing released was an electronic signal for scoring. On a real-world combat mission, a drag chute deployed on the bombs, and they would drift slowly down to the ground as the bomber escaped.

The pilots quickly changed course to the next target and pitched down to 400 feet again, creating negative Gs, and a floating sensation in the cockpit. Any unsecured objects (ink pens or my sharp pointed dividers) floated around the cockpit if we weren't careful. It was quite a roller coaster ride! About twenty minutes later the sequence repeated itself until the final simulated bomb release. After the last "Bombs away!" call-out, instead of pitching over, the pilots continued climbing the eight-engine bomber out of the low-level route and back up to high altitude for the flight back to our base. During this climb, I would drop my mask, lean back from my tabletop, and take a long swig of water from a nearby bottle. I could finally relax a bit for the flight home.

B-52 missions required detailed planning from all six crewmembers because the training route covered so much territory as the mission progressed from air refueling to high altitude bomb and missile releases to low level routes and then back to base. Planning a mission took an entire day before the actual flight. My final B-52 checkride from Castle AFB was scheduled for January 29, 1986. Mission-planning day was January 28, and as we all huddled around the charts that morning, a major walked in at around 8:45 a.m. telling us the Space Shuttle Challenger had just exploded. It was a somber moment as we let the news sink in.

We were told that if we did not feel up to taking our checkride the next day it would be understandable. Although it was a terrible tragedy, we completed the planning, then headed home to watch the news updates about the shuttle explosion and the repeated scenes of the horrific mishap. Our crew knew we were well-prepared for our final evaluation, and all showed up early the next morning to fly our seven-hour checkride. By the end of January, I was a qualified BUFF Nav and Karin and I packed up our Monte Carlo for the move to Louisiana.

CHAPTER 10
BARKSDALE B-52 HIJINKS

Photo of the 62nd Bomb Squadron at Barksdale AFB in 1986

I called my grandfather to tell him the news of my B-52 assignment earlier that year, telling him over the phone, "Papa, I'm going to Barksdale Air Force Base. That's in Shreveport, Louisiana."

He chuckled and replied, "I know where Barksdale is. I helped build that base."

My grandfather was born in 1908 and as a single 23-year-old man in 1931, he rented a small room in the Shreveport YMCA while he coordinated the MoPac train shipments of material for building the air base outside of Bossier City. This two-year project near the Red River was the job that saw my grandfather through the Great Depression. Knowing I now had a family connection to Barksdale helped shed a positive light on my less-than-ideal assignment.

Flying on a B-52 crew had its highlights. Although the B-52 may not have been a popular assignment to receive, the camaraderie of working with the same six-man team and enjoying each other's company, as well as getting to know their families, helped me enjoy my job. This was the beginning of a very gratifying Air Force career.

My aircraft commander during initial qualification training in California was Major Glenn Lunsford. We both were assigned to the 62nd Bomb Squadron (62 BMS) at Barksdale AFB, arriving in February, 1986. New crew members were typically combined with experienced crew members to form bomber crews. Major Lunsford and I were paired together as part of a permanent crew. Major Lunsford's copilot was First Lieutenant Dan McMillan, and later First Lieutenant Stan Buelt joined our crew as well. Captain Joe Wolf, six years older than I, was the radar navigator. The electronic warfare officer (EWO for short, or simply "E-Dub") was First Lieutenant Alan McGreer and finally, our gunner was Airman First Class Mike Barker.

Major Lunsford, or Glenn, as only Karin and the other spouses could call him, was a chain-smoking 35-year-old, soon-to-be-divorced Californian with thinning blond hair. He reluctantly returned to the B-52 after a Pentagon staff tour where he worked in the targeting office, planning strikes against the USSR. Even at 35-years old, he was the old man and adult supervision of our crew.

Captain Joe Wolf was the same age as my brother, Jack. Joe hailed from Baltimore, but joined the Air Force after obtaining his biology degree from the University of Tampa, which would later be our daughter's university. Joe told me early on, "You know what you do with a biology degree? Join the Air Force and become a navigator."

Joe was a lean, athletic triathlete, excelling in swimming, biking, and running. He had a narrow face with a sharp, pointed nose and wispy blond hair. Joe tackled every challenge with 110% effort. When he took up tennis, he bought the latest high-tech big-face racket and the tennis apparel to look the part. Once he became interested in golf, he immediately started making his own clubs and made my first set, too.

On a rare B-52 trip away from Barksdale, our crew flew a bomber to Tinker AFB, near Oklahoma City. Taking advantage of this rare off-base trip, Joe, Al, and I packed our golf clubs in the huge storage compartment behind the bomb bay. Once we changed out of our flight suits, we headed to the base golf course, as all Air Force officers should.

We were true golf novices but I knew enough not to tee off from the Women's red tee box markers, or the blue markers for the pros, so Al and I walked up to the Men's white tee box. Mr. Athlete, Joe Wolf, stood back at the blue markers and yelled, "Get back here, you wussies!"

Alan and I grabbed our tees and balls and sauntered back toward Joe, at the blue professional tee box. We then proceeded to spray our tee shots in quite a military fashion; our three golf balls flew left, right, and left from the intended fairway. At that moment the loud speaker from the pro shop announced for all to hear, "Will the party on the first tee please move up to the white tees." Thanks, Joe. Golf is a stupid game.

Alan, the EWO, provided our self-defense by electronically jamming enemy radar and dispensing chaff (small, long strips of metal) and flares to confuse incoming missiles. Mike, the gunner, was the only enlisted crewmember, and though sitting in the cockpit alongside the aft-facing EWO, he controlled the tail-mounted 50-caliber machine guns and had a tiny four-inch scope to hopefully track any attacking fighters behind us. His job was to shoot at any enemy fighter that got close enough for a gun kill.

We used to tease Mike, asking if he brought a roll of quarters for his video game, since that is what his gunner's station looked like. His system was so low-tech that even he knew his job was to spray-and-pray, throwing out enough lead to hopefully hit something. The gunner was a carry-over from the days before accurate air-to-air missiles were widely used. In reality, an enemy fighter no longer needed to get within machine-gun range and the gunner's position was eventually removed.

The vast majority of our training missions took off and landed from our home base. It was always known that Strategic Air Command (SAC) provided a stable family life because we were rarely away overnight. Barksdale had two squadrons of twelve B-52s (24 bombers on the base) and each crew spent one week out of every four to six weeks on nuclear alert. Sitting alert, as it was called, was similar to being a fireman on duty at a firehouse, only our rotation was 24/7 for a full week. At other smaller SAC bases this rotation was once every three weeks and could be a real morale killer. Once our crew gained experience, flying the same training missions and always returning to Louisiana started to become routine. Fortunately, our crew got a break from the routine when we were selected to head to England in the fall of 1986 for a month of flying.

Each fall, four crews and two bombers deployed to the Royal Air Force (RAF) Fairford, near Swindon, in southwest England. From there, we flew live bombing missions over the North Sea Texel Islands off the coast of the Netherlands. Other missions flew over France and West Germany to a low-level route along the East German border, or we practiced anti-shipping operations over the Mediterranean Sea. This specialized off-station training was far better than flying the same nine-hour flights over a Midwestern prairie. The annual Busy Brewer Exercise, as it was officially named, was definitely considered a Good Deal Tour at the height of the Cold War. It also came several months after our Air Force's F-111 raid on Colonel Muammar Gaddafi's bases in Libya. Pictures of our B-52s were splashed across the front pages of the British newspapers as the press speculated that we were there to conduct a follow-up raid.

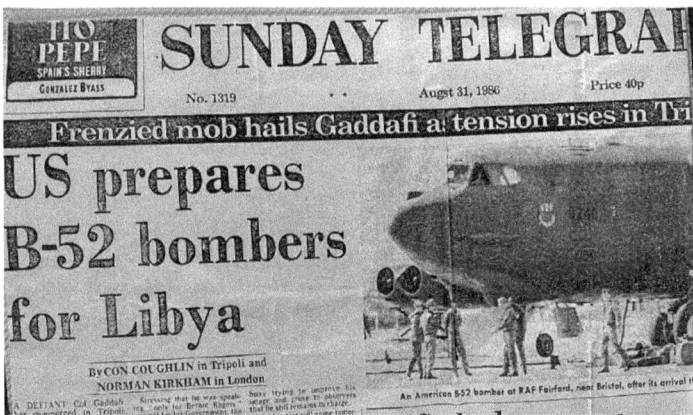

British headline the day we arrived in England for Busy Brewer

Alan and I roomed together in a small hotel room. He was one year older and married to Davilynn, a Sacramento native whom he met while at nav school. Our room phone rang in the dead of night at 0230, startling us both. Davilynn didn't realize the time zone difference and couldn't wait to share her news. Since he was away, she bought a cute little Shih Tzu puppy for $400. This was at the time when lieutenants made $800 every two weeks.

"A what?!" he asked. "I don't even know what that is!"

After hanging up, Al looked at me and said, "She bought a $400 dog! Do you even know what a Shih Tzu is?"

"It's a little white dog about the size of a football," I told him. "You should call it Wilson." And from that day forward, Alan referred to Davilynn's precious puppy as Wilson.

Meanwhile, I had two navigator friends flying the F-111 fighter-bombers from RAF Lakenheath and RAF Upper Heyford. One was Jim Thomas, my college and nav school roommate, and the other was a nav school classmate. One of them asked me if we would take the B-52 down Loch Ness in Scotland at low level the way they did. Apparently, it was allowed and even condoned, since the British loved military aviation.

One afternoon, our planned B-52 mission over central Europe was scrubbed due to bad weather. On this particular flight, our wing commander, Colonel Eugene Habiger, an experienced B-52 pilot himself, joined us. As a back-up plan, I took my F-111 friend's advice and came up with a routing, flying counter-clockwise around the east coast of England, up to the northern coast of Scotland, then down the Loch Ness at 500 to 1000 feet above the water, before returning to RAF Fairford.

Besides working in a compartment with a downward ejection seat, the navigator station also lacks windows. To give us a view of the outside world, the B-52 has two cameras under the nose. These are the two bulges or blisters seen below the cockpit in B-52 photographs. One of the cameras is Forward-Looking Infra-Red, also known as a FLIR, and the other was a low-light television, LLTV. These cameras provided night vision on television screens at both the downstairs navigator stations and on the pilots' display panels. As navigator, I had a trackball that I could use to swivel the cameras up, down, left, and right.

Our B-52 dropped down over Loch Ness and cruised over the water, slightly higher than the cliffs on both sides. I swiveled the cameras left and right, viewing the old stone buildings along the Loch. It was a quick trip down the Loch and as we climbed out of low-level Colonel Habiger said over our plane's interphone, "That was nice, but it's a bit like our Grand Canyon, so I don't think anyone else should do that." Good thing I got to see it when I did.

In the evenings, the four bomber crews would go to a local Swindon pub and enjoy this new life in England. That dark pub, with its low ceiling of heavy timbers and clouds of cigarette smoke, was my first experience drinking British ale or Strongbow hard cider. Other times I ordered a lager shandy, which was beer mixed with their "lemonade," our version of 7-Up. This was completely new to me and helped offset the bitter hoppy taste of the English lager. While in the pub one evening, one of the other crew's gunners revealed that he would be turning 21 the following week. The news made its way from the crew to the owner/bartender, Gerald. "Leave it to me," he said with a wink.

At 10:45 p.m. each night, Gerald yelled, "Last call, Gentlemen!" meaning we had fifteen minutes to finish our drinks and be out the door before the mandatory closing time of 11:00 p.m. On the following Friday, word passed quietly among the American crews to only meander toward the door but let the British patrons leave first. As the last British customer left precisely at 11:00, we stayed behind and Gerald closed the door. Todd's 21st Birthday Bash officially began, and we all raised a pint in his honor. At 11:15 there was a loud banging on the door and when Gerald opened it, in walked two Bobbies. Uh, oh. The male cop chastised us for being in the pub after closing time and asked who was responsible. Gerald pointed at young Todd and calmly said, "He is." Todd was confused, scared, and stammered, "This wasn't MY idea!"

Decked out in a British police hat and uniform blouse, the lady Bobbie walked over to Todd and commanded, "Put out your hands!" Todd stuck his hands out in front, expecting to be hand-cuffed, but she grabbed his left hand with her right and placed it firmly on her breast. Yes, catching us all by surprise, Gerald had hired a stripper for the occasion. As the celebration progressed into the night, our pudgy weather officer, a captain deployed with us from Barksdale, informed us, "It's my birthday next week, you know."

After a month in England, our crew returned to Barksdale AFB and we resumed our rotation of sitting nuclear alert. We ate three meals each day in the alert facility's chow hall and Joe and I shared a small dormitory-style room with two twin beds. The alert facility housed aircraft maintenance personnel and the eight six-man B-52 crews and eight four-person KC-135 crews. It was like a firehouse packed with up to 80 men, plus a few women from the KC-135 crews, for the next seven days. (Women joined the B-52 crew force ten years later.)

Outside of the alert facility, rows of blue Chevy pick-up trucks were parked, one for each crew, so that we could respond quickly to our aircraft when the klaxon went off. That blaring horn signified that we needed to respond immediately to our aircraft, start engines and decode an encrypted message. The message from SAC head-quarters instructed us whether or not to taxi to the runway and also whether this was a training event or the actual beginning of World War III. The wartime scenario we trained for assumed that Russian submarines had launched missiles at our military bases. We had only a few minutes to get airborne and be on our way to return fire over the Soviet Union with the cruise missiles mounted on our wings and the large bombs held in the bomb bay.

One night, the klaxon sounded and our crews responded quickly to the aircraft and started the eight engines. The decoded message stated that it was a training exercise, but we were all to taxi to the runway, as though it were an actual launch. Taxiing a heavily-laden B-52 with live weapons on board down the runway, then returning to the alert pad was a daunting task. As Major Lunsford completed the slow trip down the runway and turned back towards the alert pad, he asked our copilot, Stan, "Hey Co. Do you want to taxi the jet for a little while?"

"Sure!" replied Lieutenant Stan Buelt as he placed his hands on the bomber's eight throttles and steered the bomber straight ahead with his rudder pedals and brakes.

A few moments passed, then Major Lunsford made the dramatic statement, "Co, do you realize that you are right now in control of the world's third largest nuclear power?" Although exaggerating, he was saying that the bombs and missiles we had in our B-52 exceeded the nuclear firepower of most countries except the U.S. and USSR.

As the significance sank in, Major Lunsford said, "Wait a minute. I have the aircraft back," and he resumed control of our lumbering BUFF.

Sitting alert just one week after returning from England, our crew was told to report to the base clinic for a TB-Tine test, since we had been out of the country for a month. Of our entire crew, only our gunner Mike was still single. While in England, he met a lovely young British lady named Sally, and she eventually would become his wife. Mike and Sally enjoyed a few weeks of togetherness during a whirlwind romance before we returned home. As he and I strolled down the hallway toward our pick-up truck, Mike asked, "Why do we have to go to the clinic?"

Without any forethought, I quickly responded, "Probably to see if we brought back any sexually transmitted diseases."

Mike said, "Nooooo. Really?!" but I just let it go.

We dutifully walked into the immunization clinic and had our forearms pricked, knowing we would return three days later to have the results examined. Once back in the truck, only Joe and I sat in the bed of the pickup truck while Mike and the others all took seats in the cab. I told Joe about my "STD" comment to Mike. Joe laughed and said, "Oh that's good! We can do something with that."

The day before returning to get our tests checked, Joe called the immunization clinic and told the young technical sergeant about our upcoming prank on Mike, and he readily agreed to go along.

On the third day, our crew returned to the clinic and one by one showed the sergeant our forearms. Everyone was in the clear until Mike put his arm out.

"Oh wow. This might be a problem," the technician said.

"What?!" Mike exclaimed. "Mine looks the same as theirs!"

But the med tech did a great job of getting out a micrometer and measured the spot several times, making his arm redder with each press. The tech then asked, "Who's in charge of your crew?"

Major Lunsford, going along with the joke, quickly stepped forward and replied, "I am."

The tech looked very serious and explained, "Sir, we need to make some calls and see about getting this guy off alert."

Mike interrupted, "Whoa! We're not calling ANYBODY!"

At that point I was biting my lip to keep from laughing, so I stepped out into the hallway. There, a young mother was waiting with her grade-school-aged daughter for school immunizations. She asked me what was going on in there and I told her about the STD joke we were playing on Mike since he met someone in England. She said with a smile, "Oh, y'all are bad!"

The scam continued inside the clinic as Major Lunsford pretended to make a phone call to the alert facility to remove Mike from alert status. Moments later the whole crew came out of the clinic, Mike still thinking he had tested positive for an embarrassing disease. While I did not instigate what happened next, I couldn't have planned it better. As Mike walked past the young mom, she reached out and patted his shoulder and with great sympathy said, "Everything will be alright."

Mike looked around at all of us and yelled, "Does EVERYBODY know?!"

At that point we couldn't contain ourselves any longer and all burst out laughing. He knew he had been had. Having a young enlisted troop on our crew provided some pretty fun moments.

Capt Alan McGreer (EWO), me with headphones, SrA Mike Barker
(Gunner), and Capt Gordy Neff (Evaluator Navigator).
Standing by our Barksdale B-52G while visiting Hill AFB, Utah.

CHAPTER 11
A CRAPPY FLIGHT

Throughout my career I worked with many memorable Air Force leaders and learned a lot from several of them. Many provided positive lessons on effective leadership, while others taught me lessons on what not to do. Most of my leaders served as positive role models, but occasionally, there were those I wouldn't want to emulate.

One night we had to fly a B-52 training mission with our operations officer tagging along as the instructor pilot. For this story, his last name was Bright and he was not well thought of within the squadron, so to us his call sign was NotSo. We were flying a nighttime mission that concluded with a one-hour low-level route over La Junta, Colorado and New Mexico. With the low-level portion completed, we climbed back up to 31,000 feet for the two-hour flight across Texas back to Barksdale AFB.

Once we leveled off at high altitude, NotSo came on the interphone and said, "Guys, I'm really not feeling well. I need to clear off and use the honey-bucket." Our 1959-model B-52 was built to accommodate a six-man combat crew. There was no flush toilet. Just a stand-pipe to pee in and a metal box with a plastic-lined hole to poop in, affectionately known as "the honey bucket." The mantra among B-52 crews was, "You don't poop where you work." Taking a dump was strictly verboten … unless you're the operations officer with diarrhea. Then you get to foul up the cockpit for everyone within the twenty-foot radius of the honey bucket. That man made our eyes water, even after he tied off the plastic bag.

We still had over an hour to cruise before returning to Barksdale for the mandatory 30-minutes of approaches, allowing the pilots to practice their touch-and-go landings at 10:00 p.m. for all of Bossier City to enjoy. But NotSo had an idea. "Guys, let's drop down to 10,000 feet, depressurize, and I'll put the bag in the forward wheel well."

As described earlier, the B-52 had two levels, with both pilots, the electronic warfare officer and the gunner sitting on the upper level, and the two navigators sitting below the pilots. Behind the navigator seats in the lower level was a small door that led to the wheel well and the bomb bay beyond. After live weapons drops it was the navigator's job to crawl through the door, over the massive tires of the forward wheels and along the catwalk to peer into the bomb bay to ensure there weren't any live bombs hanging from the bomb racks or on the bomb bay doors. It's not neighborly to accidentally drop live weapons on our fellow countrymen. NotSo's idea was to open the small door and place his stinking bag of poop on the wheels with the hope that when the gear doors opened over northwest Louisiana, the offending bag would drop harmlessly from the bomber, and we would complete our training mission.

With the bag now resting on the landing gear, we repressurized the cabin, climbed back up to altitude and completed our trip to Barksdale. The gear doors opened, and the pilots both completed their obligatory touch and go landings. After the final full-stop landing, we taxied to our assigned parking spot and waited as the crew chief plugged in his headset. As the eight engines wound to a stop, we could hear the sergeant yell, "Oh my God! What the hell?!"

It seems the offending bag of poop had other ideas than to drop to the earth below. In a confounding display of fluid dynamics, once the landing gear doors opened the air swirled around and around in the wheel well like a tornado. Sadly, our sorry sack of shit managed to smear itself all over the gear well, becoming the smelliest graffiti ever. As we started to download all of the crew gear, I heard the crew chief tell NotSo, "I am NOT cleaning this up!"

We clambered aboard the crew van and went to the maintenance debrief, never knowing how that crappy night ended.

Chapter 12

Blue Ribbon Crew

Our B-52 crew continued to work together for a year and a half, rising through the crew ranks from R (Ready) crew, to E (Experienced) crew to S (Select) crew. Select crews were normally assigned to the Standardization and Evaluation (Stan/Eval) division, but Major Lunsford's S-61 crew held the distinction of progressing rapidly up the chain and became one of the few non-evaluator Select crews.

I found the saying "Timing is everything" to be quite true in both bad ways and good. My career got off to a slow start because there weren't enough pilot slots to go around. Now, thanks to the Reagan administration's military buildup, the Air Force greatly needed pilots in the late 1980's. The annual quota of navigators accepted for pilot training had just doubled from 50 to 100. Competition was pretty stiff, considering there were hundreds of navigators vying for those 100 slots. Additionally, a navigator had to serve two years as a nav before applying for Undergraduate Pilot Training (UPT) and had to be in training by age 27.

In the spring of 1986, I was one year into my B-52 navigator assignment. The 2nd Bomb Wing at Barksdale AFB was preparing for its Operational Readiness Inspection, or ORI. This was a make-or-break event in SAC, dating back to its founder, General Curtis LeMay. Jimmy Stewart's 1955 movie, *Strategic Air Command* is a great depiction of how important passing an ORI was to a bomber unit and the crewmembers who took part.

The ORI tested the base's ability to carry out its nuclear mission. Failing it resulted in the firing of the wing commander. The crews had to pass a written evaluation and selected crews were chosen to fly an inflight evaluation. At the very least, we wanted to pass. At most, we hoped to be recognized as a SAC Blue Ribbon Crew. This meant we excelled at both the written test and inflight evaluation. The test portion concluded with a scenario-based question and depending upon timing calculations, the crew had to decide whether to drop a nuclear bomb on a target or not. We could elect to withhold the release of our nuke and if the correct answer was to drop, then we just had points deducted for a wrong answer. But if we elected to release the bomb when the correct answer was to withhold, then our crew would fail, and we would immediately become unqualified air crew members. It was also likely that our entire wing would fail. Nothing like a little bit of pressure!

As we went through the scenario, we ran the calculations again and again and each time came up with the answer to Release our nuke over the target. Joe was insistent that it was the right answer, but we all had to agree on "Release" being the right answer to go for it. We opted to Release and nervously awaited the results. We were correct! What a relief.

The following day, we boarded our B-52 for an eight-hour training flight that included one and a half hours at a low-level route through both South and North Dakota. After striking the three simulated low-level targets on time, we returned home to a late-night landing. As we climbed down the short crew-entry ladder the two ranking colonels of the base leadership met us, smiling broadly. The wing director of operations (Wing/DO) shook each of our hands, telling us how proud he was of our timing and bombing results.

Days later, Crew S-61 was honored to learn we had earned the elite status of B-52 Blue Ribbon Crew during the Reagan-era Cold War. Our crew's performance contributed to the 62nd Bomb Squadron and 2nd Bomb Wing winning both the Sweeney and the Kenney Trophies for the highest bombing effectiveness results of the 1986 Strategic Air Command Operational Readiness Inspection (SAC ORI). As an instructor and Blue Ribbon Crew navigator, my application for pilot training grew stronger.

S-61 Blue Ribbon Crew
L-R: Senior Airman Mike Barker (Gunner), 1st Lt Van Heckman (EWO), me,
1st Lt Stan Buelt (Copilot), Major Glenn Lunsford (Aircraft Commander),
Lt Col Randy Wooten (62nd Bomb Squadron Commander).
Unfortunately, Capt Joe Wolf (Radar Navigator) is not pictured.

At this point in my progression, I could have opted for a quick upgrade to radar navigator or become an evaluator navigator in the Stan/Eval office. Knowing that I wanted to get to pilot training as quickly as possible, I decided that spending the next year as an evaluator probably looked better on my resume than becoming a radar nav on a newly formed Ready-crew.

I was only 25 and told Karin that the Air Force would probably try to get more time out of me as a navigator. Regardless, I built a pilot training application package that included an endorsement signed by the 7th Air Division two-star general, bolstered by my status as a Blue Ribbon crew member. I submitted my pilot training candidate package in the summer of 1987 and crossed my fingers.

In November 1987, I was paged to the squadron commander's office, where Lieutenant Colonel Randy Wooten, a 6' 4" East Texan, stood waiting. With a big grin on his face, he handed me a letter, signed by our 2nd Bomb Wing commander, Colonel Brett Dula. I stared at the official Air Force letterhead and read the words I longed for: "Congratulations on the selection of Lt Dale as a primary selection to attend Undergraduate Pilot Training."

I'm not one to whoop or holler, but with a huge smile, I thanked my squadron commander while shaking his hand. I was on my way to Vance AFB, a pilot training base in Enid, Oklahoma. Finally!

CHAPTER 13

WILD BLUE YONDER

UPT CLASS 89-05
VANCE AFB

11 FEB 88 - 16 FEB 89

To become an Air Force pilot, trainees attend a rigorous 12-month course, preferably somewhere with very few distractions ... like Enid, Oklahoma. Karin and I packed up our two cars and two dogs, a cocker spaniel and a beagle, on Super Bowl weekend in February 1988. We moved into a 1400-square-foot, $400-per-month rental house on the outskirts of Enid, a farming and oil town in western Oklahoma.

Undergraduate Pilot Training, or UPT, began with four months of aviation academics and specialized training, such as experiencing the high-altitude environment in an altitude chamber, and undergoing basic parachute training. Once complete, students head to the flight-line for flight training. Students received 80 flying hours in the T-37, an under-powered twin-engine jet, learning acrobatics and instrument flying. We then transitioned to the supersonic T-38 jet trainer for 120 flight hours of acrobatics, formation flying, and instrument flying. The biggest difference between the two was that the T-38 was a faster, more responsive jet, once used by the Air Force Thunderbirds in the 1980s.

Our class began, like most others, with thirty students, most of them second lieutenants right out of college. As a first lieutenant, I was one of three senior officers in my class. I was joined by Skip Shoenheit, another first lieutenant B-52 navigator from Minot AFB, North Dakota, and Lori, a female captain maintenance officer from McConnell AFB, near Wichita, Kansas. Lori was the highest-ranking officer, so she was the senior ranking officer, or SRO, of our pilot training class. Skip was #2 in line with a date of rank higher than mine. That was fine with me. I felt this meant I could concentrate on learning to fly and graduating.

Pilot training got off to a good start for me, probably due to my experience as a navigator and because I already had 125 hours of private flying. I was also familiar with Air Training Command written tests, and had already gone through several altitude chambers to get a sense of hypoxia and the benefit of our oxygen masks. Although I had not piloted an Air Force plane, I had begun to develop situational awareness, and I no longer felt claustrophobic wearing an oxygen mask. I could also talk on the radio without getting tongue-tied and nervous. Some of my classmates, on the other hand, had hardly ever flown before.

After completing academics, our class went parasailing in the flatlands of Oklahoma. The ejection seat sequence only takes a few seconds, but pilots have to learn how to hit the ground to minimize the impact and injury to our body. Just like the "banana" landing technique I was taught while skydiving in Austin during college, the proper sequence of touchdown was feet, side of one leg, then roll to our backs, letting our body gracefully absorb the impact. This three-step method was the textbook Parachute Landing Fall, or PLF. Its counterpart is the PFL, or Poor Fucking Landing, which consists of feet, knees, and face-plant. The objective of our Oklahoma Parasailing Excursion was to learn the PLF, and not the PFL. Once successfully completed, we headed to the flightline.

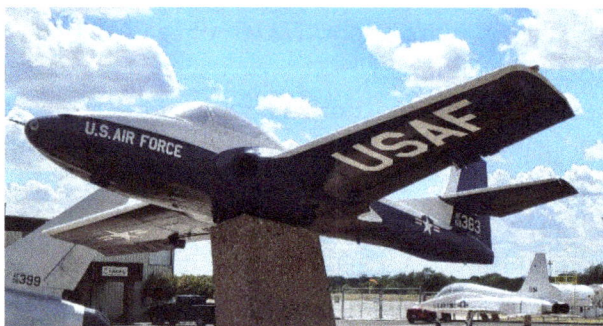

The T-37 is now a museum piece. T-38 in background.
(Photo by Dan Smallwood)

On the first day of T-37 training I met my instructor pilot, or IP, First Lieutenant "Vic" Morrow. Vic was his call sign because his last name was the same as the popular 1970's actor Victor "Vic" Morrow. At this point, it was time for everyone to receive their first Air Force call sign. Many were a play on their actual name. Lieutenant Lee enjoyed a quick promotion (in call sign only) to General. Lieutenant Kling became Static, while Lieutenant Schweinberg became Pig Mountain, then just Pig for short.

Some call signs were geographical, so a pilot from Oklahoma became Okie, while another from the Tennessee Smoky Mountains announced Smokey for his call sign before another classmate, Lieutenant Robinson, could grab it. Lieutenant Brian Robinson, our only African American in the class, went by Velcro, which I don't think would be allowed today. After graduating from pilot training, Brian later changed from Velcro to Smokey, and progressed up the ranks, now serving as a three-star general.

I successfully avoided the call sign of "There" that Karin had given me. During my previous two years in B-52s, SAC decided to include first names as well as last names on our flightsuit name tags. Our radar navigator, Joe Wolf, thought it would be funny for our whole crew to order an additional set of nametags with the last name of Yossarian, the infamous bombardier from *Catch-22*. The six of us "Yossarians" walked through the Barksdale Base Exchange (BX) making the cashiers think we were all brothers. With that precedent, I became Yossarian, then Yos for short. Kind of lame, I'll admit, but at least it wasn't embarrassing. After UPT, I never went by Yos again. Most of my Air Force friends have called me Double-D or D2. I should have gone with that call sign.

Within the first few minutes of meeting my instructor, Lieutenant Morrow, we both realized we were 1984 college graduates and I learned that he had attended the University of Colorado at Boulder. When I told him that my dad still lived in Parker, south of Denver, he happily announced, "T-37 cross-country to Colorado!"

That was a great idea! The only problem was that I had to pass three checkrides and numerous ground evaluations before the Good Deal cross-country trip could be scheduled. It certainly made for a nice incentive, though.

The first checkride in pilot training is called the Mid-Phase Contact checkride. Its purpose was to prove that student pilots could handle the aircraft by accomplishing specific acrobatics and performing a dizzying spin recovery. I was the first one in my class to take the Mid-Phase checkride, undergoing a one-hour ground evaluation, answering my evaluator's questions, followed by a one-hour, twenty-minute flight. I passed with an Excellent (on a scale of Outstanding, Excellent, and Good), so I was off to a strong start.

Each morning of training began with a Morning Briefing telling us what was to take place that day. The briefing ended with a Situation of the Day. These situations were meant to be stressful scenarios, designed to make trainees think about and state how they would correctly handle a specific emergency. The IP stood at the podium, described a flying scenario, including the weather, what the jet's instruments were reading and other important details. Then he would give a clue about the impending malfunction. We all listened intently, not knowing who would be called upon to answer. After running through the scenario, the instructor would pause and look around the room before continuing.

"Lieutenant Morgan! You have the aircraft."

Lieutenant Morgan would stand and could ask questions to verify the situation and then apply the correct checklist steps verbatim from memory. If at any point, Lieutenant Morgan said the wrong thing, the IP would shout, "Sit down!" and that disheartened student would not fly that day. A dreaded Pink Sheet would be added to his training folder, indicating a deficiency, and the IP would move on to his next victim.

"Lieutenant Smith! You have the aircraft."

Lieutenant Smith would proceed to spout out the correct procedures until the T-37 was safely back on the ground.

Having already completed Undergraduate Navigator Training, I can attest that UPT was intentionally and definitely more stressful. Navigator training focused on academics and was mainly a mental exercise. We were certainly nervous before each test or navigation checkride, but there was a different element in UPT. Pilot training was not only physical, as we controlled the airplane as it danced around the sky, but it was also purposefully stressful. This ensured we could react correctly under pressure. Those who could not were weeded out. There is a saying that goes, "Given enough time, even a monkey can learn to fly." But the military did not have an infinite amount of time or money to spend on trainees, so we had to keep up with this fast-paced flying program.

Our class was comprised of one woman and twenty-nine men, including a country boy, Nick Coleman, from Lubbock, Texas, who already owned his own Piper J-3 Cub taildragger aircraft. This kid was cool! I already had my Private Pilot License, but Nick already had his own airplane. And he spoke with a slow, West Texas drawl.

One morning, the IP described a scenario of a T-37 coming in for landing and as the wing flaps were extended, an unexpected rolling motion began. This described a condition called Asymmetric Flaps, which meant the left- and right-wing flaps were not extending equally. The correct first step is "Flaps-Retract" to stop the rolling motion, which must be stated verbatim.

The IP barked, "Lieutenant Coleman, you have the aircraft!"

Nick slowly rose to his feet and in his best Slim Pickens country drawl said, "Well. I'd get my flaps a-comin' up."

"SIT DOWN!" the IP barked. Poor Nick did not fly that day.

T-37 training continued through the Instrument phase, learning to fly in poor weather, by using the cockpit instruments and not being able to see outside. As the training came to a close, I was surprised to find out that I was the only student to not have a bust on their record. Everyone had either hooked (failed) an inflight checkride or had failed a Stand-Up scenario, all of which resulted in receiving what was referred to as a Pink Sheet in our gradebook. I survived the T-37 evaluations unscathed and even pinned on the rank of captain in early July.

At this point, our SRO, Lori, had failed a checkride and was not progressing on schedule, so she was washed back to the class four weeks behind us to re-accomplish some of her training. Washing back happened quite frequently in all classes, just as it had in navigator training. The only issue for us became who was going to move up to SRO of the class. Skip outranked me but was struggling and did not want the added responsibility, so I assumed the role of SRO. Even as a newly-pinned captain, I was still expected to salute my first lieutenant instructor pilot and call him "Sir."

I was not so hung up on rank to believe there was anything wrong with this temporary arrangement. In military etiquette, the junior officer always salutes first, then the senior officer returns this salute. Some military officers are especially rank conscious and would never render the first salute to a junior ranking officer. In my mind, that instructor pilot had the wings I wanted, so I easily played the role of cooperative student. Each morning, I gladly offered Lieutenant Morrow the first salute.

With my three checkrides completed, Lt "Vic" and I finally planned our T-37 cross-country flight. Two other crews joined us for our weekend trip to Colorado. The three T-37s departed Vance AFB on a Friday morning, June 18, and headed first to Amarillo to fly practice approaches before proceeding up to Peterson AFB, near Colorado Springs.

While the planes were refueled, Vic grabbed the paper low-level terrain charts of the nearby area and started to circle each of the well-known ski resorts west of Colorado Springs and Denver. After tracing circles around the turn points of Aspen, Vail, Copper Mountain, Breckenridge, and others, Vic drew a line connecting them all. The route headed west from Colorado Springs and eventually turned east to come over the Rockies just south of Denver, where my dad lived in Parker.

The other pilots copied Vic's route onto their own charts and, knowing that the mountains extended up to more than 14,000 feet, we decided to fly the route at 16,000 feet to avoid the terrain. With me piloting from the left seat, Vic and I took off first from Peterson AFB and climbed westward towards the Rocky Mountains.

The summer sun gleamed off snow-covered peaks as we made our way up to 16,000 feet and searched for the first ski resort turn point of Breckenridge. After 45 minutes of weaving above the mountains and overflying famous ski resorts, we headed east towards Interstate 25. The highway would lead us north toward our destination of Buckley Field on the east side of Denver. In the vicinity of Castle Rock, I descended to 1,500 feet above the flat plains to stay below the Denver airport arrival corridor and began circling to allow the other two T-37s to catch up with us. Once #3 was in sight, Vic announced over the radio, "Okay, Dave has navigation."

We headed north at 1,500 feet in search of my dad's house, on the outskirts of Parker. Dad lived on five acres of land in a two-story rough cedar house, and most of the houses looked just like his. I located the golf course and tennis court bubble I knew he used, so I was close. Then our family's hobby paid big dividends. Ever since the 1970s my family has enjoyed visiting the western National Parks of Zion, Arches, and Bryce Canyon. We camped at many of those parks in a pop-up Coleman camper. And now, in the late 1980s, my dad, stepmom, Karen, and stepsister, Alison, still enjoyed camping in a new pop-up camper. As I scanned back and forth for Dad's house, a flash suddenly appeared to my left. Looking down, I was excited to see the bright sun glistening off the top of Dad's camper in his driveway.

"There it is!" I shouted to Vic, and we gave Dad a quick low altitude fly-by.

Dad told me later that he was in his walk-out basement when he heard our jet whistle by. The Tweet was known for its shrill-sounding engines. He made it outside just in time to see the #2 and #3 Tweets cruise overhead on our way north to Buckley AFB. There, Vic and I rented a car and headed south to Dad's country house for dinner. It had taken four months to pull off, but Vic and I completed the cross-country flight to Colorado that he had promised on my first day of flying the Tweet.

CHAPTER 14

THEN THE WHEELS FELL OFF

T-38 Talon, supersonic jet trainer (Military.com)

Transitioning to the T-38 got off to an exciting start. I was now class leader and the only student in my class with an unblemished record. My instructor for the flight was our flight commander, Captain Mo Beale, a former A-10 pilot and soon-to-be Air Force Thunderbird, flying Opposing Solo (one of the two jets that cross at show center) for the Air Force demonstration team. I will never forget that first T-38 flight on a hot August afternoon. After years of flying with an instructor sitting next to me in a side-by-side seat airplane, I was now in the front seat of a tandem seat fighter trainer, sitting in the pointy end.

The Air Force Thunderbirds have flown the F-16 since the late 1980s but prior to that, they flew this model of T-38 I was now flying. Now it was my turn to push up the throttles and sink back in the seat as the twin-engine jet sped down the runway. The most memorable sensation was going into that first turn. I felt like I was in a kayak that was tipping over. The bubble canopy was at shoulder level so my neck and head felt so high up, I could see the sides of the plane as I banked left or right. And the power! It felt so nice to be in a powerful jet that didn't lag as I pushed up the throttles.

All I had to do to get my pilot wings was pass three more check-rides: Contact (basic aircraft handling and aerobatics), Formation, and Instruments. What could possibly go wrong?

The training flights in the first phase all went well. I truly loved flying the Cuban 8 maneuver – I pulled the T-38 into a 3-G loop, and as the view shifted from blue sky to brown ground while flying upside down, I quickly pushed forward on the stick and rolled the wings 180 degrees. I was now upright, but the nose never left the spot it was pointing at on the ground. I felt like I was on a bombing run in a fighter-bomber, keeping my target insight while rolling from upside down to right side up. The maneuver was repeated as I traced sideways figure-8s in the Oklahoma sky.

I performed the aerobatics and returned to the landing pattern to perform landings in an abnormal configuration. This included a landing without wing flaps extended, should a no-flap landing occur while I was flying solo. As a bit of foreshadowing, any plane landing without extending its flaps will come in at a higher airspeed to make up for the lack of lift normally created by extending the flaps, and this requires a longer final approach.

On September 12, the day of my Contact checkride, I breezed through the required aerobatic maneuvers and now it was time to head back to Vance AFB for several approaches. The Oklahoma winds had started to shift around throughout the day, and I was now faced with something I had not encountered before, a no-flap landing with a significant tailwind. Under normal conditions, pilots prefer to land into a headwind since the wind over the wing helps to generate lift. But at this point, Vance AFB had not "turned the airport around", switching to landing in the opposite direction into the wind. The rule of thumb when taking a checkride is to not do anything dumb, dangerous, or different during that evaluation. For me, a no-flap landing with a strong tailwind was very different.

I knew that I needed a long final approach from my overhead pattern, but how much, I could not imagine. The overhead pattern consists of flying straight down the landing runway at 1,500 feet above ground level (AGL) with the landing gear and flaps up, known as a clean configuration. Halfway down the runway, pilots go into "the break," throwing the plane into an aggressive 180-degree left turn at nearly 90-degrees of bank to bleed off speed. At the end of our downwind turn, we are flying parallel to the runway and offset about two miles to the side.

As the speed decreases, we extend the landing gear and flaps (in a normal configuration landing), and when the runway is 45 degrees behind our left shoulder, we begin a descending left turn to the runway. In a no-flap condition, our downwind leg is extended well beyond the 45-degree angle to the runway. This allowed the faster flying aircraft to make the turn and land still within the first 3,000 feet of the runway. Add a tailwind into the mix, and I needed a really long final to complete the landing.

At this point in my training, I had not been "issued enough judgment," or gained enough experience to understand how long of a final approach I needed to make a safe approach and landing. My first attempt overshot the runway badly, and I aborted the landing, pushed up the throttles, raised the landing gear, and went around to try again. I extended my final turn on the second attempt, but still not enough, and went around again.

The Runway Supervisor Officer (RSO), monitoring landings that day was Captain Mo Beale, my first T-38 instructor. He emphatically broadcast the winds over the radio, indicating that there was a 10-knot tailwind, which is the legally allowed tailwind limit for landing. On the third attempt, I extended my final turn even further, rolled out on final approach and the T-38 glided at a high speed down to the runway. Unfortunately, I touched down beyond the allowable first 3,000-foot touchdown zone. Welcome to the T-38, Captain Dale, you've just hooked your first checkride. It didn't help matters that as I taxied toward the parking ramp the tower announced over the radio that they were now using the opposing runways, into the headwind. I felt as deflated as an 18-wheeler's shredded tire lying on the freeway.

CHAPTER 15

WHERE'D HE GO?

Vance AFB T-38s flying in formation. (Military.com)

I successfully passed my T-38 Contact recheck on September 15, demonstrating that I could safely perform a no-flap landing and then moved on to the Formation phase. Now for the fun! If you've ever seen the Thunderbirds or the Navy's Blue Angels at an air show, then you may have heard the announcer tell the audience that all military pilots are trained in the maneuvers the team is performing. The demonstration teams just do them with a lot more aircraft and for a longer period of time while looking very cool at the same time.

Now it was my turn to learn how to do a formation takeoff, joining on the wing of the flight leader, with three feet separating our wingtips as I followed him through the skies. Where you lead; I will follow. A little later, the second plane slides into a position called Close Trail and flies just beneath the tail of Lead, and resumes the game of Follow the Leader.

Halfway through the flight, Lead switches to being the #2 aircraft and the new leader practices leading his flight of two T-38s before returning to the airfield for a formation landing. During both the formation takeoff and landing, the leader flies normally, as if flying solo, while the number two pilot focuses solely on the lead aircraft, becoming airborne and touching down only when Lead does and without referencing any other visual cues.

I rotated between two different instructors during formation, and their instruction and my subsequent performance were like night and day. My first instructor, another Captain Dave, was a burned-out First Assignment Instructor Pilot (FAIP) who had been at Vance for four years. This was his initial assignment as a second lieutenant after graduating from pilot training. Most FAIPs would serve three years before moving on to another Air Force aircraft. Captain Dave had now been at Vance four years and had been a high-level evaluator on the base. He was now "just an instructor" as he put it, grudgingly flying with new students again and wanting badly to move on to his next C-141 cargo airlifter assignment.

Dave had spent the past year giving checkrides. In other words, he focused on evaluating rather than instructing students. He was often in a foul mood and very nervous about flying with new students. I became very tense while flying with him and my performance showed. Flying in formation required small inputs on the controls, using a light touch. Being tense led to a heavy grip and erratic flying. I flew poorly with him and began doubting my abilities.

After a particularly bad, "What-are-you-doing?!"-training flight, Captain Dave berated me for what I did wrong. Being a fellow captain and about his same age, I finally told him, "You're telling me what I'm doing wrong, but you're not teaching me how to do it right."

I told Captain Beale, my flight commander, that I thought I needed an instructor change and he agreed. And along came Second Lieutenant Larry "Judas" Deist. His callsign rhymed with Judas Priest, the popular heavy metal band at the time.

Judas was a very fun-loving T-38 IP, and always in a good mood. Everything about him made me laugh. I vividly remember my first formation flight with him instructing from the backseat. I was the #2 aircraft, taking off and climbing out three feet to the left of the leader's wing. Judas exclaimed, "Oh yeah! We are Thunderbirds today!"

He later added, "You're on him like flies on shit!"

I grinned from ear to ear and because of his encouragement, I really enjoyed formation flying. Attitude is everything. After a few more training rides it was time for my Formation checkride.

The plan for my November 17 evaluation called for me to lead the formation of two and switch to the #2 position halfway through the flight. We taxied our T-38s to the Vance runway, each with an evaluator in the back seats. Approaching the runway for takeoff, Tower instructed us to hold short of the runway for an incoming emergency landing. We sat and we sat and we sat, burning crucial gas as the malfunctioning T-38 flew its long 15-mile straight-in final approach, then proceeded down the runway with fire trucks in fast pursuit. Once the airplane and trucks cleared the runway, we finally rocketed down the runway, side by side, but with a lot less gas than originally planned. I led our flight of two through the required maneuvers which included a loop, pulling the required minimum of 3 Gs, while #2 stayed tucked in below and behind me in the Close Trail position.

Once my portion was complete, we performed a lead change and I followed the leader around the skies of western Oklahoma. At the appointed time, I slipped into the Close Trail position behind Lead and he began his loop. Lead was not pulling at the required 3-G minimum and when he noticed this, he snatched back aggressively back on his control stick. Once he did that, he quickly pulled away from me, and I lost my formation position. Our flight of two had now broken up and I needed to rejoin the formation. All of this was taking more fuel than we could afford and still return to Vance with our required minimum fuel. The end result was that we returned to the airfield without completing all the required formation maneuvers. Bust #2 for Class Leader Captain Dale.

That checkride bust had major implications. By this point, I wanted to be a Strike Eagle fighter-bomber pilot in the brand-new twin-engine, two-seat F-15E. This plane seemed a bit more survivable than the single-engine F-16. Plus, it had a Weapon System Operator (WSO) navigator in the back seat and dropped bombs, like I had done in the B-52. Like any fighter assignment, it required that I be Fighter, Attack, and Reconnaissance qualified (aka, FAR'd). Two failed checkrides, one of them being formation, took me out of consideration for being FAR'd. My hopes of flying fighters crashed to earth like the Hindenburg zeppelin over New Jersey.

For my recheck, my evaluator was the lieutenant colonel Director of Operations (DO) for the training squadron. He was an experienced Air Force fighter pilot but did his best to put me at ease about the upcoming re-evaluation. With the sortie briefed, our formation took off again, this time with me in the #2 position, since that was the part of the checkride I needed to accomplish. The clouds that day were high and thick. I stayed on the wing of Lead as he climbed up to 14,000 feet. We finally popped out into the Oklahoma blue sky and continued with formation evaluation. After several minutes of required formation maneuvers, the lieutenant colonel evaluator said, "There's nothing wrong with your formation flying. Take me back home." Recheck complete.

CHAPTER 16

A MONUMENTAL EVENT

Throughout any flying training program, simulators are used both to practice emergency procedures and save the cost of fuel by perfecting skills such as instrument flying. Once a simulated emergency had been successfully handled, the instructor cleared out the malfunction and reset the simulator for the next scenario. A well-known expression was, "Okay. New day. New jet." That meant everything previously experienced was now in the past and we were starting with a clean slate. At this point I had failed the first two T-38 checkrides and was heading into the final phase -- instrument flying. "Okay. New day. New jet."

During instrument training it's assumed that we are flying in clouds and unable to see the horizon ahead or the ground and runway below. This phase took place about two months before graduation and consists of both simulator training and flights from the back seat of the T-38, relying solely on the airplane's instruments. I progressed through the training flights and in mid-January 1989 was four weeks and one flight away from my final UPT checkride.

Throughout the year, physical fitness was emphasized for us to stay in good shape to be able to sustain the G-forces encountered in the jet trainers. Plus, we were, after all, in the military. There were numerous physical training sessions throughout the week and we also played intramural sports. My downfall was pretending that I could play basketball.

One night, I attended my one and only intramural basketball game, showing my support as the class leader. Other than shooting around for fun, I had not played a real basketball game since junior high. I dressed out for the game and sat on the bench waiting for my chance. A foul was called and during the free-throws, I subbed in, assuming my place on the side of the lane. The ball went up, bounced off the rim and came in my direction. I leapt off the court for the rebound, caught the ball, and immediately came down on my opponent's foot, rolling my left foot to the side. I felt a pop and collapsed to the floor. I hobbled to the bleachers where my wife was waiting, shaking her head. Neither of us could believe that I was injured in just three seconds of playing time.

I iced my ankle at home and got ready for bed. The next morning, we looked at it and the ankle was a bit swollen. An ominous blue streak ran down the outside of my left foot, toward the little toe, and it was painful to touch. I couldn't put any weight on it without feeling a shooting pain.

I headed to the base flight surgeon and had it X-rayed. The young flight surgeon, not much older than I, and lacking any bedside manner or sympathy, gave me the verdict.

"Well, you broke your foot. Looks like we'll need to wash you back a class."

I couldn't believe it. I was the class leader of 28 guys that I had trained with for the previous eleven months. Now I was supposed to wash back to the class behind me just before graduation? I asked if there were any other options. Vance AFB is a small base without a main hospital and only a health clinic, so the young flight doc referred me downtown to the hospital, where I met a kindly, old doctor.

The gray-haired doctor looked at my X-ray and pointed to the hairline crack just below my little toe as we talked about my broken foot. I told him I was due to graduate in four weeks and had only two required flights left in the program, one training ride and the instrument checkride. I explained I was the class leader and desperately wanted to graduate with the guys I had come to know so well over the previous year.

The doctor knew all about Air Force pilot training and took pity on me. He explained that normally the crack would heal wearing only a hard shoe or boot. He then graciously offered a solution that could make us both happy.

"How about we cast it for two weeks and you stay off it completely, then we'll take another look at it. That'll give you two weeks to fly those last two flights."

During those ensuing two weeks our class held its Assignment Night. This was very similar to what I had experienced on Assignment Night in navigator training, except without any ill-conceived guesses as to what I might receive.

Our class wore flightsuits that night and our standard issue black flying boots. I pulled a large black sock over my left foot plaster cast, and our class waited in the back of the room for our introduction. The Master of Ceremonies introduced Class 89-05 and with rock music blaring, I led the class in a limping jog down the center aisle. It looked as though I was strutting to the song as the event was filmed for posterity.

It wasn't until many days later that I saw the video and realized that my whole class took up my "strut" and limped/jogged up to the front of the room, coming to attention in front of the base leadership. Since we all had the same gait, many attendees never realized my foot was broken and in a cast. Had I known the class was doing this, perhaps our introductory song should have been Aerosmith's "*Walk This Way*."

The momentous evening proceeded, with each classmate being called up individually to stand in front of a dual screen. Behind him was the Hero Shot of the pilot trainee holding his helmet and standing on the ladder next to the sleek T-38 cockpit. The MC enjoyed roasting the trainee with an embarrassing tale before finally announcing his assignment.

Top graduates were thrilled to receive an F-16, as others received A-10s, or larger cargo and refueling aircraft. One necessary but dreaded assignment was to be retained as a First Assignment Instructor Pilot (FAIP) meaning they weren't leaving Enid, Oklahoma. Those pilots would be staying at Vance AFB, flying the T-37 or T-38. They would train brand-new students for three more years before receiving a follow-on assignment to a fighter, bomber, tanker, or cargo aircraft.

This was not happy news for one young couple. As the young second lieutenant stood on the stage, the MC said the fateful words, "Tactical Air Command is going to have to wait three more years to put you in a fighter. You're staying here at Vance to fly the T-37."

Staying in Oklahoma and becoming a T-37 IP was not what he expected or wanted at all. His young bride didn't want it, either. Sitting one row behind the wing commander and squadron commanders, she stood up and drunkenly cried out, "What the hell?!" The other wives sitting nearby quickly pulled her back into her seat.

My #1 choice was the newly-built B-1 bomber. It was the latest and greatest bomber, could fly at supersonic speeds, and was known to handle like a big T-38. Behind that, I wanted a B-52 to Loring AFB in northern Maine or Andersen AFB on the Pacific Island of Guam. Those two bases focused on sea-mining operations and conventional bombing and did not have to sit nuclear alert. After two years at Barksdale, I now embraced the bomber mission and thought my career would go further if I eventually flew the future B-2 Stealth Bomber. The Air Force initially planned to use former navigators as pilots in this long-range two-pilot bomber.

My third choice was the newest plane in the inventory, the KC-10 Extender. This was a modified McDonnell Douglas DC-10, used by the military for aerial refueling and cargo transport.

Unlike Assignment Night in navigator training, I was not resigned to receiving a B-52, but truly hoped a B-1 would be my next plane. Hopefully one B-1 training slot would be allocated to our class, but that was not a given. As my name was called, I anxiously awaited my fate.

"Captain Dale, even though you placed two bombers as your top two choices, you will be returning to Barksdale Air Force Base, Louisiana to fly the KC-10."

That was certainly an unexpected surprise. It was unheard of to list an unpopular B-52 above a KC-10 and receive the new plane over the older. But it happened. I was shocked but not disheartened. I just never imagined this would be the result.

Now I just needed to pass my final Instrument checkride. Over the previous two weeks I was unable to fly with my foot in a cast, but I was given daily use of the T-38 simulator to practice my instrument approaches. That was a godsend.

The day came to return to the in-town doctor for reexamination. He removed my cast and sent me back to X-ray and we met in his office a few minutes later. With the two X-rays side by side, I could still see the hairline crack on my left foot.

He asked, "How does it feel?"

I answered, "It hurts a little, but otherwise it's fine."

"So, you think you can fly with it in your flight boot?"

"Yeah, I can do that."

He reached for the paperwork to put me back on flying status and in a slow drawl said, "Okaaay. Just don't get me in trouble," as he handed me the signed medical clearance form. I headed back to Vance AFB ready to schedule my remaining T-38 flights, with graduation just two weeks away. I was given one practice instrument flight to warm up and then scheduled for my final pilot training checkride.

On February 10, fifty-one weeks after moving to Enid, I met my evaluator and we briefed the flight. The location was up to me, weather permitting, so I planned to perform my final checkride at Barksdale AFB, my old B-52 home and future KC-10 base. Once there, I would fly a series of instrument approaches from the back of the T-38 with a cloth curtain pulled over the windscreen, blocking my view of the outside visual references around me.

As we headed toward the crew van, I noticed the evaluator also limped as he walked. In his case though, he was favoring his right foot. We boarded the van with several other pilots, all waiting to be dropped off at our respective jets. A fellow IP on the van knew both of us and said to my evaluator, "Didn't you sprain your ankle at the basketball game last night?"

"Yes," he replied. "But it's only minor."

This was news to me. Turning to me, the IP continued, "And didn't you break your foot in a game?"

"Yeah, I just got the cast off a few days ago," I replied.

"How are y'all going to fly and hold the brakes on the T-38?" he asked.

Since my left foot was cracked and his right ankle was sprained, I said, "Well, I'm going to hold the right brake and he's going to hold the left brake." I was kidding, but we hobbled off down the flightline toward our T-38.

I flew back to my old Louisiana stomping grounds, completed my three instrument approaches and then landed to refuel. We parked very close to my future 32nd Air Refueling Squadron (32 ARS), so I asked my evaluator if I could stop in for a visit and he said, "Sure."

Still wearing my G-suit and carrying my helmet bag, I walked into the 32 ARS and told the first pilot I saw that I would be coming to this squadron in a month. He said, "Well, let's go upstairs and meet your future boss!"

We headed upstairs to the squadron commander's office where I was introduced to Lieutenant Colonel Wally Dill. He shook my hand and in a friendly voice said, "Look at you with your Fast Pants on," referring to the G-suit. It was a quick visit, but I felt it was a great way to close out pilot training and start my future assignment in the KC-10.

Days after my last checkride, on a bitterly cold February day, my parents and brother arrived in Enid for the graduation activities. It was exactly one year after Karin and I arrived. I gave my family a tour of the base and Jack enjoyed flying the T-38 simulator. The ceremony culminated with Karin pinning silver pilot wings on my uniform where my navigator wings used to reside.

Once back at our house after the ceremony, my dad and I headed outside to walk our cocker spaniel and beagle around the block. My dad was a fairly quiet man. Dad was very stoic towards me and my brother, and rarely showed affection. We received handshakes instead of bear hugs and when I said, "Love ya, Dad," he would smile and say, "Right," but never uttered the word "love." I'm sure it was generational because many of my friends have said the same thing about their dads.

Dad loved to tell lots of funny stories and was very kind, but he was mostly ambivalent toward my aviation career. My dad didn't discourage me from flying, but he wasn't curious or enthusiastic about it either. On this brisk, blue-sky day as we walked the dogs, I finally realized my dream of becoming an Air Force pilot. I didn't follow in my dad's footsteps of being a lawyer, but rather my uncle's. As we walked together side-by-side something monumental happened. My father quietly said, "You know, Davy ... I'm proud of you."

This was the one and only time my dad ever said those words.

T-38 Hero Shot. UPT Graduation photo, February 16, 1989.

CHAPTER 17

BECOMING A GUCCI BOY

Barksdale KC-10, 1989.

M y KC-10 Initial Qualification simulator instructor was a
Korean War F-86 fighter pilot veteran named Jim, who
was kind of full of himself. Back in the late 1960s, after
serving as a MiG-killing fighter pilot over Korea a few years earlier,
Jim was not happy about being reassigned to the fairly new KC-135.
Instead of flying fighter sorties against the enemy, Jim flew KC-135
tanker missions during the Vietnam War.

After several weeks of academic training, I started to notice that
Jim only had two responses when I asked a question:

"Well, what does the book say?" or

"Well, it's obvious that…"

While on a break one day, and frustrated, I asked my training
partner, Randy, that if everything was either obvious or in the book,

why did we need Jim as our instructor? Randy sympathized and said, "Dave, I gave up asking him questions a week ago."

I completed my KC-10 training in the summer of 1989 at Barksdale AFB. The fleet of 59 KC-10s was divided among three bases: Seymour Johnson AFB, in North Carolina, March AFB in southern California, and Barksdale AFB. Each of the three bases had its own simulator and staff of instructors, so all training was done in-house. This was unlike other Air Force aircraft where new crewmembers went to a training base that specialized in a particular aircraft and mission.

I was paired with Captain Randy Fopiano, an upstanding guy who became my good friend. Randy was the first in his family to attend college and played tennis as a cadet at the Air Force Academy. After pilot training at Columbus AFB, Mississippi, Randy flew T-37s as a FAIP (first assignment instructor pilot) for three years before coming to Barksdale to fly the KC-10.

The KC-10 is a modified McDonnell Douglas DC-10, the long-range version of the commercial DC-10 jumbo jet airliner. The Air Force modifications added extra fuel tanks underneath the main cabin floor, plus the air refueling equipment and plumbing required to perform the midair refueling mission.

Many people step into the cockpit of a large aircraft and wonder, "What do all of those buttons and knobs do?" I would spend the next three months finding out. My impression of KC-10 training is that I had to learn how to fly the huge airplane twice. First, it is a massive 590,000-pound aircraft with three powerful General Electric engines. Randy and I came to this plane from very responsive T-37 and T-38 trainers, so we had to learn how to handle this lumbering, heavy jet. Second, the KC-10 had state-of-art automation for its time, including an autopilot, which the training aircraft did not have. Part of the 19 simulator training sessions we flew were spent learning how to use the autopilot to fly the heading, speed, and altitude, or perform the instrument approach we wanted.

KC-10s boasted a modern cockpit and were still being manufactured and delivered to the Air Force. For this reason, we were dubbed by the Air Force crews flying older aircraft as the "Gucci Boys." What started as a put-down by outsiders was actually proudly embraced by the KC-10 community. Our freshly-built KC-10s, nicknamed Big Sexy by some of the crews, even had airline-style lavatories. Such luxury! No more peeing in a metal tube or pooping in a plastic-lined box.

Randy and I also had to learn the art of aerial refueling. The KC-10 is officially called the Extender because its mission is one of Force Extension. Through our air refueling and cargo capabilities, we greatly increased the Air Force's ability to move fighter and bomber airplanes to a combat zone. The passenger plane cabin area was now a cavernous cargo hold, capable of carrying 20 passengers and 27 pallets of goods on a floor with built-in rollers for easy movement.

There was also a passenger Increased Accommodation Kit configuration available. Each kit consisted of 75 red cloth-covered seats, much like those found in the economy section of an airliner. When used, 75 seats took up the forward third of the cabin, just outside the cockpit door, still leaving room for 20 pallets of cargo for items such as spare parts or extra engines for fighter aircraft.

In theory, a formation of three KC-10s could escort and carry a squadron of 12 fighter aircraft, refueling them over the ocean with their maintainers and other support personnel riding along inside with us to the deployed location. The KC-10 could both give gas to receiving airplanes and take on fuel from other tankers, such as the older KC-135 or another KC-10. With a nearly endless supply of fuel, it was said that our GE engines would run out of oil before the jet ran out of gas. The simulator training course, therefore, had to teach us not only how to fly and operate the KC-10, but how to run a rendezvous as both a tanker aircraft to give the fuel or as a receiver aircraft taking on fuel.

Randy and I completed our simulator evaluation and headed to the flightline in late May of 1989, with my very pregnant wife about to deliver our first child. I signed in to Training Flight and a very gracious instructor pilot, Major Jerry Babbin, asked, "Isn't your wife expecting a baby any day now?"

"Yes," I answered.

"What are you doing here? Go home!" he commanded.

Daniel Joseph Dale was born June 1, 1989, at the Barksdale AFB hospital in Bossier City, Louisiana. His middle name was given in honor of my B-52 friend, Captain Joe Wolf. The tiny black and white TV in Karin's hospital maternity room showed the major story of the day: the Tiananmen Square standoff in Beijing.

On the day we thought we'd bring our son home; Daniel became jaundiced and his departure was delayed by three days. As Tank Man stood defiantly in front of a Chinese tank, our tiny son slept in his bassinet by the hospital window. Karin and Daniel stayed another three days at the base hospital and I went back to the 32nd Air Refueling Squadron 932 ARS) to prepare for my first flight.

On June 7, one week after Daniel was born, I pushed up the three throttles and accelerated down the two-mile long Louisiana runway. Seven flights later, after numerous takeoffs and landings and multiple air refueling rendezvous, I completed my initial qualification checkride on July 10.

One week later, I flew with an instructor pilot, Captain Pam Melroy, a future Space Shuttle pilot and commander. Flying just 30 feet behind another KC-10, I held our jet steady enough to successfully make my first receiver refueling contact as their boom plugged into the receptacle on the roof of our plane -- an unforgettable thrill. Receiver refueling was not a requirement for copilots to master. But it was both a challenge and confidence-booster to learn to fly in close formation with another large aircraft while taking on fuel.

The next few months were spent becoming Mission Qualified, flying several missions to overseas bases in England, Germany, out to Hawaii, and up to Alaska. The Hawaii trip ended on an unexpectedly amusing note.

KC-135R (left) and KC-10 (right)
The KC-135 is similar to a Boeing 707.
This four-engine airframe is also used for the E-3A AWACS,
RC-135, EC-135, and VC-137 referenced throughout this book.

In October 1989, we were tasked to refuel an EC-135 (Boeing 707) intelligence gathering aircraft over the Pacific as the crew monitored an upcoming Russian missile test. We departed Louisiana on a beautiful fall day for one week of temporary duty (TDY) to Hickam AFB, Hawaii. We planned to come straight back to the mild temperatures of Louisiana. Who needs cold-weather gear, right?

With our week of daily refuelings complete, our task changed to take the EC-135 and its support crews back to Eielson AFB, near Fairbanks, Alaska … in the winter. Our flight engineer for this trip was a very funny Englishman named Simon Wray. Of course, anything said with an English accent was funny, so everyone loved Simon. As a joke, he decided to complete his exterior preflight walk-around wearing only his brightly colored knee-length Jams swimsuit, popular in that day. Simon had pasty white, skinny legs, and we all enjoyed the show.

Hours later, we landed in a driving snowstorm in Alaska with snowflakes the size of quarters blowing sideways. In between each flight, the flight engineer must conduct an exterior inspection, looking for possible fluid leaks or signs of an unknown bird strike. Knowing that Simon was still wearing his Jams under his flightsuit,

I called out, "Simon! You don't have a hair on your ass if you don't complete that walk-around in your Jams again!"

His first reaction was, "Naaaah, I ain't gonna do that!" But then he thought about it, took on my challenge, and unzipped his flight-suit and said, "Well, all right."

I had to get a picture of that, so I headed down the large mobile staircase with him, into the blizzard. He did the world's fastest walk-around inspection, and I met him at the engine nacelle to get his photo. It was a common pose, showing how big our engines were compared to a human. Simon leaned against the engine in his bright orange and pink swimsuit yelling, "Take the picture! Take the picture!"

We returned home to the mild fall temperatures of northern Louisiana in time for the beginning of the holiday season. Around that same time the evening news began reporting rumblings about some guy named Noriega in Panama.

CHAPTER 18

OPERATION DENY CHRISTMAS

Air Force E-3 Sentry AWACS (Military.com)

In the fall of 1989, Panamanian dictator Manuel Noriega refused to honor the results of a recent election and he put down a second attempted coup. Members of the U.S. forces stationed in Panama were attacked and harassed on the streets. Marine Second Lieutenant Robert Paz was fatally shot in his vehicle as he fled to escape an angry mob. Navy SEAL Lieutenant Adam Curtis and his wife were detained and assaulted by the Panamanian Defense Force after witnessing the attack on Lieutenant Paz and his three military companions.

By mid-December the Defense Department completed plans for an eventual invasion of Panama in order to: safeguard the lives of US citizens in Panama; defend democracy and human rights in Panama; combat drug trafficking; and protect the Panama Canal treaty and its usage.

The KC-10s at Barksdale were placed on Bravo Alert, which required the ability to be airborne within two hours of notification. Crews were told to go home, pack a deployment bag and stay on telephone standby. Some crewmembers returned to the base to stay in the Visiting Officers' Quarters (VOQ). This placed them closer to the fueled and preflighted KC-10s on the flightline.

I headed home in the middle of the day on December 20 and told Karin I had to pack a bag but couldn't say where I was going or what I was doing. I didn't have any details to give her anyway.

That night we watched CNN together as it reported from outside of Ft Bragg, North Carolina. The reporter dutifully told the nation that C-141 Starlifter cargo planes were departing from Pope AFB, next to the Army's 82nd Airborne base at Fort Bragg, and were heading south in the direction of Panama. Karin looked at me and said, "I think I know where you're going." So much for operational security.

Our squadron's crews spent 48 hours in the VOQs on Bravo Alert, ready to depart on a moment's notice. My 48-hour shift began at noon on Christmas Day. This allowed me to be home Christmas morning and the off-going crew to get home Christmas afternoon. I was able to spend Daniel's first Christmas at home along with Karin and her parents. After lunch I loaded my deployment bag into the car and headed for the base.

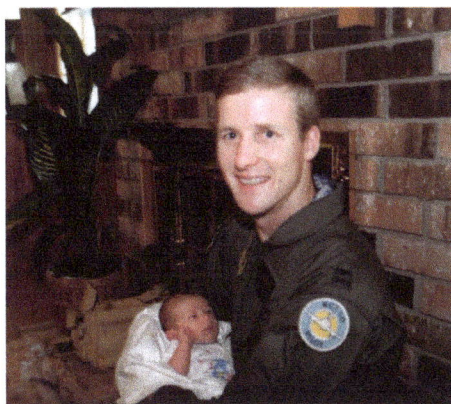

Baby Daniel Dale and I before a KC-10 flight

Several crewmembers in the KC-10 had come to the squadron from KC-135s and B-52s, and were used to sitting SAC alert, waiting for a response notification. My aircraft commander (AC), Captain Willie Waddell, had come to the KC-10 many years earlier as a new second lieutenant right out of pilot training, so he never knew the luxury, thrill, or inconvenience of sitting alert. Willie grew bored sitting around the VOQ and headed off to the gym. Timing is everything, right?

Our number came up to launch and I received the pager notification for our crew to report to the squadron as soon as possible to takeoff. I had the flight engineer and boom operator with me, but how do we track down our AC in the days before cell phones? The crew was assigned one pager, which was left with me as Willie went to the gym. After numerous phone calls to the gym, Willie was finally tracked down in the gymnasium shower and quickly met us, hair still wet, at the squadron.

During the mission briefing we were told we would be refueling the E-3A Airborne Warning and Control System (AWACS) over the Panamanian region. The AWACS is yet another Boeing 707, but with a large spinning black disk on top, providing radar coverage of an area. They are like air traffic controllers in the sky and help to manage the air traffic over a warzone, or vector our fighter aircraft towards the enemy aircraft. As described in Air Force Magazine, "an AWACS flying over New York City could manage the aerial battle as far north as Boston and south as Washington, D.C., at the same time." In an effort to show leadership by example, the Barksdale wing commander, Colonel Mudd, would fly this Christmas night mission with us.

My first operational combat support mission was an anticlimactic, quiet affair. Military aircrews maintain radio silence during combat support missions to avoid tipping off the enemy with radio chatter. We headed south toward the east coast of Panama and arrived at our prescribed refueling orbit over the Gulf of Mexico, telling the controlling AWACS over a scrambled radio frequency that we were on station. We set up a long racetrack pattern with 30-mile legs and

180-degree left-hand turns at each end. Everyone on the crew stayed off the radios as Mike, our Boom Operator, scanned the night sky out his large, aft-facing window in the belly of the plane.

Silently, the large, black and white AWACS appeared below us and slowly climbed into the refueling position, stabilizing in a position fifty feet behind us, both airplanes matched at 450 miles per hour. Mike extended the telescoping refueling boom, making contact with the AWACS refueling receptacle above and just aft of their pilots' cockpit seats. Once in contact, Mike told the Flight Engineer over the aircraft interphone to begin transferring fuel. Within twenty minutes, our AWACS received 9,000 gallons, or roughly 60,000 pounds of fuel. Once completely topped off, the AWACS headed off to continue his airborne command and control mission over Panama, while we stayed in our orbit as an on-call tanker until released to return to Barksdale.

The flight itself and refueling went as scheduled and was pretty uneventful. My main memory from the flight was that after my copilot duties were complete for the AWACS refueling, I got out of my seat to let the wing commander fly the plane from the right seat. With no other aircraft around us, Willie told him to go into a turn, and Colonel Mudd, a B-52 pilot, aggressively rolled to 30 degrees of bank, slinging those of us now sitting in the red airline seats in back to and fro. Perhaps he wasn't used to the responsive controls of the KC-10, but it got our attention. We landed twelve hours later on the morning of Dec 26.

Officially, the operation was named Just Cause, because "our cause was just." Among the crew dogs, as we called ourselves, it was coined either Operation Just 'Cause (cuz) or Operation Deny Christmas, which would happen over and over throughout the years. After watching the CNN report for this event, and those leading up to Desert Shield and Desert Storm, I began referring to the KC-10 as the CNN Reaction Force, because if it was on CNN, that's where we were going.

CHAPTER 19
GO NAVY! FOR TWO DAYS

The KC-10 was a versatile aircraft, which I grew to appreciate. My first few months in the plane were a bit boring after coming to the tanker mission from the bomber side. The B-52 crews I had been part of were combat-ready men in their 20's to 30's (no women until 1993), flying long-duration missions. All of this was during the height of the Cold War as the Reagan Administration built up our military to face down Russia's Mikhail Gorbachev. There was a real sense of purpose as we sat nuclear alert and read the news or received classified intelligence reports about anything happening in the Soviet Union. I'll always remember reading Tom Clancy's *Red Storm Rising,* which included Barksdale B-52s as part of the plot, while I sat on nuclear alert.

Now I was a tanker pilot ... sort of. My job was to "pass gas" as the tanker joke goes. But we could also receive fuel, and deliver cargo. Pretty cut and dried. But we didn't want to be confused with those that flew the old KC-135. If a pilot said they flew "tankers" that meant they flew KC-135s. But if he or she flew KC-10s, then they said "KC-10s," not tankers.

I was beginning to enjoy the ability to fly to Europe and the Pacific, instead of always taking off and landing at the same base, the way bombers operated. The KC-10 also had the ability to refuel any service's aircraft capable of receiving gas: Air Force, Navy, Marines, and some of our allies as well.

We were a multi-role tanker, equipped with a 25-foot telescoping flyable boom to refuel Air Force aircraft, and a hose-and-drogue system for the Navy and Marines. Our long fuel hose could be unreeled from the back of the fuselage and at the end was a basket that looked like a large badminton birdie. Navy and Marine fighters had a refueling probe, and it was their job to stab their probe into our drogue, where a connection would be made. Once securely fitted, we passed our fuel to them, but at a much slower rate than we could through the boom.

In March of 1990, my crew was tasked to support a naval exercise over the Mediterranean Sea. The USS Eisenhower was in the eastern Med and about to be relieved by the USS Forrestal, entering the Med from the west. Whenever the Navy had two aircraft carriers in the Mediterranean Sea, they would simulate a wargame against each other. Our KC-10 was temporarily based out of Naval Air Station (NAS) Sigonella, at the sole of the boot, near Catania, Italy. We'd provide refueling support to all takers, not favoring one ship or the other.

After our first day of the exercise refueling Navy F-14 Tomcats, F-18 Hornets, and EA-6B electronic jamming Prowlers, we received permission for an aircraft carrier fly-by. Everyone remembers the "*Top Gun*" scene where Tom Cruise zoomed past the carrier in his super-fast F-14, spilling the coffee of the officer on deck. Ours was nothing like that, let's just say.

We dialed up the Forrestal's TACAN radio navigation beam to guide us to the ship and set up for the approach as if it were a runway. Once at 200 feet above the water, we offset from the ship's centerline and flew along the port, or left side, of the ship. We then executed a low approach, retracting our landing gear and flaps, and flew back around the carrier for a high-speed pass at 250 knots (290 mph).

Our little airshow completed, we headed back to Sigonella for the day. I'll admit I was a bit nervous about flying those low passes, not for concern of getting caught or getting in trouble, but because I no longer had my B-52 ejection seat to get out of the plane if something went wrong. I told the crew that evening that at least in the B-52 we trained for low altitude flying and had a way of punching out of the aircraft. On this day, the Happy Pessimist wasn't completely comfortable with what we did. But it certainly was memorable!

Although our fairly new KC-10 was pretty reliable, this particular aircraft had a maintenance issue on Day 2 of the exercise. A vital piece of equipment for our electrical system, called the transformer rectifier, stopped working and the plane was grounded until that part could be replaced. Our KC-10 was parked on the Navy ramp near some C-2 Carrier Onboard Delivery (COD) aircraft, which were twin-turboprop small airplanes used to ferry men and equipment out to the aircraft carriers. I jokingly asked my AC, Jeff, if we could get a ride on the C-2. We figured it didn't hurt to ask.

At this point, Jeff and I were both captains, which is the third rank an officer can be promoted to in the Air Force. It's also known as O-3 (Officer Grade 3). In the Navy an O-3 is a lieutenant, and a Navy captain is an O-6, a very senior rank equivalent to an Air Force colonel. See Appendix 6 for a table of service ranks.

Jeff and I entered the C-2 squadron and found a Navy O-3 lieutenant behind the scheduling desk. I walked up and said, "Hi. We are with the KC-10 sitting out there, but it's broken today. What's it take to get a flight on a C-2?"

He looked down at his pad of paper and without any hesitation said, "I have one leaving at 1500 (3:00 p.m.) for the Forrestal. Wanna go? I can add you all to the flight manifest."

"Sure!" we answered with a smile. Jeff and I headed back outside to tell our flight engineer, Reagan, and boom operator, Russ, that we had arranged for us all to fly out to the USS Forrestal.

The C-2 crew gave us our protective headgear and inflatable life vests and showed us to the aft-facing seats in the cargo hold of the small plane. The four of us couldn't believe our luck as we took off and headed for the same aircraft carrier we had just flown by the day before.

The C-2 had very few windows and they were tiny at that, so knowing where we were in relation to the carrier was difficult. The plane entered the arrival pattern for landing aircraft and made a series of abrupt 90-degree turns, throwing us from side to side, until we finally lined up on final approach. The trap landing was very sudden and the quick deceleration after catching the cable felt like the end of a roller coaster ride when the coaster car comes screeching back into the station. It was all very abrupt.

We deplaned and looked around the massive carrier as men in their khaki naval uniforms looked down at us from the Crow's Nest high above the flight deck. One of the men was a Chief Petty Officer who volunteered to take us on an impromptu tour of the big ship.

Jeff, me, and Russ, our boom operator, aboard the USS Forrestal

We strolled through the narrow hallways, up and down numerous staircases, and into the flight rooms of the various Naval flying squadrons assigned to the ship for that sea tour. We gave our day-old copy of the *Stars and Stripes* military newspaper to a Naval aviator and he sarcastically remarked that we got to be in the Navy for all of one day. Our single day was much easier to enjoy than his six months at sea.

Eventually our tour ended up in the Flight Operations Center, where we got to meet the Air Boss, a Navy O-6 captain in charge of the launch and recovery of the ship's air fleet. He asked, "Were y'all the crew that flew by yesterday?"

"Yes, sir. That was us," Jeff answered with a grin. "What did you think of it?"

He smiled back and remarked, "Well, that high-speed pass was nothing, since we have Tomcats. But the low-speed approach and go around was very impressive! Your tail engine was shooting up a rooster tail in the water. Now that was cool."

Unbeknownst to us, our tail engine had created a giant spray in the ocean behind us.

Earlier, Jeff told us the story of a KC-10 crew doing a similar carrier flyby a few years back. The Navy audience thought that demonstration was so cool that the Naval commander sent an 8X10 photo of the KC-10 "airshow" to the Air Force wing commander as a thank you. That crew got in trouble. Jeff asked politely that no photos be sent back to our Barksdale wing commander.

The Air Boss then asked, "How long will y'all be onboard?"

Jeff replied, "We have to get back to Sigonella today to coordinate the repair of our KC-10."

Due to the time-zone difference, the maintenance personnel back at Barksdale were not even aware at this point that our jet was broken.

The Air Boss then remarked, "That's too bad. If you stayed the night, I'd probably be able to get you a Tomcat (F-14) ride in the morning."

We couldn't believe that opportunity, but really had to get back to shore since our plane was preparing to depart. As we crossed the carrier's flight deck, I told Jeff, "It would almost be worth the Article 15 (military punishment) to stay the night and get that flight!"

We strapped into the back of the C-2, and the enlisted crewmember briefed us on what to expect during the catapult launch, or "Cat Shot." Because we were facing backwards, we needed to cross our arms across our chest and cross our feet at the ankles, then brace for the departure. Otherwise, the instant G-forces of the launch would make our arms and legs fly out uncontrollably in front of us.

We did as told, and heard the two turboprop engines rev up to takeoff rpm. In a flash, the plane lurched forward, and we could feel the blood rushing to our cheeks and eyes as we strained to keep our arms and legs close to our body. Within seconds, the rapid acceleration ended and we were airborne in what felt like a calm, floating sensation after that violent takeoff. I looked at my friends' faces and we were all bright red from the rush of blood created by the G-forces. Within an hour we were back on terra firma and Jeff placed a call back to Barksdale to explain our maintenance issue.

The good news for our crew was that the replacement part would be sent to us on a C-141 cargo plane leaving the States and flying a routine resupply mission throughout the Mediterranean region. This meant our broken KC-10 would remain on the ground for another four days. Enough time to tour southern Italy and go on another C-2 flight!

The four of us toured Palermo and walked on Roman ruins, then enjoyed authentic Italian pasta and pizza with glasses of red wine each evening. Quite a cultural and worldly experience for guys in their late-20s.

We headed back to the C-2 squadron and scheduled another flight, but this time to the more modern USS Eisenhower. The landing and tour were very much like the first event on the Forrestal, but I wanted to experiment on the next catapult takeoff. I purposely relaxed my arms and legs, resting my hands on my knees. As the C-2 shot forward with me facing the back of the plane, my arms and legs involuntarily flew out in front of me, parallel to the floor. With all my strength I could not bring them back close to my body until the rapid acceleration subsided. We all looked at each other again, red-faced and laughing like kids at a carnival.

CHAPTER 20

SOS

All military officers take part in Professional Military Education (PME) for career advancement. Leadership training continues throughout our careers, first with Squadron Officer's School (SOS) for captains, followed by Intermediate Service School (ISS) for majors, and finally Senior Service School (SSS) for lieutenant colonels and colonels. Each of these schools is a competitive benchmark for those hoping to lead at the next higher level.

By July 1990, I was on my way to attend SOS in residence at Maxwell Air Force Base, near Montgomery, Alabama. My selection to attend in residence was better than simply completing the course by correspondence. And it helped pave the way for promotion to my next rank of major. SOS was a six-week course, which I attended from July to August 1990. Although it was a privilege to attend, when the class was asked to write down our goals for the six-week course, I vowed to not spend a single weekend in Montgomery, Alabama. I failed once, but fulfilled that goal the other five weekends.

Of the weekends I spent away from SOS, I played beach volleyball with my ROTC classmate, Captain Bobber McMurry, near Eglin AFB in the Florida panhandle. I water skied and partied with SOS classmates at our AC-130 gunship classmate's condo near Hurlburt AFB - also in the Florida panhandle - and was lucky enough to attend the Talladega 500 free of charge.

Just weeks after the course began, I met a classmate who was also a big NASCAR fan, having been born and raised in Daytona, Florida. After talking about the upcoming Talladega 500 race, he called my room one night to say that he won two raceway tickets as part of a local Montgomery radio contest and he invited me along. For $2 each, we rented two sleeping bags from the Morale, Welfare, and Recreation office and slept in the bed of his pickup truck the night before the race. The roar and thunder of the heavy stock cars rumbled my feet as the race began with us standing just three rows from the track. I'll never forget how brightly colored the cars were, the neon colors so much brighter than could possibly be captured by television.

The other monumental event involved rendezvousing with Karin and our 13-month-old son halfway between Shreveport and Montgomery at a Jackson, Mississippi Holiday Inn. After a Saturday spent swimming in the pool, we were thrilled to watch Daniel take his first steps ever in our hotel room that evening. Not a bad way to escape Maxwell AFB, even if for just a few days.

Daniel's first steps, August 1990, in Jackson, MS

Our SOS class was comprised of twelve captains from various backgrounds: pilots, navigators, engineers, missileers, administrative support, and an Air Force Reserve chaplain named Norris Burkes.

The requirements for the class, in addition to physical fitness and teamwork, were three written point papers (not to be confused with college English papers) and three speeches. Our chaplain's speeches were memorable. This extremely nice Baylor graduate came off as overly polite while talking informally, but put him behind a podium for a speech, and he became a different person. It was as if the Director called, "Action!" as Norris launched into a dramatic and moving speech, without actually preaching to us. At the end of his allotted time, he would step away from the front of the classroom and resume his meek and mild demeanor. It was an amazing transformation to witness. That man had a commander's voice, and my kids would tease me about my commander's voice several years later.

During a class break one day, a female classmate asked an F-15 pilot in our class if he could fly any airplane. He gave a memorable answer, "If I can start it, I can fly it." Every airplane has a unique sequence for starting either the jet or propeller engine. But once the engine is started, the flying principles remain the same: Add thrust until takeoff speed; pull back and the houses get smaller; push forward and the houses get bigger again. It helps to know the proper speeds for landing, too. But I've always remembered his quote.

Our SOS class was due to graduate on August 10, 1990. On August 2, Saddam Hussein's Iraqi forces invaded Kuwait, and our world changed forever. Several students were recalled to their units for immediate deployment. All of us in aviation hoped we would get that recall notification. Send me back and let me fly! By this point we had not flown in over 30 days so we were all non-current and would need a proficiency flight to regain our takeoff and landing currency.

Some of the F-15, F-16, C-130, and even C-21 Learjet pilots were recalled to their units, but the rest of us had to stay put. We ground out the next week of papers, speeches, and a war-gaming exercise. The aircrew members watched the nightly news reports and called our squadrons, begging to be recalled.

The night before the course ended, I called Chaplain Burkes's room and asked if he would give a blessing for our class the next day. After our instructor gave her final debrief of our class's performance, we all stood in the middle of the classroom. Bowing our heads, Chaplain Burkes asked God to watch over us as we parted ways and prepared for our expected upcoming deployments.

CHAPTER 21

DESERT SHIELD

Big Sexy at Seeb Air Base, Oman

I returned to Barksdale in mid-August to find the ramp empty of its nineteen KC-10s. The planes and crews were busy moving people, planes and equipment all over the world. The squadron was deployed everywhere; from the Arabian Peninsula, to England, Spain, Germany, and the islands of Guam in the Pacific and Diego Garcia in the Indian Ocean. For the time being, I was a Non-Mission Ready copilot because I had not flown in more than six weeks and there were no KC-10s or instructor pilots around to requalify me.

A KC-10 and instructor were finally available August 15, and our four-man crew set out on a mission supporting a B-52 deployment. My requalification flight took place on a three-hour sortie from Barksdale to the B-52 base in Loring, Maine. From there, we flew ten hours to Hickam AFB, Hawaii to spend the night. We then continued the next morning for another seven hours to Andersen

AFB, on the island of Guam, about halfway between Australia and Japan. Although thousands of miles from Iraq, this is where some of our B-52 bombers were now stationed. After delivering the bomber support cargo and personnel, we stayed overnight before getting up the next day for the 13-hour return flight back to Barksdale. After completing this five-day mission, I was now designated as Mission Ready for any upcoming missions.

I spent most of September in Zaragoza, Spain with several other KC-10 crews. We were placed there as an Air Bridge, meaning we were ready to provide air refueling support to any long-range bomber missions in the event the U.S. needed to strike Saddam Hussein's Iraqi forces as our military build-up continued in the desert. American B-52s eventually flew 30-hour roundtrip bombing missions from the U.S. These missions were made possible by the refueling tankers over the Atlantic Ocean and Mediterranean Sea.

By October, after I returned from Spain, the ability to fly the KC-10 dropped off again as the planes were already deployed to bases in Oman, Spain, and Italy, along with an adequate amount of crew members. Fortunately, the Air Force had a flying program allowing copilots to gain flying experience when not flying the KC-10. The Accelerated Copilot Enrichment (ACE) program allowed two SAC copilots to sign out a T-37 trainer - the same small two-seat jet that we first learned to fly in pilot training - and fly around the U.S. to gain airmanship experience.

At first glance, this might sound like a boondoggle just waiting to be exposed on *60 Minutes*. In reality, it allowed two young copilots the chance to plan flights and make decisions about weather and safety, and not be overruled by an over-protective aircraft commander. Cloud-dancing was a favorite activity in the nimble Tweet. We weaved and bobbed around the cumulus clouds above the Arkansas/Louisiana/Texas region. I spent most of October flying to small airports, grabbing a burger in Ardmore, Oklahoma, College Station, Texas, or New Orleans, Louisiana.

While I was busy supporting the local economy of small airport restaurants, my KC-10 copilot friend and fellow former Barksdale

B-52 navigator, Kirk Shepherd, settled into the tent-city at Seeb Air Base outside of Muscat, Oman, on the eastern edge of the Arabian Peninsula. He was in the second wave of crews dispatched to the threadbare desert base in mid-August just weeks after Iraq invaded Kuwait. Those first crews arrived at a camp that was built using the prepositioned supplies deployed during the Reagan administration years before.

Quonset huts of materials contained 10-man canvas tents, a chow hall, and even never used 1984 camouflaged Chevy Blazers with keys inside. Just add oil, gas, and a battery and they were ready to go. The initial crews rotated home in late November and Kirk arrived as part of the four new crews manning two KC-10s. Within a few days he called back and said, "Dave, you've got to get over here. The flying is great!" Our wives were best of friends, and Karin knew I wanted to be over there helping out.

I asked Kirk and his wife, Colette, if he needed anything; after all, we were bringing a huge KC-10. Remember the part about being a Gucci Boy? Kirk gave me a shopping list: power strips, microwave, TV, VCR, and told me what I should pack for the three months. While Army and Marines troops deployed with what they could carry, and smaller Air Force cargo planes arrived with the bare essentials, our jumbo KC-10s made it to the desert with most of the modern conveniences of the early 1990s. The other services would agree, that's pretty Gucci.

My KC-10 simulator partner during initial training, Randy Fopiano, completed his upgrade to aircraft commander on November 1 with me serving as his copilot. His previous flight time as a T-37 instructor counted toward the 1,200 hours required for upgrade, whereas my navigator time didn't count, so I needed to build more hours before I could move up to aircraft commander. This deployment would provide those needed flight hours. On November 29, Randy and I became a crew, along with flight engineer (FE), Sgt Mike McKittrick, and boom operator (BO), Sgt Eric Thomas. We set off for Mildenhall Air Base, England for an overnight stop before heading down range to Oman.

Karin and I celebrated Christmas very early that year and she gave me a blue and green striped, long-sleeve rugby jersey. It was the right shirt to wear on a cold November night at the Mildenhall Officers Club. There was a lot of drinking going on that night as we all knew we were heading for a war zone. I drank a pint of English ale at a table with other Barksdale pilots as a group of loud, staggering drunk guys from another base started drinking Afterburners -- a flaming shot of liquor.

I didn't actually know what happened next, but I saw the effect. A swaying young stud behind me attempted to throw back his flaming shot, but only proceeded to throw the blue flaming liquid on his face. In the dark British pub, I sensed a glow behind me and turned to see what looked like a flaming jack-o'-lantern; all flames from the neck up.

I jumped out of my chair, tackled the big guy to the ground and started swiping my new rugby jersey sleeves over his face until the flames went out. I held my arms over his face and wondered what I would see when I removed them. I slowly pulled my arms away; he looked at me with singed eyebrows and a blistered lower lip.

In a low, gravelly voice he said, "Whoaaah."

Fortunately, most of the fire was just burning the alcohol; his skin didn't actually burn. Within minutes the air base medics and police responded to look after the young party animal and my crew headed to bed.

The next morning, December 1, 1990, we took off for Oman, flying across the Mediterranean region, through Egypt, and across Saudi Arabia. The accents of the foreign controllers were very difficult to understand as we headed eastward. Suddenly, when we were handed off to Doha Control over Qatar a perfectly understandable American voice acknowledged my radio check in.

After reporting my altitude and confirming we were in radar contact, I asked, "Are you military or a contractor brought in for the airlift?"

"Nah," he said. "I'm one of Reagan's boys."

He was a former U.S. air traffic controller who had gone on strike in 1981. When the government was unwilling to negotiate, he and others were fired by the Reagan administration for conducting an illegal strike. I told him it was a relief to hear his American accent. We flew south out of his airspace and as he handed us off to the United Arab Emirates (UAE) controllers he signed off, "Good luck to you boys. Be safe."

We landed at Seeb International Airport in the capital city of Muscat, and proceeded to our tent city, named Camp Nacirema, alongside the runway. Not everyone in the international community supported our coalition's build-up and military plans. There was a bit of contention about Americans being in the region to help one Muslim nation prepare to fight another. It was hard to stay low key during such a massive military buildup, but we were told not to be too flashy, which included no displays of American flags.

Proudly displaying the Texas flag outside our tent,
because American flags were not allowed.

Camp Nacirema was built in late August, soon after the Iraqi invasion of Kuwait, using prepositioned war materials intended for a possible conflict with Iran. The innovative first inhabitants came up with the camp's name, NACIREMA, which was AMERICAN spelled backwards. It was never changed during the entire military operation.

Sgt Mike McKittrick, Sgt Eric "ET" Thomas
Me, and Captain Randy Fopiano

Randy, Mike, Eric, and I settled into a large tent along with Kirk's four-man crew. Everyone was assigned a green canvas folding Army cot and had about four feet by eight feet of personal space, but the tent itself was an open style barracks without dividers. Our tent mates were happy to see our supply of power strips, large television, VCR, and microwave, just as requested. Karin sent me off to war with a cardboard powder-blue fold-out, three-drawer dresser for my clothes, on which I taped Polaroid family photos. We each brought a sleeping bag, sheets and a blanket, since the desert could get cold at night.

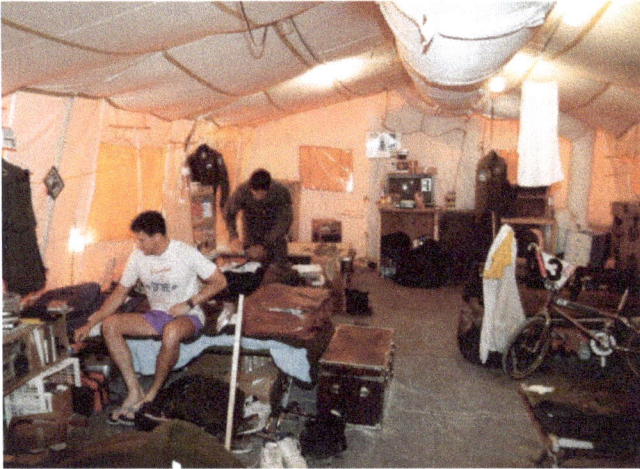

Randy and Kirk in our home away from home,
December 1990 to February 1991.

The camp had shower and lavatory tents at one end with ten
toilets in one tent and eight showers in the other. Advised to stay
hydrated in the desert, we initially drank two liters of water per day.
After my first 3:00 a.m. run to the bathroom with a near-bursting
bladder I gave up on the desire to stay overly hydrated.

At the opposite end of the camp was the chow hall, serving
cafeteria-style meals. Outside were two large trash cans of hot, soapy
water and clean cold water for cleaning out our mess kit after each
meal. This was 1990, but the conditions were similar to any TV
episode of the 1970s comedy *M*A*S*H*.

Creativity flourished after the basic necessities were taken care
of. The civil engineering unit out of Travis AFB, California did a
marvelous job building the Muscat Rose Saloon, complete with
wooden sidewalk and swinging doors. The benefit of being based in
Oman instead of Saudi Arabia was that alcohol was permitted, to a
limit. Because of our round-the-clock operation, each crew member
was allowed two beers within two hours of landing and each person
had a punch card to track their daily allotment. This didn't prevent
the non-drinkers from "loaning" you a beer, though. Two hours

after landing, we were back in Crew Rest to be rested for the next flight. Beer drinking could start at 10:00 a.m. if we landed from an all-night mission.

Unused scrap lumber was free game for camp members. Industrious crewmembers created lounge chairs, tables for card games and even a mock stockade to chastise offenders of informal camp rules: showering too long, snoring, farting, you name it.

Three days after getting settled into Camp Nacirema, our crew took off on our first five-hour mission. Kirk's aircraft commander, Captain Pat Heatherman, served as our guide for this orientation to the military operations. Our area ranged from Oman up to Saudi Arabia, just south of the Kuwaiti border, and the skies over the Persian Gulf. This included the area just off the Kuwaiti coast, where Saddam's forces loomed. Our mission this day was to refuel four 4-ship formations of F-16s, for a total of sixteen fighters. We would do this over a one-hour period while orbiting over the northern Saudi desert.

With our refueling assignment complete, we headed southeast to Oman at 27,000 feet. Randy needed to take a restroom break and left his seat to use the lavatory, just outside of the cockpit. In the few minutes he was away, the plane suddenly yawed to the left, with the tail swinging abruptly to the right a few degrees. Mike, the flight engineer, and I looked at the three columns of engine instruments. To once again quote that memorable children's song from *Sesame Street*, "One of these things doesn't look like the other."

The engines on any plane are numbered from left to right, so the #1 engine is on the left wing, our #2 engine was mounted on the tail, and the #3 engine was on our right wing. Our engine instruments, in the days before glass displays, were round dials with needles. Each engine had its own column, or stack, of gauges. Engines #2 and #3 both had their needles pointing toward the right, indicating good rpm, fuel flow, oil pressure, and exhaust gas temperature. The needles of the #1 engines were all pointing left, like a fuel tank running on empty. Our left, #1 engine had flamed out.

Every KC-10 pilot and flight engineer went through emergency training in the simulator four times a year. We knew the procedures inside and out for dealing with an engine failure and how to land with one engine out. My first step, however, was not in the checklist.

I pushed the PA (public address) button which was broadcast throughout the empty cabin and lavatory and calmly announced, "We just had an engine flameout." Randy quickly finished his business, and I turned off the autopilot and autothrottles to manually fly the plane while Randy got back in his seat to assess the situation.

An engine flameout is very rare, and we didn't have an explanation for why it happened. There was never a sense of panic but more of a reaction of, "Hmm. What caused this?" Years earlier a KC-10 flying out of Riyadh, Saudi Arabia had contaminated fuel, resulting in sand clogging all of the fuel filters. The crew had one engine flameout but was able to get the airplane back on the ground before the other two engines flamed out. That was a real possibility in our case, too, and their incident raced through our minds as we continued back to Seeb Air Base.

Some of the questions we wrestled with were: Should we divert to another foreign base without KC-10 maintenance support? Or should we continue over the 8,000-foot mountain range between us and Seeb?

"*What could go wrong next? Plan for the worst, but hope for the best,*" thought the Happy Pessimist.

The #2 and #3 engines, on the tail and right engine, were operating normally. Randy and I both remembered our simulator instructor's encouraging words, "This three-engine plane is designed to fly normally on two engines." Knowing that, Randy re-engaged the autopilot, and resumed flying while I declared an emergency with the air traffic controllers. This was not a shouting, "Mayday, Mayday, Mayday!" call as seen in the movies, but an advisory call to the Doha air traffic controllers.

"Doha Control, Esso 1-0 is declaring an emergency. We have one engine shutdown and need to proceed directly to Seeb Airport."

"Esso 1-0, Doha copies your emergency. State souls on board and fuel remaining."

This is a routine question during any emergency, for their incident paperwork.

"Doha, Esso 1-0 has five souls on board and three hours of fuel remaining."

"Esso 1-0, you are cleared direct to Seeb Airport. We will notify them of your emergency."

There are times in life when I've adopted a technique that I call micro-prayers. Sometimes, when entering a stressful situation, I simply ask, "LORD, please help me to say and do the right thing."

Other times, like during an aircraft emergency, I employ Alan Shepherd's Astronaut Prayer, "DEAR LORD, please don't let me screw this up." Apart from wanting to save my own neck and those of my crew, it's admittedly a selfish prayer to ensure I'm not blamed during an accident investigation.

Our flight engineer, Sgt McKittrick, read aloud the checklist steps for Engine Failure Inflight, which we completed step by step. Oman was notified of our emergency, and we safely crossed the small mountain range north of the airport. Randy brought our large jet in for a flawless one-engine out landing. Welcome to desert flying! We all certainly enjoyed our two beers that evening.

The KC-10 maintenance crews at Seeb discovered a bad fuel control unit for the #1 engine, but the fuel itself was fine. The control unit was replaced and the aircraft was put back into service the following week.

Our crew flew again three days later, refueling Navy F-18 fighters and EA-6B Prowler jamming aircraft in Exercise Desert Force, a show of force to let the Iraqis know we were in the region and ready to strike back aggressively if they pushed south from Kuwait and into Saudi Arabia during General Norman Schwarzkopf's military buildup.

A few days later, we closed out our first week of living in the new region by flying a Navy support mission, refueling F-18s and A-6 Intruder attack aircraft from the USS Midway. The carrier was located in the Persian Gulf, across the Straits of Hormuz from Iran. During Navy refuelings, Eric, our boom operator, extended a long refueling hose from the aft belly of the KC-10 and monitored the refueling as the Navy fighters stabbed our refueling basket with their refueling probe.

One of the dangers of this method of refueling is that if the fighter hits our basket with too much speed, it can create a sine wave with the hose that whips up and down violently enough to snap off the basket. The KC-10 would then have the equivalent of a fireman's hose spewing fuel and wagging uncontrollably behind us, perhaps even striking our tail. In that event, the boom operator needs to shut off the fuel and sever the flailing hose with a guillotine switch. This clamp and sever operation of the guillotine mechanism is like cutting an umbilical cord for a newborn, and it takes only seconds to complete. But this emergency situation requires a boom operator in his boom pod to keep us safe.

A heavily armed Navy F-18 refueling from
the KC-10 hose and drogue system.

By this point early in our deployment, Eric's stomach was not enjoying international chow hall food. After completing the assigned F-18 refueling, he called over the flight interphone, "Pilot? Boom. I'm not feeling too good. I need to come forward to the bathroom." Randy said he was clear to come forward and we could hear his flight boots running up the cargo floor. The door to the airline lavatory slammed just outside our cockpit.

A few seconds later, the amber annunciator light on our dashboard lit up stating, "Drogue Engaged." This meant that a Navy fighter had plugged into our refueling basket. In his haste to leave his refueling station, Eric never retracted the hose and now we had an unknown customer attached. Mike, the flight engineer, was in charge of the refueling pumps that delivered the fuel to our waiting customers. He was a little unsure what to do.

"What should I do?"

I laughed and replied, "He has to be one of ours. Give him some gas."

Meanwhile, Randy hit the PA button (why do things always happen while in the lavatory?) and said, "Boom! Someone is on the drogue!"

SLAM! THUMP, THUMP, THUMP, THUMP.

We heard Eric dash out of the bathroom and run down the 50-yard wooden cargo deck and down the stairs to his station. By the time he looked out the large aft window our mysterious Navy customer had disconnected and was pulling away.

Eric came on the interphone and announced, "Well. It was an A-6."

Chuckling, Randy said, "Boom, if you need to come back forward, please stow the drogue."

Back in Camp Nacirema, the off-duty flight crews, support personnel, and security police gathered at the Muscat Rose Saloon for beers under the cool, black starlit sky. Kirk and his crew returned from a mission and treated us to a low-altitude KC-10 flyby, using a legal circling approach maneuver.

A circling approach is a landing maneuver used when an airport has an instrument approach to get below the clouds but not to the runway of intended landing. If the winds are out of the south but the only approach available is to the north, the crew will fly the northbound approach until below the cloud layer, usually not lower than 500 to 1,000 feet above the ground. Once clear of the clouds, the crew breaks off the northbound approach and turns 30 degrees right or left and flies to the north end of the airfield, then begins a

180-degree turn, keeping the field in sight and completes the landing to the south. It's a visual maneuver flown below the clouds once the airport runway and surrounding environment are in sight.

Many crews had accomplished this approach, which conveniently overflew the camp's saloon at 700 feet above the ground. Right on schedule, Kirk's huge KC-10 appeared in the night sky, heading right for us. As they overflew the camp, their boom operator turned on all of their underbelly refueling guidance lights. This is a collection of red, yellow, and green lights in two parallel rows used to tell a receiver aircraft if he was too close, too far, or in the correct refueling position. At the same time, the boom operator lowered the flying boom and wagged it left and right, as Kirk banked the airplane left and right, in a wave to the crowd below. We all cheered and raised our cans of Smithwick Irish Ale, Newcastle Brown Ale, or O'Doul's non-alcoholic beer.

Our wing commander, not amused by the display, announced that Kirk's was the last fly-by to be flown over our camp. We protested, saying they were just flying a practice circling approach. He was in no mood to change his mind.

"It was a circling approach right up until the wing-wag. Then it became an airshow. No more!"

As the military build-up continued, air crews routinely monitored BBC broadcasts over the airplane's High Frequency (HF) radio to keep up with the diplomatic efforts and ensure we were aware if war broke out in the middle of our eight-hour missions. The HF radio also came in handy for calling our families back home.

The Military Auxiliary Radio System (MARS) is a volunteer organization that uses U.S. amateur (ham) radio operators to complete calls to our military dependents. From our KC-10 flying high over the Arabian Peninsula, we contacted a radio operator in the States and he or she patched us through to our home telephone in Louisiana. Before beginning the conversation, the radio operator explained that they would be monitoring the call and had to switch a dial from Receive to Transmit to carry out the link between the two parties. At the end of each statement my wife or I had to say,

"Over," to let the radio operator know that the other person would now talk. The brief conversations went something like this:

"How are you doing, Karin? Over."

"All is fine here. Over."

"I love you. Over."

"I love you, too. Over."

The touching conversations became memorable for the slogan, "I love you. Over."

We closed out 1990 with an outdoor Christmas celebration where I sang in the choir on a wooden stage complete with a fake decorated Christmas tree. I remember thinking that we were in the Middle East, surrounded by dry desert sand and not far from that Little Town of Bethlehem.

Operation Desert Shield provided just what the name implied. We provided a protective air shield over the Arabian Peninsula while ships full of combat personnel and equipment offloaded in ports throughout the region. Our country and allies completed the largest military buildup since World War II in record time.

CHAPTER 22

MOGADISHU, PART I

AC-130 Gunship (Military.com)

O ur country mainly knows about Africa's Somalia and its capital Mogadishu from the 2001 movie, *Black Hawk Down,* about a downed Army helicopter during the 1993 Battle of Mogadishu and the daring rescue operation that followed. Although I would eventually deliver those same Army Rangers into Mogadishu, my first encounter with the capital city actually started a few nights before Operation Desert Storm kicked off.

While based at Seeb Air Base in Muscat, Oman, our crew was pulled away from our Desert Shield refueling missions as the military buildup in Saudi Arabia continued. We scrambled as an Alert Tanker to support the evacuation of the State Department workers in the Somali capital of Mogadishu as the city fell to rebel soldiers. Our task was to refuel an AC-130 gunship off the coast of Somalia as they provided air support during the evacuation.

Taking off at 3:00 a.m., we flew 1,700 miles south from Oman in just under four hours to rendezvous with the gunship as the sun rose on January 4, 1991. The AC-130 had rapid-fire gun barrels and cannon protruding from its side, and refueled at the very slow speed of 220 knots (250 mph). In comparison, the relatively slow A-10 fighter refueled at 250 knots but most of the other aircraft we refueled flew at 280-300 knots, so 220 knots seemed quite slow.

The heavily loaded AC-130 pulled up behind us at dawn to start the air refueling process. They had difficulty closing the distance between us because they could not penetrate the bow wave coming off our aircraft. The bow wave is a cushion of air between airplanes, and it requires a little extra power from the trailing aircraft to penetrate and proceed into the refueling position. The heavy AC-130 just couldn't generate enough power to break through this air cushion.

Their pilot asked us to slow to 210 knots, which we did. They asked again for us to slow some more, so we slowed to 200 knots. We were so focused on helping them get onto our refueling boom that we didn't realize we were now flying so slowly that we should have partially deployed our wings' trailing edge flaps to create more lift and help to lower our nose closer to a horizontal, level attitude.

We finally realized that our deck angle was abnormally high and told the AC-130 to maintain their distance while we deployed our flaps a few degrees and safely slowed to 200 knots. Once slowed, we began a slow, gradual descent called a Toboggan maneuver, allowing the heavy AC-130 to use the descent to gain enough speed for them to complete their contact and receive the fuel they needed.

With the refueling complete, the gunship peeled off to the west, toward Mogadishu. We stayed in the refueling orbit over water for four hours, monitoring the radios to keep abreast of the situation over the crumbling city.

Suddenly, we heard the Navy Super Stallion helicopters, sent from the USS Guam to retrieve the State Department workers, calling for air support from the AC-130. There was no reply from the gunship as the helicopters made repeated radio calls. After listening to the unanswered calls, I radioed the AC-130 on the same frequency.

Because we were flying at 25,000 feet, much higher than the other low-flying helicopters and gunship, we could hear all of them, but they could not hear each other. I quickly became a radio relay between the two-ship helicopter flight and their gunship support.

The helicopter pilots painted a verbal picture of the situation in the city, saying there were roving patrols of rebels driving around the city in station wagons with rifles sticking out of the windows. I thought about the dichotomy of our American airborne gunship bristling with cannons and machine gun barrels, and this Somali "rebel gunship," probably a beat up 1970s station wagon with AK-47s protruding from its windows. While Randy flew from the left seat, I relayed the position of the roving rebels to the AC-130 crew for them to lend their aerial support to the evacuation below.

In July 1992, Malcolm McConnell wrote an excellent account of this operation for *Reader's Digest*, entitled "Rescue at Mogadishu." Of that day's mission he wrote:

"The city of Mogadishu spread before the helicopters, a confusing white-washed sprawl. Finding the embassy on their outdated map would not be easy. They were flying at rooftop level now and had to keep a sharp watch for power lines. Suddenly, the lead pilot spotted the embassy's distinctive mushroom-shaped water tower. As they sailed toward the compound's southern perimeter, men with rifles and rocket-propelled grenades were climbing the ladders set against the outside walls. The pilot hauled back on his controls to rear the big chopper just above the wall. The rotor wash blew away the looters and their ladders as if they were made of paper. He then eased the chopper forward to land inside the compound. An hour after landing, the two Super Stallions departed with the first 61 evacuees, including all of the foreign diplomats and private U.S. citizens in the compound." *

By the end of the day, 61 U.S. State Department personnel were extracted from the U.S. Embassy compound by the two Navy Sea Stallion helicopters and safely evacuated to the USS Guam. Once

---

* Malcolm McConnell, "Rescue at Mogadishu," Reader's Digest, July 1992, page 68.

the AC-130 completed its air support mission over the city, they returned to their base in Kenya. We flew north late that afternoon, logging 12 hours and 45 minutes of combat support time. Assisting in the safe evacuation of the State Department workers gave our crew immense satisfaction -- right place; right time.

CHAPTER 23

DESERT STORM

KC-10 taking off from Seeb Air Base, Muscat, Oman

Our time in the desert took place before cell phones, the internet, or email. I wrote and received a lot of letters, most to and from friends and family in the States, but others were exchanged with kind-hearted Americans writing letters addressed "To Any Serviceman." These were pen pal-type letters written by school kids, military veterans and even another David Dale that I wasn't related to.

Camp Nacirema had one telephone tent with phones placed in wooden cubicle-style booths. A camp member could sign up for a 10-minute time slot and call home collect. The trick to holding down the cost was to call my family, give them my international phone number in Oman and have them call me back quickly at the cheaper rate. I spoke to my mom in Houston on January 15 and called my dad in Denver at 9:30 p.m. Oman time (10:30 a.m. Mountain Time) on January 16. I spoke briefly to him, relaying my number and hung up, then waited for the callback. I sat by the quiet phone for my allotted ten minutes but it never rang.

Once my time slot closed, I headed back to my cot and off to sleep. Meanwhile back in the U.S., my dad couldn't get the call to go through, so he called Karin in Louisiana. What they discovered is that he was dialing 001 followed by the phone number, but 001 is for calls going to the States. He needed to dial 011 followed by my number in Oman. This was all figured out once I was in bed. Two hours later the telephone tent was shut down for what would turn out to be two weeks.

Sometime after midnight, Lieutenant Colonel Jan Swickard, our DO, stepped quietly into our tent of eight sleeping crewmembers and gently woke up Randy, Eric, Mike, and me. We were chosen to fly our camp's first mission of Desert Storm. We slipped on our flightsuits, pulled on our boots, and I quickly wrote out what might have been a last letter home to my wife and stuck it in my deployment bag.

Last Letter Home, January 16, 1991 (fortunately, never mailed)

My Dearest Karin,

This is it. Randy & I were just notified that we will be flying the first real mission in support of the offensive. Everyone has studied, and our crew is one of the best prepared here. Randy has read and asked a lot of questions about tactics. Mike has been a real positive influence on the crew with his "let's do it" attitude. Eric is a good boom operator who takes his job seriously in the air.

Randy and I proofed the flight plans for the operations folks and pointed out pretty useful corrections. Except for our wedding day and the birth of Daniel, this has been one of the most important times of my life. I've been able to make real contributions at a time when they really count.

I'm so sorry we're not together. I honestly have not had a single day in the last 49 days when I have not thought of you and our great son Daniel. No matter how mad I've ever gotten at you in the last 6 years, you have always been one of the most beautiful women I've ever met. I thank you for the fantastic support you've given me, especially in the tough times. Our year at UPT seemed to be our best.

I hope Daniel continues to grow big and strong. He is the pride of our lives. Tell him I LOVE HIM more than anything in the world.

Take care always.
Love Forever,
David
Mom, Dad, Lucy, Hannah, and Jack:
I LOVE YOU ALL

We gathered in the operations tent for the mission briefing and signed out the necessary communications gear, enabling our KC-10 radios to make and receive encrypted radio calls undetectable to the Iraqis. We piled into the blue Air Force pick-up truck and drove out to our waiting KC-10 to begin the preflight. In our haste to get moving, we forgot our bag of protective chemical gear. We needed it if we returned to a base that had received a chemical attack while we were gone, which was a real possibility. The Supervisor of Flying, or SOF, quickly brought us the large green canvas bag of gasmasks, large black rubber gloves, and green rubber boots.

We took off in the dead of night and headed northwest to refuel F-15s from the 1st Fighter Wing, deployed from Langley AFB, Virginia. Our mission that night lasted seven and a half hours and was all accomplished in radio silence. Other than checking in with the E-3A AWACS providing air traffic control in the sky that night, it was pretty quiet on the radios. The F-15s provided a Combat Air Patrol, or CAP -- a protective air cover to the warfighters in the desert below. Like hummingbirds returning to a feeder, the four fighter jets came to us two at a time throughout our mission as we orbited in a left-hand 30-mile racetrack over northern Saudi Arabia.

By the time we landed at sunrise in Oman, we weren't really certain that the war had actually begun. We completed our mission debrief and turned in our classified communications gear, then headed to the TV Tent to watch the CNN coverage of the beginning of Operation Desert Storm.

Like everyone in the U.S., we watched the reports from Bernard Shaw and Wolf Blitzer showing the snaking green anti-aircraft tracers arcing over Baghdad, something we would eventually see ourselves. For now, it was time for breakfast and sleep.

Two missions later, on January 19, there was a miscommunication in the tasking order. Our crew briefing stated that our KC-10 would take off as the fifth tanker behind four of our base's KC-135s. This 5-ship tanker package was to refuel a large number of F-16s before and after their bombing missions. Our mission was officially referred to as Pre-strike and Post-strike refueling. Before we departed for our aircraft, word came down that the mission was canceled. The four KC-135s remained on the ground and our KC-10 was directed to take off and head to an orbit to serve as a back-up tanker. We were on station in case anyone needed emergency refueling.

We arrived on station in the daylight in an area just south of the Kuwaiti border and took up our racetrack pattern of left-hand turns. All was very quiet again on the radios when suddenly Randy looked over his left shoulder and said, "I have four F-16s closing on our wing."

I looked out my window and said, "I've got four on the right."

Eric, our boom operator, looked out his large window in the bottom of the plane below the tail and called out, "I've got eight back here!"

Without warning, our flying gas station was swarmed by sixteen F-16s that had just released their bombs over Kuwait. They came screaming southbound out of the combat area and were now low on fuel. The leader of each four-ship flight prioritized his receivers according to lowest fuel state and Eric began quickly plugging his boom into the receptacles of the thirsty fighters over the next 22 minutes.

I radioed AWACS and said we needed other tanker support in this area, and they quickly vectored other tankers our way. In all, Eric refueled 14 of the 16 F-16s, giving them each 1,000 pounds, or about 150 gallons of gas, in just 15 seconds per airplane. Two of the sixteen couldn't wait any longer and diverted to another tanker or a nearby runway below us.

It was later determined that only the pre-strike refueling mission should have been canceled. The strike package of four F-16 four-ship flights either took off with enough fuel to get to their targets, or they refueled from other tankers. Our five-ship tanker package should have been on station for the post-strike refueling. Fortunately, Eric managed to handle most of it single-handedly, refueling 14 F-16s in just 22 minutes. Those fighter pilots were thankful that our boom operator performed so well under pressure!

Me (center) watching Captain Kirk Shepherd (right) load flight gear and Meals Ready to Eat (MREs) for an upcoming mission. Our intelligence officer is pictured to the left.

Our missions were pretty evenly split between refueling Navy fighters off the east coast of Kuwait and refueling Air Force jets south of Kuwait. In an impressive demonstration of the firepower the U.S. could gather, our crew would typically be one of three KC-10s, flying one mile behind each other and each plane 500 feet above the preceding tanker. Alongside each KC-10 were eight Navy fighters, four on each wing. The strike packages consisted of F-18s, F-14s and A-6s. Each KC-10 topped off their eight "chicks," then the entire strike package peeled off northwest toward Kuwait and we awaited their return.

The Iraqi Air Force soon realized their outdated Russian-made MiG fighters were outmatched by our F-15s and F-16s and they began to flee to Iran in the hope of surviving the war. To prevent their escape, we began escorting F-15s deep inside Iraq where they would chase down the fleeing MiGs. Again, our crew was selected for the first refueling mission into enemy-controlled Iraq.

We were the lead tanker of a two-ship KC-10 flight assigned to refuel four F-15s. As we crossed north into Iraq, we turned off all our external lighting - per our mission directive - so the enemy ground forces 30,000 feet below us couldn't see us. Everything was done in radio silence with the fighters easing up alongside us in the pitch-black sky.

Ninety miles south of Baghdad, we could see the red anti-aircraft tracers snaking up in four wavy columns into the sky below us but burning out before reaching our altitude. Two interesting facts about tracers: Although depicted on CNN's night-vision cameras as green, they were actually red. And although the tracer rounds burn out at 20,000 feet, the lead bullets fired as part of the AAA gun burst continue climbing much higher. We were blissfully ignorant of this, not realizing the lead bullets came much closer to us than the tracers ever did.

Why were we seeing anti-aircraft fire below us? I got my answer as we went into a left U-turn and saw that the #2 tanker in our formation still had his red anti-collision beacon flashing. This is the same light people see in the night sky as airliners pass overhead. I couldn't believe it.

"Kill your beacon!" I yelled to #2 over our interplane formation frequency.

Night missions afforded what I called the "Light Show" below us in Kuwait. We saw the series of bomb flashes go off as B-52s and coalition fighter-bombers dropped their loads on the Iraqi Republican Guard. Many of us in the KC-10 had previously flown the B-52. Although we were happy to be flying the modern KC-10, we felt nostalgic and missed performing the combat bombing operations for which we had trained.

This five-week air campaign was meant to reduce the Iraqi ground forces before our Army moved north. On daytime missions we could see what looked like long clawing scratch marks on the Saudi desert floor as massive amounts of Allied tanks and armored fighting vehicles moved into place along the southern Kuwaiti border.

The U.S. Army had long-range artillery known as the M270 Multiple Launch Rocket System (MLRS). These fired using either a long-range, low-altitude profile or a short-range, high-altitude profile. We encountered the latter. After completing our assigned refueling west of Kuwait, our flight plan called for a southbound leg before turning eastward toward Oman. It was a quiet night, and we thought we'd take a shortcut southeast, skirting the border of Kuwait. Our cockpit suddenly lit up as a stream of MLRS missiles came screaming up toward the left side of our cockpit. The only words I could manage were, "Whoa! Whoa! Whoa!" as I pointed across the cockpit to the rising tower of flames. I'm certain our Army's rockets were miles from us, but in a pitch-black sky, they certainly looked uncomfortably close. We turned to the right and back to our proper southerly course.

Our base continued these F-15 refueling missions into Iraq for three more nights. We soon realized it's not a good idea to fly the same combat support mission in the same area night after night. Eventually the enemy will see a pattern. On the fourth evening a crew was refueling on a partly cloudy night when suddenly the clouds around them lit up as bright as day. An enemy surface to air missile had been launched and flew through the tanker formation, but fortunately no one was hit. That ended the series of refuelings over Iraq.

The threat came not only from the enemy, though. In the densely packed combat airspace, mid-air collisions were a real danger. One cloudy night we were assigned a Navy refueling mission over the Persian Gulf refueling eight F-14s that were providing air protection to the carrier fleet below. Our assigned altitude of 25,000 feet was still in the thick of the clouds. The Navy has a smaller version of our Air Force AWACS, called the E-2 Hawkeye, with its own smaller spinning radar. Their mission was to provide air traffic guidance to the planes in their area. I called the Hawkeye and requested a climb to 27,000 feet to get above the cloud layer so that the F-14s could pick us up visually to refuel.

We completed our first set of nighttime refuelings as we skimmed in and out of the top layer of clouds. I started to hear a whining sound from the right and looked out my window as a KC-135 popped out of the clouds and zoomed right over our cockpit, missing us by 500 feet. I knew it was close when I heard it before I saw it.

I shouted at the E-2, "Who just came through our area?!"

He replied, "I'm not painting any targets in your area."

I yelled back, "Well, we almost just got hit!" Apparently, another tanker crew thought it was a good idea to take a shortcut home.

The support we received from home during Desert Storm was phenomenal. Total strangers and school children continued mailing us letters by the stack. Organizations big and small sent us care packages and a supply of current magazines for our camp's recreation center. Our refueling missions lasted up to eight hours, so I often grabbed a magazine to read on the one-hour return leg home after things calmed down. Before one evening's sortie, I spied a recent issue of *Skin Diver* magazine and threw it in my helmet bag, telling Randy I'd show him an advertisement in it later.

My childhood friend, Larry Leonard, now lived in the Cayman Islands and was the marketing director for a dive shop called *Parrot's Landing*. Larry finished college during a recession, so he answered a job ad in 1988 for a bartender in the Cayman Islands. His whole family were scuba-dive certified, and now he could bartend at night and dive during the day.

His bartending work had run its course by 1990, and with the help of his future wife, Shelley, Larry met Greg, the owner of *Parrot's Landing* dive shop. Greg was in need of a marketing guy and Larry was itching to use his business degree and entrepreneurial skills for this small business. Larry realized that the way to fill dive boats was to sell dive packages, so he created one-stop shopping for hotels, airfare, and diving, using a new innovation called the internet. Over the next several years *Parrot's Landing* grew from a single boat to a fleet of seven off-shore diving boats.

To gain exposure, Larry placed advertisements in *Skin Diver* magazine, and I brought along this latest issue only to show my crew a small ad for *Parrot's Landing* and to brag about my friend.

With our refueling complete, we turned southeast for Oman, and I dug the magazine out from my helmet bag. I flipped through the pages, searching for the dive shop advertisement when I suddenly saw a picture of Larry… with a parrot on his shoulder. I couldn't believe it. A random issue of *Skin Diver* that I grabbed from a stack of magazines in Oman had a three-page article about *Parrot's Landing* and their pioneering marketing director, Larry Leonard. The world just keeps getting smaller.

One month after the air war began, I completed my 20th combat support mission on February 16, 1991, during a flight that demonstrated the versatility of our "Big Sexy" KC-10. The tasking was to refuel Navy F-14s and F-18s from the USS America off the coast of Kuwait. As the copilot, one of my duties was to monitor several radio frequencies, including an emergency air refueling (A/R) frequency in case there was an urgent need for gas.

As we continued to refuel the Navy using our hose and drogue system, I heard a call on the emergency frequency.

"Any Tanker. Any Tanker!"

I answered the call and discovered it was an F-16 desperate for fuel. He was part of a two-ship Hunter/Killer F-16 flight. One wingman would remain at high altitude to spot enemy targets and then guide his wingman down to the target for the kill. The fighters had gotten so wrapped up in their mission that this pilot was now dangerously low on fuel. He asked if we had a boom or a drogue on this mission, since the KC-135 could do one or the other but not both. I told him, "We're a KC-10. We have both. Come on up."

I gave the F-16s our location and told them we were currently refueling Navy fighters, but they could join our formation. Randy then told the Navy receivers that the F-16s would be joining up soon. I was able to snap a photo of three multi-service jets on our wing: two Air Force F-16s, and a Navy F-14. It had to be a pretty cool sight for both services to watch as Eric reeled in the hose and lowered the boom to complete the impromptu Air Force refueling. The F-16s thanked us for the gas and resumed their mission over Kuwait. As I monitored the refueling frequency, I heard him say, "Hey, if anyone needs gas, there's a real friendly KC-10 off the coast."

Refueling Air Force F-16s and Navy F-14s on the same mission.
"Flexibility is the Key to Airpower!"

After thirty days of nearly continuous flying, our crew hit the safe maximum flying hour limit of 150 hours in 30 days. Additionally, our KC-10s still had to undergo routine scheduled maintenance back in the U.S. to maintain their FAA certification. Many of these checks had been delayed as long as possible but the planes still needed to be swapped out. Our base used a first in, first out (FIFO) schedule, so Kirk's crew departed a week earlier, and our crew would be next to head home. Without the ability to fly KC-10 missions due to our excessive flight hours, I decided to go on a joyride, flying with a KC-135 crew. That was almost a mistake.

The KC-135 crew made their way up to their assigned Persian Gulf orbit to refuel Navy A-6s with the small hose and drogue assembly attached to their boom nozzle, dangling very much like an elephant's trunk. I followed their boom operator back to his station, and we laid on our stomachs, each on a thin bed mattress, our chins resting on a support and looking out of the small rectangular window. An A-6 appeared from below in the night sky and closed toward the drogue basket. I don't know if the naval aviator was excited or nervous but he closed at a high rate of speed. He undershot the basket and continued to close on us as the boom operator commanded the emergency procedure.

"Break Away! Break Away! Break Away!"

This is the standard command during a botched refueling attempt and the tanker accelerates up and away from the receiver at the same time as the receiver pulls power and dives below to avoid a collision. Given the momentum of the A-6, his round bulbous grey nose rose toward our glass window like a SeaWorld Shamu coming up for a herring treat. Although it did no good, the boom operator and I both backed up as far as we could in the cramped refueling station. Much like Goose's quote from *Top Gun,* I could just hear the military telling my wife and mom, "The Defense Department regrets to inform you that your son is dead from being stupid, joy-riding in a KC-135 during wartime." Fortunately, the A-6 didn't hit us and I returned to the base to prepare for the homeward journey.

We landed at Barksdale AFB the night of February 21, 1991, after an overnight stop in Mildenhall, England. We were home again after 85 days of living in the tent city. In total, I completed 30 combat support missions, 10 during Desert Shield and 20 during Desert Storm. On February 27, I rocked our eighteen-month-old son in my lap, and listened to President George H. W. Bush tell our nation that the Iraqi forces had surrendered.

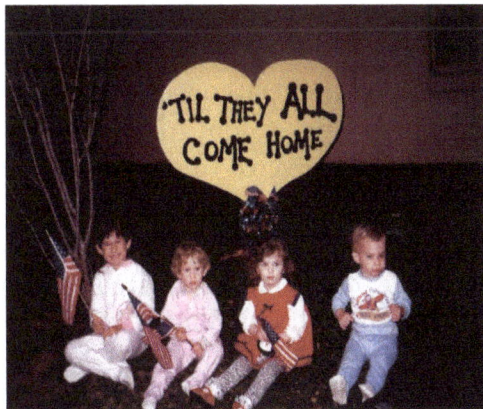

Daniel, far right, on the night I returned from Operation Desert Storm.

143

CHAPTER 24

BARKSDALE IS THAT WAY, I RECKON

Bringing the F-117 Stealth fighter home.

Although the combat operations had ended by March, there was still a lot of work to do. All of the combat airplanes and crews that we delivered to the desert bases now needed to come home. My days of tent-living were over, but I deployed to Morón Air Base, Spain, in May 1991. From there I made numerous trips back to the desert, retrieving F-16 cargo from Al Minhad Air Base in the UAE bound for Hill AFB in Utah, and B-52 supplies in England that we delivered to Loring AFB, Maine.

In May, we flew to Khamis Mushait in southern Saudi Arabia, the wartime home of our F-117 Stealth fighter bomber. After arriving, we received tours of the Black Bat Stealth fighter and were shown combat film footage from their airstrikes in Kuwait and Iraq.

Given the limited visibility from the F-117 cockpit, each of our three KC-10s only escorted two fighters as we brought them back to the U.S. We had one on each wing, instead of the usual flight of four. We started the long deployment to their base in Nevada with overnight stops in Mildenhall, England, and Seymour Johnson AFB, in North Carolina, before finally touching down at their air base near Tonopah, Nevada.

The Nevada desert winds were howling that day, buffeting the airplanes as the support crews deplaned and the cargo was off-loaded. Once empty, we were ready to turn and burn, wanting to head back home to Barksdale as soon as possible. Because the Tonopah airfield was classified, we had very little geographic information available to align our inertial navigation system (INS), and the aircraft buffeting from the high winds did not help the situation.

Our plane was the second of the three KC-10s and our INS, consisting of a spinning gyro, failed to align itself on the first attempt. The lead tanker got his system to align properly and decided we would all head home separately, so he said, "See y'all back home," and departed. Our INS aligned on the second attempt and we taxied out for takeoff.

There are various pieces of navigation equipment onboard the KC-10, and this was all prior to the highly accurate GPS units we have today. The first, dating back to the early days of aviation were radio beams that planes can track from station to station. Second was the onboard INS system with its gyro. The INS allowed planes to fly directly to a set of geographic coordinates. We routinely cross checked the accuracy of the INS by flying over a radio beacon and ensuring both systems were guiding the plane to the same spot.

This didn't happen in Tonopah. As soon as we lifted off, the INS needle indicated that we needed to turn right, but the radio beacon needle pointed to the left. We started flying to the right, because INS is our primary navigation source, and the departure controller quickly broadcast that we needed to turn left. We knew right away that we had a navigation issue. It appeared we would be flying from one radio navigation beam to another, like Charles Lindbergh and other mail carriers in the 1920s.

We continued to climb into the peaceful Sunday morning sky and were told to contact the Los Angeles Control Center, the air traffic controllers for that region of airspace. Unbeknownst to us, when our lead tanker had checked in earlier, he told the controller that we had just returned from a desert deployment and were heading home. When I checked in with Los Angeles Center, he cheerfully greeted me with, "Good Morning, Deuce 5-0! Welcome home, boys. You're cleared direct to Barksdale."

It was a very nice favor to allow us to short-cut across the southwestern U.S. That is, if we had a functioning navigation system. I looked at the aircraft commander and harkening back to my navigator days said, "Well, it should be a 090-degree (easterly) heading."

We proceeded to use dead reckoning as our means to get home. Eventually, we saw that Albuquerque, New Mexico was coming up and we had the geographic coordinates available for that airport. Flying our plane directly over the Albuquerque airport, I entered the airport's latitude and longitude coordinates into our INS, providing a manual update to its waywardness. Two hours later, we found Barksdale just where we left it one week earlier.

Chapter 25

Covering All of My Bases

WARNING: "Because of the magnitude of interrelated aerodynamic effects, flying two aircraft in close vertical proximity is not safe. — KC-10 Dash 1, Operating Manual
(Photo by MSgt Harold Wenner)

Four lights danced in the ink-black night sky up ahead of us. A red rotating beacon pulsed rhythmically, and three small white position lights formed a perfect triangle just above the red beacon. The lights seemed to float in space, drawing us in like a June bug to a porchlight. I was flying 1,000 feet below the still-invisible KC-135R and one mile behind. From that trailing position, I pushed the three KC-10 throttles with my right hand, adding power to climb an uphill slope of 100 feet for each tenth of a mile. From a half mile behind and 500 feet below, the old, gray tanker loomed into view and the roar of its four large CFM-56 engines could now be heard.

With my left hand on the control yoke and my right on the three throttles, my hands began to sweat inside the green Nomex flight gloves. The gloves included a small patch of gray leather for the fingers and palms, like the tracing of a ten-year old's hand. This provided enough traction despite the nervous sweat. I eased the throttles back gently about two inches, stopping the escalator-like ascent to the refueling position. I was now in the pre-contact position, just 50 feet away from the tip of the boom's nozzle, pointing at me with a white light like a policeman's flashlight in my front windscreen.

Eighty feet farther ahead, just below the boom attachment point, I could see the face of the KC-135 boom operator through his wide rectangular window. His face was illuminated by a soft red light inside his boom pod. Inside the tanker, the young airman lay face-down on a thin, narrow mattress, his chin resting in a tiny, padded T-shaped support, taking the strain off his neck. In his left and right hands, he gripped two small black control sticks for the "flyable boom" dangling between us. With his right hand he controlled the up, down, left, and right movements of the 28-foot-long boom. With his left, he could extend the telescoping boom to place it inside our rooftop receptacle once I arrived at the correct position.

I stopped my closure rate and now matched the tanker's speed of 480 miles per hour, or eight miles per minute. From the Pre-contact position I pushed the transmit button near my left index finger, "Cajun 2-1. Stable, Pre-Contact."

"Cajun 2-1, Bolt 3-3. You're cleared to contact." the boom operator replied.

"Copy. Cleared to contact." I squeezed the three throttles to move them forward a fraction of an inch.

The tip of his boom passed over our cockpit and the rush of the outside air grew louder as we crept slowly toward the refueling position. The telescoping portion was like the white stick poking from an old tire pressure gauge. It could extend from the 28-foot boom housing and had a sweet spot of 12 feet extension. This meant that I would be sitting approximately forty feet from the boom operator in the plane ahead of me. But the boom could maintain a contact from as close as 8 feet extension and out to 16 feet. It could also safely swing left and right eight degrees each direction. Ideally, the boom dangled at a 30-degree angle, but could rise up to a 22-degree angle or drop down to 45 degrees. This was my box of airspace, and it was my job to stay inside that box.

The air current rushing over the KC-135's wing spilled downward and encountered the large, blunt nose of our heavy KC-10. This created the bow wave, preceding us and pushing on the tail of the tanker flying above us. I closed in toward the center of the refueling envelope when I suddenly saw the nose of the KC-135 dip down, his fuselage growing larger in our windscreen. His antiquated autopilot was unable to keep up with the changing trim conditions caused by our bow wave and abruptly kicked off.

"BREAKAWAY! BREAKAWAY! BREAKAWAY!" commanded the young boom over the radio as he recognized that his plane was descending into our huge airplane just outside his window.

I snatched the three throttles back to idle and pushed forward my yoke, beginning an immediate collision-avoiding descent. Simultaneously, the KC-135 pilot aggressively pushed the power up on his four large engines, grabbed his yoke and pulled back to climb away from us.

Once we were safely separated below him and drifting aft, I added power to stabilize my position. The KC-135R returned to its assigned refueling altitude of 30,000 feet and I climbed back to the Pre-contact position for another attempt. Such was the thrill of night air refueling behind a KC-135R. I really didn't care for it very much.

Two months earlier, after the F-117 return mission to Tonopah Air Base, Nevada I had accumulated the required 1,200 flying hours to enter the aircraft commander upgrade course. All the trips to the desert had accelerated every copilot's upgrade that year. Air Force flight crews typically flew 300 to 400 hours per year, which is much lower than an airline pilot's usual total of 800 to 900 hours per year. I closed out 1991 with 550 flying hours.

I entered the upgrade program in September 1991, beginning with a brief academic overview of KC-10's system and a series of seven simulator sessions. The academics portion was similar to my initial qualification training two years earlier. In 1989 I soaked in the information, but it was mostly rote memorization and theoretical. Now, I had two years of applying that knowledge, so studying it all a second time really made the details more understandable. I envisioned the knowledge sinking in deeper and not just bouncing off my Teflon brain.

During the four weeks of simulator training, I was paired with another upgrade candidate, Captain Drexel Kleber, who we all simply called Drex. He was a tall young man with thick, black hair. I remember him as a nice family man. He shared that he and his wife made it a point to get a baby-sitter once a week and go out on a date. Karin and I took his advice to heart years later.

The hardest part of the upgrade training was physically transitioning from the right seat to the left and retraining my brain to do everything with the opposite hand. It's comparable to the mental gymnastics of an American renting a stick-shift British right-side-drive car. The American driver must get used to driving with the right hand and shifting with the left hand. My transition became a bit of a "rub my stomach and pat my head" exercise for the first few simulator sessions.

Once my brain adjusted to the new control inputs, I began the most physically challenging portion of KC-10 flying: receiver refueling. As a copilot, I was never expected to take on the fuel behind a tanker, but we did practice from the right seat to get used to making the very slight control and throttle inputs required to remain in position. Now it was my responsibility to get into the contact position and stay thirty feet behind the KC-135 or KC-10 as the fuel was transferred into our plane. Although almost everyone mastered this mission capability, the inability to complete the receiver refueling portion of training was grounds for disqualification and could potentially lead to a permanent assignment as a First Pilot in the right seat.

The high-fidelity, full-motion simulator was a large white box lifted by four hydraulic arms, containing a life-size replica of the

KC-10 cockpit. It included a viewscreen ahead of us, projecting a realistic depiction of the sky and ground. The training provided extremely realistic scenarios in how to handle KC-10 emergencies, both on the ground and in the air. Although we practiced the normal procedures for our role as both the tanker and the receiver in a refueling situation, the primary focus during each four-hour session was practicing our emergency procedures.

The week of simulator sessions culminated with a stressful two-day evaluation, each session lasting four hours. During the first four-hour session, I served as Drex's copilot as he handled a loss of electrical generators and a high-speed engine failure on takeoff, requiring that the takeoff continue with one engine inoperative. Drex did a great job performing all of the required maneuvers and managing the emergency situations.

On Day 2 it was my turn in the hot seat. After performing our role as both tanker and receiver, it was time for our evaluator to play Dial-A-Disaster. My emergency scenarios (not all at one time) consisted of a dual hydraulic system failure, losing two of our three systems, another high-speed engine failure on the takeoff without the ability to abort, and an engine fire at altitude with a return to the runway with one engine out.

The concentration was intense throughout the entire session, knowing that my every move and decision was being watched by an evaluator sitting just three feet behind us. After four pressure-packed hours, the simulator box gently settled down on its hydraulic legs as the full-motion sim became still and quiet. I felt a wave of relief, knowing our evaluation was finally over. Our evaluator for both sessions, the chief of the evaluation branch, complimented both of our performances during his one-hour debrief.

With the simulator evaluation behind us, it was time to return to the flightline and receive actual refueling practice. I spent the month of October logging six training missions and refueling behind the KC-135 and KC-10. The two most challenging refueling activities were refueling at night behind a KC-135 and receiving my heavy-weight onload of 150,000 pounds of fuel behind a KC-10.

The KC-10 could carry more fuel (340,000 pounds) than a KC-135 weighed.

Refueling behind the KC-135 could be nerve-wracking, but I completed the three KC-135 refuelings without any problems. I always remained leery approaching the old tanker, not trusting its autopilot to behave. I much preferred refueling behind the more stable KC-10 and believe most pilots felt the same way.

The heavy-weight onload refueling behind a KC-10 was especially challenging, though, due to the long duration of formation flying. It required staying in position for more than 25 minutes as the tanker offloaded 23,000 gallons of jet fuel at 900 gallons per minute. This was a true confidence-booster for me to be able to match the other jet's speed and turns for the duration of a TV Sitcom. I now knew I could successfully accomplish any overseas airlift mission and not have to divert for a lack of fuel.

"10-on-10" Refueling behind another KC-10
(Photo by SSgt Katlin Hubbard-Allen, 32 ARS, 2019)

I passed my aircraft commander flight evaluation on November 4, leading a two-ship formation of KC-10s, then refueling behind a KC-135 for 15 minutes. The tanker portion involved conducting slow-speed refueling for a C-130, just as I had done as a copilot the previous year off the coast of Somalia. My evaluator closed out my evaluation report, noting, "Captain Dale demonstrated excellent aircraft commander abilities during this complex mission."

There are many milestones throughout a pilot's career but upgrading to aircraft commander (AC) is a pivotal moment. Our military stresses two factors: leadership and mission accomplishment. I was now entrusted to be the leader of my own KC-10 crew, capable of fulfilling our worldwide Air Force mission.

On the evening of November 6, I commanded my first training mission as an AC with a slightly unusual crew complement. In addition to my flight engineer and boom operator, my copilot was a designated squadron safety officer, who conducted quarterly briefings on safe aviation principles. As we briefed our night-time local training sortie, I learned that both the hospital's flight surgeon and the base chaplain needed to log their required quarterly flights and asked to come along. There was certainly no harm in that.

As we proceeded off to the flightline for our scheduled 5-hour night mission, I was certain I was covered for all eventualities. I had alongside me a safety officer if a mishap occurred, a flight surgeon if it involved injuries, and a chaplain if things really took a turn for the worse. I wondered if all new aircraft commanders were sent out the door in this fashion.

CHAPTER 26

TESTIMONY

Shelby Marie's christening, 1993

Neither of our children were much for on-time arrivals. Both kids were due in May, but three years apart. Daniel arrived at 12:30 a.m. on June 1, 1989. Raising Daniel had been challenging for us as young parents. A colicky baby, he battled reflux, breathing issues, and an occasional fever, sometimes as high as 104 degrees.

Our daughter, Shelby, greeted us bright and early on April 25, 1992. Now we had our little girl to complete the son-and-daughter set. Ten days after she was born, we set out with squadron friends, Captain Scott Mitchell and his wife, Caroline, for a Shreveport Captains minor league baseball game. We had our newborn daughter with us, wrapped in a blanket. Coincidentally, we saw our pediatrician in the stands that night, too.

On Friday morning, May 8, Scott and I, now both aircraft commanders, set off for a week-long Pacific cargo and refueling mission with our copilot, Captain Stu Archer. This was a long-range mission, requiring three pilots (called an augmented crew), which enabled us to work up to 20 hours per duty day. The usual two-pilot duty day limit was 16 hours.

Our first stop was Travis AFB, 50 miles northeast of San Francisco, to upload cargo bound for Hawaii, Japan, and Korea. From there, we proceeded to Hickam AFB, Hawaii, carrying 60 passengers and 50,000 pounds of cargo. Upon arrival, military airlift crews always checked in with the Military Airlift Command (MAC) command post -- often referred to as "Mother MAC" -- to see if there were changes to the mission. When we checked in, I was told to call home. This was still in the days before cell phones and email, so important communications could sometimes be really slow.

Before I took off from Hawaii on Saturday morning, I called Karin to find out what the message was all about. She was already in the hospital with Shelby. Hours earlier, while I was sleeping, Karin had taken Shelby to see our off-base pediatrician because our baby had a fever of 102. This was the same doctor who was at the ballgame with us just a few nights earlier. The doctor was alarmed at the high fever in a newborn and quickly admitted Shelby into the hospital; Karin stayed with her.

The informal wives' network of caring military spouses at Barksdale immediately sprang into action, looking after our 3-year-old son until my mother-in-law arrived. I asked if I needed to come home, and Karin said she didn't think so but would keep me posted. Scott, Stu, and I departed Hawaii for Kadena Air Base in Okinawa, Japan the next morning.

After a night's stay in Japan, we flew 65 passengers and more cargo to Osan Air Base, Korea. Because Karin reassured me that she didn't think things were that bad with Shelby, I joined the rest of my crew for some power shopping in the district just off-base where knock-off products were sold cheaply: Adidas and Nike tennis shoes for the guys, Gucci and Dooney & Bourke "Duck" purses for our wives.

At this point, we were the farthest point west our trip would go, and I was 7,000 miles and many hours from home. That's when Shelby's condition worsened. By Monday morning, she was having seizures and her fever would not go down. It seemed her temperature rose the farther I got away. I called Karin from the payphone in the Visiting Officers Quarters hallway, and through her tears, she told me that Shelby was now in the Pediatric Intensive Care Unit (PICU) at the Shreveport Hospital. Now we were both worried.

The commander of our 32nd Air Refueling Squadron (32 ARS) was Lt Col Dennis Dolle, a great leader who I had known for a few years. He had been a major during the 1990-91 Gulf War and was the Assistant Director of Operations for our small deployed unit in Muscat, Oman. Since then, he had been promoted and given command of the 32 ARS, leading one of the best air refueling squadrons.

He and his wife, Suzanne, epitomized what a squadron commander and spouse should be and both served as our role models in the years to come. Lt Col Dolle and his wife were at the hospital with Karin when I called. He asked Karin to let him talk to me. In his usual low, calm, voice, he spoke to me from halfway around the world.

"Dave, I think it's time to bring y'all home."

Shelby's condition was pretty dire, perhaps a form of meningitis, but still unknown at this point. Lt Col Dolle assured me that Suzanne and other wives were visiting Karin and Shelby at the hospital, while our neighbors, Heather and Joann, helped my mother-in-law, Barbara, take care of Daniel. He then asked me to put Scott on the phone.

Given my daughter's serious condition, Lt Col Dolle was concerned about my ability to concentrate during the remaining flights back to the U.S. He told Scott that I shouldn't fly and to leave the remaining flying to Scott and our copilot, Stu. Scott hung up and relayed the commander's directive. That night, I went to bed praying for both Shelby and Karin and hoping the doctors would find an answer.

The crew continued the planned mission the following morning. Scott and Stu flew eastbound, refueling four F-15s enroute to

Elmendorf AFB, Alaska. At first, during the seven-hour flight, I alternated between sitting in the red passenger seats just outside the cockpit, and lying in one of the four bunks positioned just aft of the passenger seats. I came to the realization that being 6,000 miles from home and worried about my baby daughter, there was only one thing I could do: pray. Those prayers had a calming effect and allowed me to doze off a few times during the long flight.

Finally, I went up to the cockpit and told Scott that it wasn't doing me any good to just sit in the back and dwell on the situation at home for what would be a 19-hour duty day. He agreed, and I started to rotate into one of the two pilot seats every few hours. As we approached Alaska, Scott radioed to ask how much cargo we needed to upload for our remaining flight to Louisiana. From overhead Shemya Air Base, Alaska, in the Aleutian Islands, Scott contacted Elmendorf Command Post and told them we would like to spend minimum time on the ground, just uploading the required fuel for our next leg home. The command post said this was fine since there wasn't any cargo scheduled to go with us. We would "turn and burn" to Barksdale. Meanwhile, an unusual development was taking place at Barksdale AFB.

Unrelatedly, both of our children's births occurred at the same time major events took place in our Communist adversaries' countries. For Daniel, it was the uprising in Tiananmen Square, as he lay jaundiced in the Barksdale hospital on June 4, 1989. Shelby was born in April 1992, after the Berlin Wall came down. Relations with Russia had warmed to the point that there was a visiting Russian Air Force IL-76 cargo plane parked on the Barksdale ramp, visible from Karin's maternity ward window.

One month earlier, in March, two Barksdale B-52s and a KC-10 visited a Russian air base for the first time ever. Now, in May 1992, Barksdale AFB hosted two Russian Tupolev Tu-95 "Bear" bombers, an Antonov An-124 "Condor" transport, and 58 Russian airmen. The Russian delegation was visiting our SAC base, home to the Cold War B-52s, KC-135s, and KC-10s. The Soviets had been invited to attend SAC's annual Bombing and Navigation Competition (Bomb

Comp), hosted each year by Barksdale AFB. Our Louisiana air base was now officially closed to landing traffic during this international visit. All of this was unknown to Scott, Stu, and me, as we flew eastward toward Louisiana. Fortunately, once the Barksdale wing commander heard of Shelby's medical emergency, we were granted special permission to land.

The flight from Alaska to northern Louisiana took six hours and again was filled with quiet time for prayer. Each time I prayed, I felt the Holy Spirit provide a sense of calm, allowing me to not dwell on negative possibilities. We landed at Barksdale and were directed to park not on our usual cargo ramp near our squadron but on the old B-52 alert pad near the end of the runway.

Lt Col Dolle immediately met our crew and released me from any crew duties and I drove home as quickly as possible. I walked in the door to find Daniel and Barbara having lunch. After giving him the glove I bought in Korea, I joined Karin at the Shreveport Hospital. We began alternating 12-hour shifts watching over Shelby, who was now receiving phenobarbital for her mild seizures. She was so tiny and her pitiful cry was hoarse and scratchy. It made my heart break to see our daughter afflicted that way.

I took the night shifts because I can't stand watching daytime television, and slept in a chair next to Shelby's bed. The nurses came in every two hours to check on her, sometimes waking her up from a sound sleep. After 17 more days in the hospital, Shelby was released to recover at home.

One year later Shelby was baptized, with Scott and Caroline Mitchell standing beside us as her Godparents. She made a full recovery and grew to be a 5' 10" high school basketball and flag-football player. Shelby combined her compassion for others and sports and is now a collegiate athletic trainer.

Our family enjoyed a wonderful church life years later in Tampa, Florida. On some Wednesday evenings a midweek service was held and our pastor asked for anyone willing to share their testimony. This prayerful Pacific trip was the testimony I shared one evening. I've always reflected on that week-long trip as Shelby's condition worsened, and especially the 19-hour long day from Korea to Alaska to Louisiana and my time spent in prayer. I told my son years later that at some point in life we all may be brought to our knees and realize that without control over a situation, all we can do is pray.

Scott Mitchell with Shelby at age 1.

CHAPTER 27

SOUTHERN WATCH, THE NO-FLY ZONE

GUCCI BOYS GO BACK TO THE DESERT

No sooner had Desert Storm ended in early 1991, when Saddam Hussein started making trouble again in his region. After overcoming a failed coup attempt, the Iraqi Air Force bombed, strafed, and gassed Shi'ite Muslims in Southern Iraq. The United Nations passed a resolution on April 5, 1991, "to ensure that the human and political rights of all Iraqis are respected."

By the summer of 1992 it was obvious to the United States and United Kingdom governments that Saddam had ignored this UN resolution. To prevent any further actions by the Iraqi Air Force, the U.S., U.K., and France established two no-fly-zones to keep Saddam's air force on the ground, stopping his aerial harassment. The Northern No-Fly-Zone was relatively small and protected the Kurds in northern Iraq. The much larger Southern No-Fly-Zone protected the Shi'ites below the 32nd Parallel in Iraq.

I was at home on leave (vacation) on August 27, 1992, the official start date of Operation Southern Watch. A squadron scheduler and friend, Captain Ricky Sobrino, called to ask, "Dave, I know you're on vacation, but we are leaving in 24 hours for a deployment to the desert. Want to go?"

"Yes, I do, but let me talk to Karin," I replied.

"It's the standard, 'Pack your bags for 60 days' and we'll tell you more in the squadron," he said as he signed off.

Like many of my military pilot friends, I wanted to go where the action was and take part in anything meaningful. I told Karin what was happening and that I really wanted to be part of it. With her blessing, the next day I was in the 32 ARS going through the mobility processing line. The KC-10 crews, in single file, walked down the line of tables in the building across the parking lot from our squadron. Our shot records were checked and any required shots were given on the spot. I needed the dreaded typhoid shot, which made my arm so sore I could barely raise it for two days. The trick was to get the shot in the left arm because if given in the right, saluting was very painful, if not impossible.

The legal team was there to update any wills or powers of attorney, if necessary. And finally, the chaplain sat at the last table, passing out little green New Testaments and asking how we were doing. Once the mobility processing line was complete, we carried our 30-pound, large green canvas deployment bags out to a pallet to be loaded onto one of four KC-10s departing that night. I wasn't flying a jet over, but joined many other crewmembers in the 75 "Red Seats," designated for troop transport and located in the forward section of the KC-10.

We arrived in Abu Dhabi, United Arab Emirates (UAE), on August 28 and set up operations on Al Dhafra Air Base. This was a UAE Air Force Base for Mirage fighter operations, along with being a helicopter training base. One hangar was made available for our operation and we quickly got to work, clearing out unnecessary equipment. We then moved in pallets of our gear: large KC-10 wheels and tires, cans of oil, maintenance kits, plus bottled water and Meals Ready to Eat (MREs) to serve as our inflight meals.

Sections of the hangar were divided into the necessary offices for the air operations staff and intelligence shop, where we would receive our classified preflight briefings from the intelligence officer. In an odd bit of irony, the intel office was cordoned off with a plywood door. On the door, a gruff, no-nonsense sergeant had scrawled in thick black permanent marker "OFFICAL BUSNESS ONLY". Yes, our military intelligence office had two misspellings on their high-security plywood door.

Having completed my upgrade to aircraft commander in November 1991, I now had my own four-person crew. Our team consisted of my copilot, First Lieutenant Kreg Lukens, a very good pilot who came to the KC-10 as a second lieutenant three years earlier. He was due to pin on his new rank of captain within a few weeks. Our flight engineer, Curt Hawn, was a very quiet and reserved sergeant. At the other end of the spectrum (and the airplane, for that matter), was rock and roll guitar-jamming Senior Airman Jose "Hozer" Martinez, our boom operator.

My Southern Watch crew on the day Kreg Lukens
pinned on captain bars.
Sgt Curt Hawn (FE), Colonel Art Lichte (458 OG/CC),
Captain Kreg Lukens, me, and SrA Jose "Hozer" Martinez

This short-notice deployment to an austere airfield required immediate housing for our aircrews, since a tent-city was not yet available at this location. In typical Gucci Boy fashion, as any other Air Force crew member would tell you, it came as no surprise that our quarters would be the 21-story high-rise Holiday Inn in downtown Abu Dhabi, complete with rooftop swimming pool. In an effort not to highlight our presence in the UAE, our Group Commander,

Colonel Art Lichte, advised the crews to close the curtains of the bus as they transited to and from the hotel.

This deployment was the epitome of "Gucci Boys in the Desert." The restaurant served any item imaginable, including a 20-ounce Chateaubriand and other fine items, all purchased with our government meal allowance. One deployed member from the Air Force Reserve KC-10 squadron was a massive Cajun boy named Pirough ("Peer-O"). When not serving as a boom operator in the Air Force, his day job was as a heavy-equipment operator on construction sites in Louisiana. He was more at home in a sleeveless T-shirt and overalls than a flightsuit. Pirough loved to order the Chateaubriand and was dismayed when we told him it was meant to be shared by two people.

We never expected to be staying in a downtown hotel when we packed for this deployment. We assumed we'd be back in a desert tent city and packed casual shorts and T-shirts to wear when not on flying duty. We discovered that Abu Dhabi was a very westernized city, complete with bars and restaurants. For a $3 cab ride, a crew of four could run down to JBJ's Bar and listen to live rock bands and drink beer. Many of us didn't pack the right clothes for the occasion. Additionally, on the first floor of the hotel was a convenience store, much like a 7-11, and also a barber shop, manned by three Pakistani barbers.

In a phone call to Karin, I told her about what the city had to offer and that we could buy a flat of 24 eight-ounce Cokes and 7-Ups in the hotel store, if only we had booze to make mixed drinks. One week later, another KC-10 arrived with more deployment supplies, and brought care packages from our families back home.

In my opinion, Karin earned Squadron Wife of the Year honors by sending me a large box with collared polo golf shirts and a pair of khaki slacks rolled around a large gallon plastic bottle of Seagram's 7. Now we were in business! I had clothes for downtown and we could screw the top off a small bottle of Coke or 7-Up, add an ounce of whiskey, and walk around the hotel with a mixed drink. That's pretty Gucci, I have to admit.

A few days after our arrival I decided it was time for a haircut and headed downstairs to the barber shop. My Pakistani barber did not speak English, so I decided to use a bit of sign language. I always kept my hair within regulation, never touching my ears or collar, but never as short as a Marine high and tight haircut. Holding my finger and thumb one-quarter inch apart, I said, "Just cut off this much." My intended message was not received. He saw the one-quarter inch signal and that's all he left me with. My blond hair, no longer parted on the left side, looked more like a white Wimbledon tennis ball. I told my friend, Scott Mitchell, "I might as well stay here two months. I can't go home 'til this grows out!"

Our refueling missions began September 1, when we refueled an E-3 AWACS, just as I had done over Panama during Operation Just Cause, and during Operations Desert Shield and Storm. We refueled a wide variety of U.S. and Allied aircraft in support of the Southern No-Fly Zone operation. Besides the AWACs, our Air Force customers over the next two months included the air-to-air F-15C Eagle, two-seat F-15E Strike Eagle fighter-bombers, air-to-air and air-to-ground F-16C Falcons, EF-111 electronic jammer Ravens, RC-135 reconnaissance aircraft, and the F-4G Wild Weasel missile-killing Phantom.

The Navy receivers consisted of F-14 Tomcats, A-6 air-to-ground Intruders, EA-6 electronic jammer Prowlers, S-3 anti-shipping Vikings, and the versatile F-18 Hornet. Finally, from the Allied coalition, we refueled French Mirage 2000s and British fighter-bomber Tornados, both of which used the same hose and drogue system that our Navy and Marine jets used.

Throughout the deployment, the four-person crews were paired off in rooms, with pilots sharing one room and the boom operator and flight engineer in another. Adjustments were made so that our female crew members could share a room, regardless of their crew positions.

Kreg and I shared the two twin-bed room, and on the early morning missions, he ordered a cappuccino from room service. On a particular bleary-eyed 3:00 a.m. wake-up, often referred to as 0'Dark-thirty, I thought that sounded like a good idea, so we both ordered double cappuccinos to give us a jolt. As a 31-year-old, I was not yet a coffee drinker. During the dark, quiet bus ride to the airport the caffeine kicked in on my empty stomach and I had the caffeine shakes the rest of the morning. This was a totally new and unusual sensation for me, and I didn't know what to think or how to make them stop. I backed off the double cappuccinos after that.

CHAPTER 28

DEATH OF A FRIEND

Mid-afternoon on September 18, I was napping in the hotel room before our 10th mission later that night. Kreg came flying in the door yelling, "Son of a bitch!"

"What happened?" I asked, startled.

"Ken Reed just died in a crash!" he exclaimed.

Since I was coming out of a sound sleep, I was confused because one of our fellow deployed pilots in Abu Dhabi was Jim Reed. I thought Kreg was telling me that a KC-10 had just crashed.

I jumped out of bed and asked, "We lost a plane?!"

"No. Ken Reed crashed in a T-37 back in the States," Kreg clarified.

Captain Ken Reed was a good friend of ours and a Barksdale KC-10 copilot still back in the U.S. with his family. He had been on a T-37 cross-country trip with another copilot, building up flying time in the ACE flying program back at Barksdale. Because the KC-10 is a non-combat aircraft and we weren't being fired upon by enemy forces, Ken's death was one of the few times our tanker crews experienced the active-duty death of a friend.

My close friend, Captain Lee "Ice" Icenhour, recalled that day:

"My mom called me in Abu Dhabi because my Shreveport neighbors, who lived three houses from Ken, had called her in North Carolina to let her know. I remember being down in the hotel lobby, getting ready to go fly and seeing Ken's close friend, (Captain) Greg Ray. He looked so lost. I knew he knew, too. When my crew showed up at the base for our mission, Dub (our Detachment Commander) told us we didn't have to fly that day ... but we did."

Our commander for this deployment was Lt Col "Dub" Splawn, a devout Christian and a very caring leader of his airmen. Lt Col Splawn posted a comforting letter the following morning notifying everyone of Ken's death. (His letter can be found in Appendix 2.)

Lieutenant Colonel "Dub" Splawn, our deployed commander.

A few days later, Dub led a meaningful, somber memorial gathering in a hotel conference room for those of us deployed in the desert. We pulled our folding chairs together in a circle as Dub read passages from his Bible. After a quiet moment, we shared fond memories of life experiences with Ken and prayed for his wife and young children. Ken's death served to remind us all, currently in our late 20's and early 30's, that we were not invincible. The service helped us process his death as we continued to fly our missions.

Chapter 29

The Mission Continues

On September 23rd, we completed a five-hour nighttime refueling of the intelligence-gathering RC-135, giving them 10,000 gallons of fuel. We returned to Al Dhafra Air Base to find the instrument approach system was out of service. This was not normally an issue because the nice desert weather usually allowed for a visual approach to the landing runway. This air base did not have an Approach Control radar facility to help crews line up for an approach.

Normally during flight operations around the world, there is a high-altitude controlling sector known as Air Route Traffic Control Center, and then closer to an airport and below approximately 18,000 feet, there is an Approach Controller using radar to sequence the planes to a runway for landing. Finally, the crews are handed off to the airport's tower controller for permission to land. In this area of the UAE, there was only the high sector center and the tower, but not a mid-altitude approach controller. Crews were cleared by the air traffic controller to the airfield, and it was up to the crew to establish themselves on the instrument approach in this non-radar environment.

On this particular night, in the days before GPS, there was not an instrument approach available for us to fly – the systems were down. Once cleared for a visual approach, I flew toward the runway, hoping we would see it. I descended as low as 1,000 feet, but the runway never came into view. I executed a go-around, adding power, and retracting the landing gear and flaps as we prepared for another landing attempt.

Although there was not a ground navigation aid in service, there were other KC-10s on the ramp undergoing preflight checks for their next mission. I radioed the Supervisor of Flying (SOF) who oversees ramp operations from a pick-up truck equipped with a UHF radio, and asked if a KC-10 was powered up on the ground. He confirmed that there was, and I asked him to bring up that airplane's air-to-air TACAN frequency to channel 92. We dialed our TACAN to the inverse, selecting channel 29. This channel pairing gave us a distance and bearing to the plane parked near the runway. I asked my crew if they were comfortable flying this unauthorized, makeshift approach down to the approach minimums of 400 feet above the ground. They all agreed that they were. By substituting the stationary KC-10's TACAN for the inoperative ground equipment, we flew the course to runway and broke out of the clouds at 500 feet above the ground and landed. Our unconventional, ad-hoc instrument approach successfully completed our 12th mission.

The Holiday Inn had a house-band from Poland, consisting of two women, Anna and Margaret, plus Robert on guitar. They performed '80s rock music (Dire Straits, Fleetwood Mac, Billy Idol) each night in the hotel lounge and spent each afternoon sunbathing by rooftop pool. The aircrews that had a day off could also be found poolside, flirting with Anna and Margaret.

U.S. troops can sometimes develop a reputation of being Ugly Americans while serving overseas. While our deployed crews were by and large respectful and well-mannered, I'll admit we did pretty much take over the hotel's rooftop swimming pool. Despite Colonel Lichte's directive upon arrival, we were not maintaining a low profile. We took the long blue and white nylon rope attached to the lifesaving ring and strung it across the pool to serve as a makeshift volleyball net. A volleyball was purchased from a downtown shop and the water volleyball tournament was born.

Playing water volleyball at the downtown Abu Dhabi Holiday Inn.

Our hotel not only housed American aircrews, but also the flight crews of international airlines, such as those from Singapore and Indonesia. Their crews also enjoyed the pool and joined our water volleyball games. One day, a young overzealous Indonesian flight attendant went to spike the volleyball with his fist. The ball careened off his wet knuckles, sailed over the 20-foot cement wall surrounding the pool and dropped 21 stories to the sidewalk below. Fortunately for all of us, nobody was hit or injured, but the young man had to perform the Walk of Shame, riding the elevator down in his wet swimsuit to retrieve our ball from the street below. Not to be deterred by this little misfortune, the water volleyball tournaments continued.

Our 23rd mission on October 15, showcased the versatility and capability of the KC-10. Our crew was #3 in a 3-ship cell that would refuel F-15C air-to-air fighters and F-15E Strike Eagle fighter-bombers. Other tankers launched with our 3-ship tanker package that night, providing us with additional fuel for the eight-hour mission.

Before reaching our assigned refueling orbit in northern Saudi Arabia, I pulled up behind another KC-10 for a heavyweight refueling, just as I had accomplished in upgrade training. This night's mission began with me staying connected to their boom for thirty minutes as our fuel load increased up to 345,000 pounds, or 51,000 gallons. Our KC-10 now weighed 585,000 pounds, just 11,000 pounds shy of our maximum gross weight.

Once the fuel transfer was complete, we continued to our assigned refueling orbit, a large racetrack pattern with 30-mile straightaways. Our formation leader guided us to our assigned refueling orbit and reported to AWACS that we were on station. My crew took up our position as #3 in the group. While the lead KC-10 flew at 28,000 feet, the #2 KC-10 took up his position 500 feet above and one mile aft of Lead. My crew flew at 29,000 feet, another 500 feet above #2 and one mile behind him. From this cell formation our receiver fighters, often referred to as chicks, could safely join the formation.

The fighter pairings arrived in groups of two or four and took up a position on the left wing of their assigned tanker. Each fighter took turns sipping from our boom, then moved to our right wing once complete, allowing another customer to take a drink. The formation of F-15Cs and F-15Es waited until everyone had their fill, then departed our formation off to the right. The aerial armada of tankers and fighter jets looked impressive from our Tail End Charlie vantage point.

We remained on station as the fighters returned throughout their night-time no-fly zone sortie. After off-loading 130,000 pounds (20,000 gallons) of fuel, we were released by AWACS for our return to Al Dhafra Air Base. Although this mission was similar to those I had performed as a copilot during Desert Storm, this time I felt the gratification of mission accomplished as the aircraft commander.

On October 17, days before our deployment came to an end, the Holiday Inn hosted a Romanian Fashion Show and Dinner. Luckily, by including the "and Dinner" portion on the ticket, we were able to use our government meal allowance to buy tickets for the event. This high-class affair was held in the Marina Club Ballroom and was attended by well-dressed Abu Dhabi citizens. Guests included Middle Eastern men in white flowing robes and red and white checkered turbans, held in place by a coiled black rope on their head.

Our steak dinner was first class and the young Romanian models were gorgeous, in emerald green and floral-patterned dresses, strutting down the middle of the ballroom along the catwalk dividing the 24 tables. The Americans, wearing our polo shirts and slacks, were seated at Table 23 and 24, in the back corner.

Romanian Fashion Show "and Dinner" in Abu Dhabi.

It was a fitting way to close out this KC-10 deployment. In the previous two months, Kreg, Curt, Jose, and I enjoyed serving our country, flying 25 combat-support missions and logging 140 hours over the Arabian Peninsula. But deploying to Abu Dhabi was certainly not a hardship tour. The modern, westernized city treated us to such entertainment as jet boat races, televised on ESPN by low-flying helicopters for the folks back home. We were entertained nightly by either the hotel's Polish rock band, or the local rock band at JBJ's bar. Even our boom operator, Hozer, was invited to join them on lead guitar. After two months of desert flying, it was time to turn the operation over to another KC-10 unit.

Senior Airman Jose "Hozer" Martinez in his boom pod.
It must've been Casual Friday.

Our crew departed Al Dhafra Air Base on October 23, stopped in Bahrain to pick up westbound Navy cargo, then proceeded to Naval Air Station Sigonella in southern Italy for the night. The next day we continued a Navy resupply mission, stopping in Rota, Spain, then spending the night in Lajes Field, on the Azores islands in the Atlantic. We completed the trans-Atlantic trip, offloading the Navy's cargo at Norfolk Naval Air Station, Virginia, and arrived home in Louisiana on October 26. I now had the required amount of flying time and experience to upgrade to KC-10 instructor pilot.

CHAPTER 30
MOGADISHU, PART II

Mogadishu, Somalia (Google Maps)

In December, 1992, I entered the instructor upgrade program, learning to instruct new pilots in the KC-10 while performing landings or air refueling from either the right or the left seat. During instructor upgrade, it becomes a coordination exercise to land and refuel from either seat all while providing instruction to the student in the opposite seat.

I completed my six instructor simulator sessions, three in the left seat and three in the right. Just before Christmas 1992, Lt Col Dub Splawn, our commander during Southern Watch and the Chief of our Evaluation Division, conducted my simulator evaluation, as my partner Greg and I demonstrated slow speed air refueling for both

A-10s and C-130s. I was home for the holidays, but my inflight instructor training was interrupted by another trip to Mogadishu.

Our mission began on December 31, 1992, flying from Barksdale to March AFB, in California. Located 60 miles east of Los Angeles, March was one of the three KC-10 bases in the United States. After arriving, we joined the long list of KC-10 crews awaiting our airlift tasking to support the new international relief mission called Operation Restore Hope, supporting U.S. humanitarian peacekeeping operations in Somalia after the country's government collapsed during a vicious civil war.

Instead of heading down-range immediately, our crew was first tasked with flying from southern California up to Travis AFB, near the Bay Area to retrieve more eastbound cargo. It was an evening flight on January 3, and I had time to watch my Houston Oilers take a commanding lead over the Buffalo Bills -- the score was 28-3 by halftime. Their lead would be 35-3 by the time we took off and headed north. Ninety minutes later, we landed at Travis AFB, and I learned that my Houston Oilers were the victims of the greatest comeback in NFL history, losing 41-38.

Once back at March AFB, we resumed our place at the bottom of the list of crews heading eastward. On a densely foggy January 5 morning, our 7-man "augmented" crew, consisting of three pilots, two flight engineers, and two boom operators, departed March AFB for a 16-hour flight direct to our staging base of Taif, in Saudi Arabia. We were the last mission to depart the United States for this wagon train of supplies heading for Mogadishu. The concept was that once a crew arrived in the region and downloaded their cargo, they entered a crew rest period. When another plane arrived, the rested crew flew that new plane back to the U.S. The inbound crew then entered crew rest and waited for the next plane. As we crossed over Kansas, I posed a question to the crew, "If we're the last KC-10 crew and no one is following us, how will we get home?"

Nobody could think of an answer, so using the UHF military radio, I contacted our Barksdale AFB Command Post and was patched through to our squadron. Captain Ricky Sobrino, the same pilot who told me about going to the UAE for Southern Watch, answered the phone. I posed the same question to Ricky, and he didn't have an answer. I said, "Well, don't forget about us!" and we continued eastward.

The long-range mission required three aerial refuelings over the U.S., Atlantic Ocean, and Mediterranean Sea to take on the required fuel to make it to Taif, Saudi Arabia, near the Red Sea and Mecca. We spent the night in a dilapidated, condemned hotel, sleeping four to a room on old, metal bunk beds. The springs were so worn out that they sagged like a hammock.

On January 7, 1993, almost exactly two years after my refueling of an AC-130 gunship off the coast of Somalia, we departed Taif for the three-hour flight to Mogadishu. The country was trying to rebuild after international troops, led by our U.S. Marines, helped the Somalis battle the warlords, in an attempt to re-establish a stable society. Nighttime was chosen for our missions, due to the safety of using the darkness and a lights-out configuration to avoid being detected by rebels in and around Mogadishu. It's not easy to disguise a 500,000-pound KC-10, but we took precautions to not preannounce our arrival. We landed at the Mogadishu's airport, bringing in 80,000 pounds of supplies to support Operation Restore Hope.

The runway was an eerie sight as we came in to land. Much like a scene from the movie *Apocalypse Now,* the runway was lined with 55-gallon drums spewing smoke and flames. We touched down and taxied to our assigned parking spot. Once the door was open the smell of the camp hit us. We learned that the flaming barrels were full of Marine shit, from the camp's lavatory tents. That aromatic runway lighting system watered our eyes.

We delivered our cargo and returned to Taif with eight Navy personnel, waiting for a ride home. The KC-10s originally belonged to Strategic Air Command (SAC), who, along with KC-135s and B-52s, focused on nuclear war during the Cold War. During that time, cargo airlift operations were assigned to Military Airlift Command (MAC), using mostly the large C-141 and C-5 cargo planes from the 1960s and 70s. Our KC-10 was a hybrid aircraft capable of delivering large quantities of both fuel and cargo, so we lived in a SAC/MAC world but mostly played by SAC rules.

With the fall of the Berlin Wall and the end of the Cold War, our Air Force reorganized into Air Combat Command (ACC) for all fighters and bombers and Air Mobility Command (AMC) for all refueling and airlift airplanes. We now had to learn and live by the old MAC rules, as the new AMC largely adopted all of the old MAC policies and procedures at the outset. Fortunately, the flight engineers (FEs) on our KC-10s came from MAC airlifters and knew the rules of this Airlift Staging operation. My FE said we were on Crew Orders and that enabled us to hitch a ride on any cargo plane transiting the area if there was space available.

On January 8, we tried this idea of hitching a ride out of Taif and boarded a C-130 leaving for Riyadh, Saudi Arabia. The seven of us deplaned in Riyadh, completely unexpected and unannounced, and asked their Operations Officer when the next flight to the States would be. He was bewildered to see us and declared, "I don't know who you are or what you think you're doing, but you need to get off this base ASAP."

We had stumbled into Riyadh just days before a major offensive operation against Saddam Hussein's belligerent forces, who had fired upon our patrolling fighter aircraft. The lieutenant colonel told us, "You need to be on the next plane out of here." And we were … on a C-130 … heading back to Taif. Well, that didn't work!

Fortunately, on January 10 a massive C-5 Galaxy, commanded by one of my former Vance AFB T-37 instructors, came through Taif. I asked Captain Dave Armstrong, "Can we get a ride out of here with you?"

"You bet, Dave." he answered. We took up our aft-facing seats in the upper aft level of the C-5 and headed northwest.

Eight months later my crew would again travel to Mogadishu, this time bringing in the U.S. Army Rangers that would become the focus of *Black Hawk Down*.

CHAPTER 31
1993 AIRLIFT RODEO

irlift Rodeo is an annual competition among the squadrons of AMC and our international allies, grading items such as cargo loading, aerial refueling, rendezvous timing, and taking on fuel in mid-air in an exact amount of time. It was a specifically designed competition for airlift and tanker aircraft to parallel ACC's William Tell Competition among F-16 and F-15 fighter squadrons, and Bomb Comp for squadrons flying B-52 and B-1 bombers.

Our 458th Operations Group commander, Colonel Art Lichte, oversaw two active-duty squadrons, the 32 ARS and the 2 ARS. Colonel Lichte selected Captain Will Nugent from the 2nd, and me from the 32nd, to pilot Barksdale's KC-10 Rodeo Team. We were joined by boom operators Scott Konieczka and Jeff Sidles, and a flight engineer.

The competition began with a precise, on-time arrival at Little Rock Air Force Base, Arkansas, the host of the June, 1993 event. Crews flew an arc-to-radial instrument approach and had to touchdown within 5 seconds of their assigned timeslot or be deducted penalty points. Of a complete 360-degree circle, 13 miles from the airfield, the planes only flew about a 30-degree portion of that circle before joining the final approach, rolling out nine miles from the runway. The trick was to track our timing along the arc.

From my navigator days, I knew about the Rule of 60. Everything in navigation revolves around the number 60. There are 60 nautical miles in a degree of longitude and latitude. The compass has 360 degrees, which is divisible by 60. Because of this, tracking an aircraft's timing is easier if dealing with a multiple or divisor of 60. Instead of flying the 13-mile arc, I proposed we deliberately fly a 12-mile arc. Because 60 divided by 12 equals 5, we covered one nautical mile in every five radials on the arc. Flying only one mile inside the prescribed arc still kept our airplane within the allowable tolerance for flying the arc-to-radial approach, and made the math much simpler.

I plotted out the approach starting from our landing time at the runway, and worked back along each mile of the approach to the point where we intercepted the arc. By precisely controlling our airspeed, I guided the KC-10 to each mile marker, making small airspeed adjustments to meet the next mark. The other competition pilot, Will, flew our KC-10 from the left seat, as I navigated from the right.

During our training approaches at Barksdale, we had this system down to perfection, touching down within the first 3,000 feet of the runway exactly on time. On competition day, either I called for the turn to final approach too early or the shifting winds pushed us closer, but we were going to be 10 seconds too early with only nine miles to touchdown. Will slowed our plane and we configured it to a full 50-degree flap landing, allowing the slowest possible approach speed. He then flew a series of S-turns to kill more time.

I don't think Colonel Lichte, Lt Col Dolle and our other passengers in the back enjoyed that part of the flight. I checked my watch as we flew over the approach end of the runway and told Will to land long. Any landing outside the 3,000-foot touchdown zone was a disqualification, so as he glided down the runway, I watched for the 3,000-foot white painted marker stripes on the runway. With 200 feet of legal distance to go I said, "Put it down," and we touched down 5 seconds early. Not bad, but not perfect.

Our competitors from Seymour Johnson Air Force Base, North Carolina were flying the newest KC-10s, now equipped with GPS. They relied on their new-fangled gadget to guide them to the runway and missed their mark by 30 seconds. Score one for the old B-52 navigator.

Our boom operators, Scott and Jeff, endured several busy days. They were scored on their ability to load 50,000 pounds of cargo, correctly and on-time, plus offload the fuel during the aerial refueling competition. For practice, our team flew training cargo missions during the previous months, enabling Scott and Jeff to work with loading various cargo shipments. One of our April training flights was from Biggs Army Airfield, near El Paso, Texas up to Elmendorf Air Force Base, outside of Anchorage, Alaska. We landed in Elmendorf, and as usual, Will and I made plans to check the weather forecast for the return flight and file the flight plan to get us back to Louisiana. Knowing there was a Burger King on base, I asked the boom operators and flight engineer if they wanted anything to eat.

Scott, in his typical dry humor, said, "Sure. Bring me a cold cheeseburger and a warm Coke."

I tilted my head and asked, "Why do you want that?"

He laughed and replied, "Because that's what you're going to bring me anyway." We fulfilled his order.

Back at Little Rock during the Rodeo competition, the loading portion didn't go as well as the two boom operators had hoped, and they were dinged a few points for their cargo load. We were now in third place going into the aerial refueling competition. This took part over two days and the KC-10s would be graded on their ability to both give and receive fuel with the 20-minute refueling contact beginning exactly on time at the Air Refueling Control Point (ARCP).

There were six total KC-10 teams in the competition. One active duty and one Reserve team from each of the three bases: Barksdale AFB, Seymour Johnson AFB, and March AFB. For the refueling portion, we were paired with the March active-duty team, piloted by Captain Milt Jordan and Captain Mike Hindes. Milt and I knew each other because he had been based at our 32nd Air Refueling Squadron prior to moving to California. Like me, Milt was also a former navigator.

The competition was overseen by a KC-10 evaluator from March AFB. This evaluator briefed all six teams on the Rules of Engagement, assigning the rendezvous times to each team and stating that the receiver had 20 minutes to take on the allotted fuel load. The weather forecast showed a small storm further up the northbound refueling track. This would become a factor once the tanker and receiver were in contact and beginning the fuel transfer.

I raised my hand and asked if random refueling was permitted. Random refueling takes place when the aircraft receives permission from Air Traffic Controllers to refuel on one compass heading for a certain distance, and not on a prescribed air refueling track. The evaluator, based at March AFB in the heart of very busy Los Angeles airspace, sarcastically replied, "Sure. If you think you can get it." That's all we needed to know.

For the first day of refueling, Will and I were the tanker, giving gas to Milt and Mike, our receivers. We ran a perfect rendezvous, west of Little Rock on the northbound track, and Milt's KC-10 pulled up behind us. Milt held his KC-10 in the refueling position as Jeff guided the refueling boom over the receptacle. As we crossed the ARCP at the air refueling control time (ARCT) Jeff plugged his boom nozzle into the KC-10 below him and started the 20-minute transfer of JP-4 jet fuel.

We were operating in Fort Worth air traffic control airspace and with the small storm looming ahead, I radioed, "Fort Worth Center, Deuce 48, Request."

The Fort Worth controller responded, "Go ahead with your request."

"Deuce 48 requests random refueling on a 090-degree heading for 120 nautical miles."

"Standby," the controller replied.

To avoid the oncoming cumulus clouds while linked together during refueling, I was asking to turn east, away from the weather and complete the 20-minute contact in clear weather. After a moment, Fort Worth Center responded, "Deuce 48, random refueling is approved on a 090-degree heading for the next 120 nautical miles."

With our boom nozzle engaged, we could now transmit through the boom interphone to the receiver behind us without communicating over an open radio frequency. I told Milt, "We are coming right to 090," and proceeded in the clear blue sky across Arkansas.

We landed an hour later, hitting all of the required marks, and earning 1277 out of 1300 possible points. We crossed the control point precisely at the control time and we had no disconnects during the 20-minute fuel transfer. Our cocky Seymour Johnson competitors weren't so lucky. They made their refueling contact and then barreled into the turbulence of the clouds, resulting in two disconnects and penalty point deductions.

The following day, Will guided our KC-10 into the refueling position behind Milt's KC-10. Once an on-time refueling contact was established, we heard Milt say over the boom interphone, "Standby for a right turn to 090." Our teams again enjoyed random refueling in smooth air, thanks to the obliging controllers at Fort Worth Center. As the receiver this day, we received 1286 points, just 14 below the max possible. The rules would be changed in future years that all refueling had to take place within 30 nautical miles of the prescribed refueling track. The competition officials couldn't believe that we deviated 120 miles off course to remain in smooth air, but it wasn't against the rules … yet.

In the end, our preparation and ingenuity paid off. Our 458th Operations Group active-duty Rodeo team flew home on June 12, 1993 under the callsign of Victor 458 with two trophies for Best KC-10 Air Refueling Team, Best KC-10 Aircrew, and we were awarded the General Richard H. Ellis Trophy for Best KC-10 Unit.

CHAPTER 32

MOGADISHU, PART III

The Horn of Africa: Mogadishu, Somalia, south of Djibouti
(Source: Google maps)

The United States Transportation Command (USTRANSCOM), responsible for the operation of all U.S. military transportation assets, has the ability to task civilian airlines to support military operations by transporting troops through the Civil Reserve Air Fleet, or CRAF. In the 1990s, many airliners still flew the Boeing 747, but an issue arose with the carriers' insurance not covering flights into an active warzone. Intelligence agencies reported there was still a threat of small-arms fire and shoulder-fired SA-7s around the Mogadishu airport.

For this reason, KC-10s deployed to Cairo, Egypt on August 21, 1993. The Gucci Boys had the hardship assignment of billeting at the Mena House Hotel and Casino, across the street from the famous Egyptian pyramids. This luxury hotel and casino looked like it belonged in a James Bond movie. Life was rough, but somebody had to do it.

The 747s were loaded with Army Ranger combat troops and departed the U.S. for the Middle East. We timed our departures from Cairo as the 747s flew across the Mediterranean Sea to meet them in the tiny country of Djibouti, just south of the Red Sea. After the airliners landed, the Army Ranger troops walked down the tall portable airstairs exiting the 747, crossed the tarmac, and climbed up the stairs of our waiting KC-10s. For this operation, each KC-10 had a temporary FAA authorization to carry 225 troops, triple the amount of our usual 75-passenger load.

My first mission for this operation departed Cairo late at night on August 30, 1993. Captain Don Barnes flew as the aircraft commander in the left seat. Our copilot, First Lieutenant Dave Denman, flew in the right seat. As an instructor/evaluator, I could fly in either seat, but sat in the passenger seats as Don and Dave flew the flight into Djibouti from Cairo. We parked on the nearly empty ramp and waited as the large civilian 747 taxied to a stop and the Army personnel deplaned. 115 U.S. Army Rangers carrying their combat gear climbed the staircase to our waiting KC-10. Once fully loaded, we departed after midnight for the two-hour flight to Mogadishu with Don flying from the left seat and me sitting in the copilot seat.

Upon arrival, Don flew a combat arrival, overflying the coastal city at 20,000 feet, then spiraled down over the Arabian Sea to 300 feet. From there, he made a short, right-hand final turn to the runway. This tight approach avoided flying over any nearby buildings since our intelligence reports stated there could be SA-7 ground-to-air shoulder-fired missiles in the vicinity.

The Mogadishu runway was long but did not have taxiway exits at both ends. There was only one midfield taxiway, meaning the only exit was halfway down the 10,000-foot runway. If the plane was not slow enough to exit at this taxiway, then the crew had to go to the end of the runway and execute a U-turn, which was very challenging in a large KC-10 on Mogadishu's narrow runway.

Our flight manual says the KC-10 has a 143-foot turning radius and on narrow runways crews have been known to drop their nose-wheel off the pavement and into the dirt halfway through the 180-degree turn. The Mogadishu runway was only 148 feet wide, leaving just a five-foot buffer, and that assumes that the crew is starting their turn with the right-side tires up against the right edge of the taxiway.

The other restriction faced by many aircraft is that they shouldn't land with a tailwind greater than 10 knots. Pilots always try to take off and land into a headwind to enjoy the benefit of more air moving over the wing, creating lift. A tailwind landing is fine, but the pilot must carry additional power throughout the landing to prevent dropping the plane firmly onto the runway. The increased groundspeed on landing also increases the stopping distance during deceleration. This would not be a factor when using the whole 10,000-foot runway, but it certainly makes stopping by the midfield taxiway, 5000 feet down the runway, quite a challenge.

Don flew the approach, and I noticed on our short final that we had a 13-knot tailwind, slightly above the 10-knot restriction. The only other option would have been a circling approach, heading parallel to the runway, out over the water and then turning left for a southwesterly approach over the city. This was riskier than a tailwind landing because of the rebel's shoulder-fired missiles. We agreed that the tailwind landing was the safer option.

As an experienced instructor and evaluator pilot at this point, I didn't have a problem with executing a tight 180-degree turn on a narrow runway. But the only steering for the KC-10 nose wheel is for the pilot in the left seat and I was sitting in the right seat. After Don's landing, I expected him to taxi to the end for the U-turn, but instead he slammed on the brakes to make the midfield taxiway.

Now, Don and I got along great and have spent many hours laughing at each other's stories, so I wasn't mad at him, but with the roar of the engines' reverse thrust I had to yell to be heard, "Roll to the end! Roll to the end!"

Don yelled back, "No way! I'm not doing a 180!" He brought the big beast to a screeching halt in time to turn off at the midfield taxiway and proceeded to the cargo ramp near the control tower.

Safely on the ground, we now faced a serious issue. After aggressive braking, the brake temperatures can rise rapidly and the excessive heat buildup could result in a fire or tire explosion. To prevent the tires from bursting, the wheels have fuse plugs that will melt at 400 degrees Celsius, allowing the air from the tires to release at a controlled rate and not explode.

If this occurred, the plane would be grounded until another aircraft with parts and equipment could be flown in to replace any faulty tires and brakes. At an austere location like Mogadishu, this was a huge problem. Our KC-10 had a brake temperature gauge which the flight engineer monitored nervously. The temperatures climbed beyond 350 degrees Celsius, but luckily, we didn't blow any tires. That would have stranded us in the garden spot of Mogadishu, Somalia.

Still before sunrise, our Army Ranger passengers filed down the staircase and marched off down the dark tarmac. We talked to our ground support personnel and gave them our *Stars and Stripes* newspapers and large green bottles of Stella Artois beer. During this operation, the Barksdale personnel were dispersed to each location from which we operated. Some were in Cairo and living the high life at the Mena House Hotel and Casino. Some were in the former French colony of Djibouti, staying at the Intercontinental Hotel along with airline crews from around the world. One of our maintenance officers had the good fortune of dating a beautiful German Lufthansa flight attendant while proudly serving his country in Djibouti. The further south our missions went, the worse the conditions became. The unlucky third group lived in tents on the dilapidated Somali airfield, surrounded by barbed wire and machine guns. Bringing them free 24-ounce Stella Artois Belgian ale was the least we could do.

Next to our large KC-10 sat a small U.S. Army C-12 King Air turboprop plane, capable of carrying ten passengers. As the sun began to rise, the warrant officer pilot joined us at the top of the mobile staircase, talking about our planes and mission and watching a thunderstorm brewing offshore to our left.

In the distance, toward the approach end of the runway we just landed on, we heard a low thump, thump, thump, and then saw columns of black smoke rising. Moments later we heard a repeated whomp sound. Curious, we shouted down to a sergeant to ask what was going on. He came up the stairs, reporting that Somali rebels were shelling the far end of the field, and the Romanian United Nations troops were returning fire with mortars. None of this was very loud, and we could only see the smoke rising about a mile away.

The flightline became a beehive of activity as suddenly hangar doors began sliding open and small black helicopters on wheeled dollies were rolled out of the hangars and into the open. The MH-6 Little Bird, also known as the Killer Egg, was similar to what Tom Selleck flew on *Magnum, P.I.* in the 1970's television show. Each helicopter had its blades folded backwards, pointing towards their tail. As each helicopter was wheeled to an open section, Army troops unfolded the blades while their aircrews boarded the small attack helicopters, each armed with rocket launchers on both sides of the aircraft. Within minutes the rotors were spinning, and I thought it looked like a hoard of angry mosquitos as the lethal small black helos lifted off. The Army C-12 warrant officer looked toward the departing helicopters in front of us and the growing dark thunderstorm not far off-shore and said, "Well, I'm out of here."

It didn't take but a few minutes for him to start his engines and taxi away to the runway. It took quite a bit longer for us. I told my crew we needed to get out of there, too, so we verified that our boom operators had completed offloading the Army cargo. We brought enough fuel onboard for the roundtrip, so we didn't need any aircraft services from the airport. We just needed someone to monitor our engine start.

Our crew all quickly got into their assigned positions, and it was my leg of the trip to fly in the left seat, with Don now sitting in the right seat. We started the three engines and I taxied to the northeast end of the runway and executed the U-turn for a southwest departure. The helicopters swept the departure path in front of us, ensuring there weren't any rebel forces under the departure corridor as we lifted off.

Meanwhile, the storm to our left continued to close in on the airfield. Under normal conditions, we weren't supposed to take off with storms closer than ten miles from the field. By this point, the winds and lightning were only five miles away and closing in. The choices we faced were to remain on the ground with smoke and mortar fire to our right and a thunderstorm bearing down on us from the left, or to get the heck out of Dodge. We agreed to disregard the Air Force's storm limitation and get out of there.

I pushed the power up to Maximum Takeoff thrust, and we began rolling down the runway. A three-ship helicopter escort consisting of two Army Cobra attack helicopters and one MH-6 Killer Egg flew ahead of us along both sides of the runway. As we gained speed, Don with his usual inappropriate timing yelled, "All I know is, the next time I need a checkride, I want you to be my evaluator!"

With the thunderstorm closing in on our left and columns of rising smoke to our right, we retracted the landing gear and I started an immediately left turn out over the ocean, just 300 feet above the waves. We landed in Cairo four hours later and settled in for three more weeks of round-robin trips.

During our down time in Cairo, many of us pilots rented camels for a guided tour around the famous pyramids and Sphinx. A young boy on a small horse took our drink orders and galloped off, then returned with large bottles of Stella. We also found time to tour the inside of the pyramids where I was struck by the number of homeless people gathered in the cool stone entrance and recessed pockets of their national treasure. It seemed similar to Americans finding a homeless camp in our Grand Canyon. I made three more round-trip flights into Djibouti and Mogadishu before returning home to Louisiana in mid-September.

CHAPTER 33

GOING DUTCH

During my deployment to Cairo, my KC-10 friend, Captain Kirk Shepherd, was back home in Louisiana reading the latest issue of *Air Force Times*. There was a job posting requesting a KC-10 Instructor Pilot to serve as an Exchange Officer with the Royal Netherlands (Dutch) Air Force. Kirk and his wife, Colette, had Karin over for dinner while I was gone and he told Karin I should apply for the job. Or, they joked, she could apply for me and not even tell me.

Karin liked the idea of living overseas and told me about the job opportunity on our next phone call. It sounded interesting to me, so I talked it over with my squadron commander, Lieutenant Colonel Tom Stickford, who was deployed with us in Cairo. He said it sounded intriguing but wasn't sure if it would be good for my career. He suggested that I talk it over with Colonel Art Lichte once we got home.

After returning to Barksdale on September 12, 1993, I called Colonel Lichte, who was now on the Headquarters AMC staff at Scott Air Force Base, east of St. Louis. Colonel Lichte felt that the foreign exchange assignment would only have a neutral effect on my career, not positive or negative. In his opinion, I would work hard in a foreign country but none of it would be known to our Air Force. In the realm of military promotion, there's a saying that goes, "What have you done for me lately?" Colonel Lichte was concerned that I would basically become invisible to the U.S. Air Force as I served with the Dutch. I appreciated his thoughts but the idea of moving to Europe was too appealing to skip.

I submitted my application to the Air Force Personnel Center (AFPC) and campaigned hard for the assignment. The KC-10 contact at AFPC was Major Jim Kotowski, a former 32 ARS KC-10 pilot whom I knew well. I spoke to Jim about the Dutch assignment, and he said my main competition was an instructor/evaluator pilot named Rich from March AFB, California. Rich was the early favorite for the assignment, but by rule the job opportunity had to be advertised for 30 days. During the selection process I had a few items to bolster my resume, and continued to update Jim on these events.

On October 13, I was chosen to fly a VIP mission, showcasing the KC-10 capabilities to the first female Secretary of the Air Force, Dr. Sheila Widnall. We picked up Dr. Widnall at Scott AFB in southern Illinois after she visited Air Mobility Command headquarters. She had toured the expansive Tanker/Airlift Control Center and received briefings about the command's airlift capabilities from four-star General Ron Fogelman. As luck would have it, Colonel Lichte now served as General Fogelman's executive officer and we chatted out on the flightline while waiting for Dr. Widnall.

From Scott AFB, my crew flew her back to McGuire Air Force Base, in central New Jersey on a chilly fall day. During the three-hour flight, I refueled behind a KC-135 over Kentucky, with Dr. Widnall sitting just behind me in the observer's seat. She watched the tanker's boom hovered over her head before plugging into our receptacle. The day after returning to Barksdale I called Jim at AFPC.

"Hey, Jim. I just flew the Secretary of the Air Force from Scott AFB back to D.C. Can you please add that to my record?"

Two weeks later, our base underwent an evaluation from 21st Air Force, the next echelon above our wing. As a squadron evaluator pilot, I received my inflight checkride from the chief KC-10 evaluator of 21st Air Force, Colonel Larry Leturmy. Colonel Leturmy was highly respected in the community and was one of the original KC-10 pilots when the program began in the early 1980s. My flight evaluation, refueling an EC-130 intelligence-gathering aircraft, went well and afterwards he reported that I was a top-notch instructor/evaluator.

My checkride performance directly helped our KC-10 operations group excel during this major inspection. Within a few days of updating Major Kotowski of my checkride performance, I was awarded the job as the first exchange officer for the Royal Netherlands (Dutch) Air Force KDC-10 program. While our KC-10 friends moved on to staff assignments or other flying assignments, Karin and I were moving overseas! We had spent a total of seven years near Shreveport, Louisiana and made many life-long friends. But a chance to see real windmills in Holland and learn a new language was too good to pass up.

The Dutch Air Force, officially known as the Royal Netherlands Air Force (RNLAF, pronounced "Ren-laugh") has always supported NATO operations with several squadrons of fighter aircraft. Their aviation fleet in 1995 consisted of numerous F-16s at bases spread across the country, two C-130s, one recently procured G-IV Gulfstream for their Queen Beatrix, and several Fokker F-27 twin-engine turboprop light transports. All but the F-16s were based at Eindhoven Air Base in the southeast corner of the small country.

When the Gulf War occurred in the early 1990's, the Dutch were not able to send their F-16s because there were not enough refueling airplanes to deliver their jets to the desert operation. The United Kingdom participated because they had two varieties of tankers to deploy their Tornado and Jaguar fighters. Having missed out on joining the international coalition, the RNLAF procured two tankers for future refueling and cargo missions.

I spent my remaining six months at Barksdale AFB in the Combat Crew Training School (CCTS) schoolhouse. I taught new students fresh out of Undergraduate Pilot Training to fly the KC-10, upgraded copilots to aircraft commanders, and trained aircraft commanders to become instructor pilots. My final Barksdale KC-10 flight took place on April 13, 1994, on a six-hour training mission, helping two new pilots learn the KC-10 mission.

Just three days later, on April 16, we loaded up our silver Chrysler minivan and my Chevy two-door Z-24, with two small kids, plus a cocker spaniel and a beagle, and headed west for Dutch language school. We set out in our two-car caravan and stopped in Tucson to see my aunt and uncle. My uncle had retired as an Air Force colonel after serving 30 years and they returned to the Arizona house they had owned since he was an A-10 squadron commander at Davis-Monthan Air Force Base in the 1970s. At their suggestion, we booked a cabin near the Grand Canyon for one night and were able to show our kids the magnificent colors of the vast canyon at sunset.

We pulled into Monterey, California on Sunday, April 24, the night before Shelby turned two years old. After settling into our temporary quarters, we bought a small birthday cake for the occasion. Since we were only traveling with clothes but no household goods, Shelby got her slice of cake on a paper plate. She proceeded to lie face-down on the kitchen floor, eating her cake without a fork or spoon.

The next six months were very special for our marriage and family life. Karin and I had been married ten years and were busy raising a 2 and a 5-year-old, who was preparing to enter kindergarten. Because I would be the first Dutch Exchange Officer for this KDC-10 program, the Air Force considered Karin and I both to be ambassadors of our Air Force, so she received a seat in the language school course as well.

We made daycare arrangements with a very nice Army wife living two doors down from our base house on Fort Ord. In a picturesque family setting, we walked the kids down the sidewalk to Susan's house each morning, and then Karin and I drove along the Pacific Coastline to the Presidio of Monterey to the Defense Language Institute (DLI).

Our multi-service class of ten consisted of two Army soldiers, two Navy officers, two Marines, plus myself from the Air Force, and three spouses. The Army personnel were a captain Foreign Area Officer (FAO) specializing in the Netherlands and a young enlisted woman serving in intelligence. The Navy officers were both lieutenant O-3s, the same military grade as me, a captain in the Air Force. Lieutenant Tim McElligatt flew the sea-surveillance P-3 Orion, and Lieutenant Tom Gonzalez was a ship navigator. The Marines were a captain intelligence officer and Gunnery Sergeant Mike Endicott. Mike was a hard-core poster child of a Marine, who had served on the front lines of Desert Storm as a sniper facing Saddam's Republican Guard. All of us would join Dutch units, with the exception of Lieutenant Gonzalez, who would serve with the Belgian Navy, just south of us.

Our instructors were a Dutch lady, Mevrouw (Mrs.) Johanna Cornelissen, raised in Indonesia, and an elderly Indonesian man who we called Meneer (Mister) Ron Kwee ("Quay"). Both had experienced loss at the hands of the Japanese during World War II. Meneer Kwee witnessed gun battles as a young child hiding under the porch of his house, while Mevrouw lost her Dutch father on a forced labor crew much like that depicted in the movie *Bridge Over the River Kwai.*

Our Monterey, California Dutch Class, 1994
Karin is in the front row on the right and
I am in the center of the back row.

We attended class from 8:00 to 4:00 each day, learning Dutch vocabulary and grammatical rules. From what I learned, the Dutch language lies directly between German and English, just as the Netherlands lies between Germany and England. We could see and hear a lot of similarities in Dutch and both of the other languages. Each Monday we received a list of 60 to 100 Dutch words, and would be tested on those words by Friday. The first two months were an intensive grammar class, where we conjugated verbs and diagrammed sentences. Once we had the foundation down, we started to practice simple conversations together for two hours each afternoon. "How are you?' "Where are you from?" "Can you help me, please?"

I found it very interesting to watch our progress over the six-month course. Our two-year-old daughter was just beginning to talk, so I could see our Dutch skills progressing from that of a two-year-old up to that of our five-year-old son. As our son was learning to read basic "See Spot Run" stories, Karin and I read Dutch kindergarten books about the adventures of two kids, Yip and Janneke.

As we had been told during the orientation class on day one, I started dreaming in Dutch; a true sign that I had internalized the lessons. My listening comprehension was never very good, though, and that was frustrating. Each Friday, we had a listening comprehension test, in addition to the written test. A television with a VCR was wheeled to the front of the class and a bath towel was placed over the screen. Meneer Kwee played a short news segment, like any seen on the evening news. The story would only last two minutes, but we had to decipher what the story was about. To me, the Dutch mumbled a lot and I rarely got it right, only catching a few phrases here and there. After our guesses were given, Meneer Kwee rewound the tape and played it again with the towel removed so we could see and hear the story together. That was an aggravating exercise.

Living on Fort Ord, near John Steinbeck's seaside city of Monterey, California, was a great way to relieve any classroom frustration and proved to be a turning point for our marriage. Karin and I were together 24 hours a day, which for some couples may not sound ideal. But after so many extended absences, it was just what we needed. Some married couples say they married their best friend. That wasn't the case for me. I married a hot Texas sorority girl after only dating her for three months. Once married, I whisked her away to Sacramento, California and we settled into Air Force life and then started to get to know each other.

We lived on a cul-de-sac of eight houses and could see the ocean from our driveway. The Army post had recently been slated for closure by the Base Realignment and Closure (BRAC) commission. Its massive 7th Infantry Division was deactivated, and the expansive Pacific Coast base now only had the housing area and commissary open … plus two 18-hole golf courses, one of which was a PGA-qualifying course. Across the street from us lived an Army colonel, who was studying International Affairs at the Naval Postgraduate School nearby. Their family included a 14-year-old daughter, soon to be our babysitter.

At least once a week, after class and getting the children home, Karin and I hired our teenage babysitter to watch our kids for two hours while we played nine holes of golf for $12 at the post's Black or Gold golf courses. The golf course was picturesque, and similar to nearby Pebble Beach, had views of the crashing waves and powered ultralight gliders cruising up and down the coastline overhead. Some of the golf outings included our kids, and they enjoyed chauffeuring us in two golf carts. Two-year-old Shelby loved the cool wind blowing back her wispy blonde hair.

From April through October 1994, we dropped off Daniel and Shelby at 7:30 two doors down the street with Susan. She would walk Daniel and her 5-year-old daughter, Allie, to kindergarten. She then took care of Shelby and her own small son throughout the day. Karin and I attended class and enjoyed lunch around the city of Monterey, either with classmates or just by ourselves.

Our favorite spot was eating at the famous Monterey Aquarium while watching seals and otters play in the ocean. The cold sea breeze was trapped by the coastal mountains surrounding the town, so Monterey was cool all year long, with highs typically only in the low-60s, even in the summer. Tourists arrived in their shorts, T-shirts, and flip flops from the surrounding 90-degree Golden State and immediately sought warmer clothes. I joked that in retirement I could return to Monterey and sell sweatshirts to the freezing tourists.

Our Dutch fluency progressed to the point that in the last two months, September and October, our instructors organized debates on Fridays. It was an intriguing method to truly learn a language. The instructors picked a controversial topic, like gun control, abortion, or the current Haitian immigration crisis unfolding that year. The idea was to become so engrossed in the topic, truly arguing at some points, that we didn't wait to think in English and translate to Dutch, but instead just blurted out our Dutch argument, sometimes heatedly.

Because our Dutch fluency was progressing at the same rate within the class, the ten of us could understand each other's sloppy "Monterey Dutch," but the instructors were often bewildered with what we were saying. Our Marine captain was from South Carolina and truly sounded like Gomer Pyle with his southern accent. One day, as he struggled for the right words to make his point, he asked Meneer Kwee for assistance. Meneer smiled and said, "I haven't understood a word you've said." The Marine replied in his southern twang, "I'm speakin' Dutch, Muh-neeer!"

People have often asked how fluent we became. My answer is that I could talk like a 5-year-old, comparing my skills to talking to Daniel at home. You can converse with a 5-year-old, but sometimes they make small grammatical errors in past or future tense or can't find the right word. I discovered that I could think quite well in Dutch, but engaging my tongue to speak often made me self-conscious.

Over the six months, our class informally divided by military service into two groups. Each Friday after class, the two Marines and the Army officer changed into their running clothes and ran the eight miles from the Defense Language Institute back to Fort Ord. Leaving that to the "ground-pounders," the two Naval officers, Tim and Tom, and I drove home with our spouses, changed into polo shirts and shorts, and headed for the golf course just as the sweaty runners arrived on post.

One summer afternoon, the Naval aviator, Tim, and I talked about how we used to be in such good shape. Tim played lacrosse at the Naval Academy in Annapolis, and I was ten years removed from my last triathlon in college. We decided right then to start running together so we could join the ground pounders on the last Friday before graduation.

Tim and I tackled the hills of Fort Ord on three- to four-mile runs and eventually ran two 10k (six-mile) runs among the wooded California hills. On the final Friday of class, after the closing well-wishes from Meneer and Mevrouw, Tim, Tom, and I joined the three ground-pounders and ran eight miles along the coastal town and hard-packed beach for a final trek back to our "seaside village."

After six months of 40-hour weeks learning a new language, we graduated with students from two other six-month courses in German and Spanish. Each class designated a spokesperson to deliver an address in their new language. Of course, only the fellow classmates could understand the address, but Tim gave his short commencement speech in Dutch. We were now qualified to speak the language of a country half the size of South Carolina with only 15 million people, but at least that also included beautiful KLM flight attendants and tourists in Aruba.

Karin and I now had a code-language to speak with each other around our kids. We could talk openly about Christmas and birthday gift ideas or weekend plans without them understanding. Our conversations were usually interrupted with yells of, "Stop speaking Dutch!"

CHAPTER 34

MOVING ACROSS THE POND

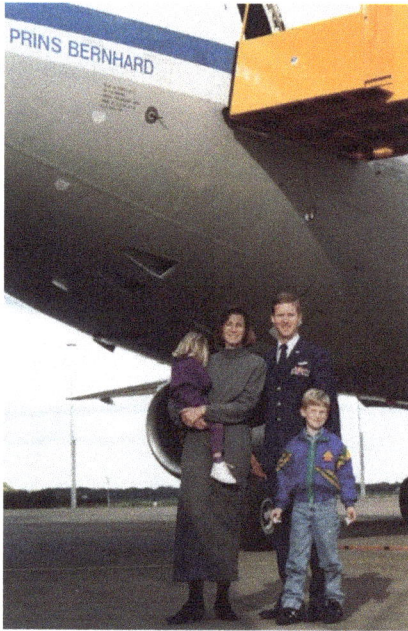

Karin, Shelby, Daniel, and me in front of the KDC-10

The contract to convert two Martinair DC-10-30s into KDC-10s was awarded to KLM Airlines, with the work conducted at Schiphol Airport in Amsterdam. The process was tedious, to say the least. McDonnell Douglas engineers in Long Beach, California, drew up the designs for the parts required to create a refueling tanker out of an already produced and functioning passenger jet. Engineering schematics and parts were shipped from

California to Holland and work began in 1994, while Karin and I attended Dutch Language School. Airplane Part A didn't always fit into Airplane Part B, so the project fell way behind schedule.

After graduating from language school in October, I was told by the Dutch squadron not to report to the Netherlands until January, so our family enjoyed a relaxing Thanksgiving and Christmas holiday in the United States. In November 1994, I took a fact-finding trip with another KC-10 evaluator pilot, Major Bob Bruton, who would also train Dutch pilots for the first year of our tour.

Major Bruton was selected to lead a four-man KC-10 crew on a two-year contract to train the Dutch crews and help get their operation started. The contract crew consisted of instructor pilot Captain JT Anderson, flight engineer Master Sergeant Mike Stinson, and boom operator Master Sergeant Steve "Slobo" Slobodnak.

JT was a tall, thin, "All American" young man with thick black hair and a long chin. He had recently married his beautiful young bride, Nikki, a trained psychologist and equestrian rider with short bobbed blonde hair. They began their married life together overseas, far from their family back home. That would certainly be an adjustment for them both.

Mike was a calm, chain-smoking southern gentleman from Mississippi. He had thinning sweptback hair and often wore a sport coat and a turtleneck when off duty. With his coat, ever-present cigarette, and swept-back hair, he could've passed for a Mafia body guard – until he opened his mouth. His southern accent and boisterous laugh didn't fit the bad-guy mold.

Our boom operator literally rounded out the crew. Slobo was short and round, and spoke in a soft, thoughtful tone.

Of the five of us, I was the only one who received language training. While the contract crew only existed for two years, my exchange officer position continued for other KC-10 instructor pilots for many years to come. Together, the five of us made up the American training contingent that helped the Dutch crewmembers make their new KDC-10 unit operationally capable.

Bob and I arrived in Eindhoven on a chilly November day to scope out the housing and school prospects for the other American crew member families. Eindhoven is in the country's southeast corner, not far from both the Belgian and German borders. We stayed at the Eindhoven Officer's Club, each of us in a small white room with a twin bed. In a scene right out of an IKEA store, the guest quarters were white-walled units with white dressers and desks, and a small twin bed with, yes, a white comforter. It was simple by American standards, but met our needs.

Every day that week, we explored the vast industrial city, home of Philips Electronics, as we searched for housing options and schools for the American school-age kids. Each weekday afternoon, we returned to the squadron bar to enjoy authentic Dutch Heineken beer and plates of Gouda cheese. Bob murmured to me, "We are going to put on so much weight over here!"

On Thursday morning, we joined the thirty other members of 334 Squadron at 8:00 a.m. for their morning routine of drinking coffee or scalding hot tea in the same squadron bar. We were told to be sure to return by 4:00 p.m. because Crown Prince (now King) Willem Alexander would be in the squadron. The son of Dutch Queen Beatrix was a qualified Air Force pilot, flying the twin-engine Fokker F-27 light transport. Bob and I made note to attend and headed out for Day 4 of our housing tour. By 4:00, we took our place around the crowded, smoke-filled bar and were introduced to Prince Willem -- a very nice 28-year-old blond man, five years younger than I was.

Friday morning started out the same as the previous few days, with coffee and one last tour of Eindhoven and the surrounding villages. By 3:30, Bob said, "We better get back to the squadron for Beer Call." And we headed back, assuming the weekend would kick-off with more Heineken and Gouda.

We arrived at 334 Squadron to find it open, but dark and quiet. Well, it's Friday, so they must all be at the Officer's Club, we thought, just like we would do back in the States. We hopped in our rented blue Opel hatchback and drove around the runway to the Officer's

Club, where we lodged each night. Bob and I strolled into the Officer's Club bar to find the bartender alone, drying glasses with a rag.

"Where is everyone?" Bob asked.

The bartender didn't understand and just said, "They've all gone home."

I asked, "Why aren't they here on a Friday night?"

He replied, "On Fridays, everyone goes home for the weekend. Nobody stays late."

Well, this was certainly a cultural change of events. In the U.S., aircrews go home each Monday through Thursday evening, but stay and drink on Friday nights. In the Netherlands, the opposite occurred and by 4:00 p.m. on Friday the weekend began with their family. Bob and I had a beer with the lonely bartender and flew back to the States the next morning.

In January 1995, I left my family behind and flew to London, England to in-process for my exchange tour. The Exchange Program for all of Europe was run by an Air Force colonel based in London. Due to quarantine rules, if our cocker spaniel landed in the U.K., she would be placed in quarantine for six months, even if she was just transiting to the Netherlands. Karin and I agreed that I travel first and Karin, Daniel, Shelby, and our dog would join me a week later. I certainly got the better part of that bargain. After a one-night stay in London and my paperwork completed, I flew into Eindhoven and checked into a Center Parc lodge, which would serve as our temporary housing until we found a house to rent.

One week later, with near historic rains and flooding throughout the Netherlands, Karin arrived in Amsterdam, with 5-year-old Daniel, 2-year-old Shelby and our 12-year-old cocker. The nine-hour international non-stop flight from Houston via Atlanta with all three was a trip she never wanted to repeat.

With my week-long jet lag overcome, I now had a confused two-year-old waking up at 2:00 a.m. each day, as her mom and brother slept soundly. I assumed the nighttime babysitter duties and we all struggled for sleep for a few more nights.

We stayed temporarily in a family recreation area, complete with water park, numerous fully furnished bungalows, and bicycles to borrow. This made for great temporary housing while we waited for our household goods to arrive. Daniel had learned to ride his first bike without training wheels in the grade school parking lot at Fort Ord. As he struggled with the hilly California terrain, I told him not to worry because Holland was flat. Now, sitting on his borrowed little Dutch bike, I gave him a push to start him on his way on the Center Parc paved trail. After several yards he came upon a speed bump, which the Dutch called "drempels." He hit the asphalt bump, fell over, and cried at me, "You said there weren't any hills here!" Welcome to Holland.

Chapter 35

Small Country, Small World

The Netherlands is twice the size of New Jersey
(Source: Google Maps)

Holland or the Netherlands? Which is it? Here's a brief explanation. The Netherlands consists of twelve provinces, two of which are North Holland and South Holland, on the North Sea coast. Two-thirds of the country's 17 million population live in these two provinces, which encompass the population centers of Amsterdam, The Hague, and Rotterdam. Therefore, for more than 11 million Dutch men and women, it is a true statement to say that they live in Holland. But the remaining third of the Dutch citizens live outside of North and South Holland. While the city of Eindhoven and its air base lie in the southeastern province of Brabant, many have just found it simpler to say Holland rather than "the Netherlands."

To occupy our time during the KDC-10 conversion process, several of us Americans visited some of the F-16 units we would eventually refuel and toured the military radar facility, called "Dutch Mil." These were the controllers who would control the airspace for our refuelings over the North Sea. As we quietly watched the military air traffic controllers monitoring their radar in the dark control center, I saw an aircraft with the callsign of JAMBO 52. JAMBO is the radio callsign adopted by the 62nd Bomb Squadron at Barksdale AFB, Louisiana, where I was once a navigator.

I asked the controller if that was a B-52. He placed his cursor over the box on the radar to expand the information and confirmed that it was. I then informed him, "He's from my old unit in Louisiana."

Pulling up the bomber's flightplan, the controller shook his head and murmured, "No. He's returning to his base in England."

Knowing the B-52 was taking part in this year's Busy Brewer Exercise, just as I had done in 1986 and 1987, I explained, "Well, he's temporarily assigned to RAF Fairford, but he's based in Shreveport, Louisiana."

"Would you like to talk to him?" the controller offered, taking off his headset and handing it to me.

"Sure!" I replied and placed the headset and microphone on my head.

I held the Transmit key and in my purely American voice called, "JAMBO 52, Dutch Mil."

"Uh. Go ahead for JAMBO 52?" he replied in a quizzical voice.

Thinking of the famous Bossier City seafood restaurant, I asked, "How are the mudbugs (crawfish) at Dudley and Gerald's these days?"

"Who is this?!" the puzzled bomber copilot asked.

"I'm a former navigator from your squadron, living in Holland now." I answered, without revealing my name over the open frequency.

It's unprofessional to chatter away on an air traffic control frequency, so we just watched the blip of the B-52 fly west, toward the English Channel. As my old bomber proceeded away from Holland, I gave him the radio handoff to England, stating "JAMBO 52, Contact London Mil on frequency 293.5," relaying the contact information for the English military sector. We watched him disappear off the left of the radar scope and I handed the headset back to the controller. What an amazing small world coincidence to have seen the Barksdale B-52 on the Dutch military radar at that brief moment.

By 4:00 we were dutifully back at the 334 Squadron Bar, drinking with other Dutch aircrew members. I relayed the story of the Busy Brewer Barksdale B-52 on the Dutch Mil radar and then recounted another story.

Back in 1987, I returned for my second trip to RAF Fairford for Busy Brewer, only this time as a staff navigator. My job was to help the crews plan their bombing runs, using both simulated and live weapon drops over ranges in central Europe. I served as the assistant to the 2nd Bomb Wing's top radar navigator, Major Nick Manginelli. The live bomb releases took place on the Vliehors Bombing Range, on the Dutch North Sea coast, about 80 miles north of Amsterdam.

Using American navigation charts of that area, Nick and I obtained the coordinates of the bomb target, a series of 16 worn-out military trucks laid out in a "+" sign pattern on the beach in groups of four, extending north, south, east, and west. Any bombs falling within the plus sign was a hit, or "shack."

The first Barksdale bomber crews took off from England bound for Holland with a load of live Mark-82 500-pound bombs in their bomb bay. After crossing the English Channel, the B-52 descended to a low-level altitude of 400 feet above the ground and began their bomb run. The B-52 copilot radioed their position to the Dutch bombing range controllers, monitoring from a nearby metal observation tower.

During any live weapon release in the United States, if there is a problem, the range controllers issue a command to "WITHHOLD! WITHHOLD! WITHHOLD!" and the bomber crew aborts the weapons release. The radar navigator disconnects a large cannon plug over his head, preventing the signals from completing a bomb release.

As our Barksdale crew rolled in on the intended target of old trucks, their position was off by several hundred feet and they were lined up directly on the control tower. The Dutch officer saw the large bomber bearing down on him and calmly said over the radio, "I think you might want to withhold."

Onboard the B-52, a few of the crew members faintly heard the word "withhold." Someone asked over the intercom, "Did he say 'Withhold'?"

The copilot queried the range controller, "Say again?"

The Dutch officer repeated, "I think you might want to withhold."

The B-52 crew now heard the key word and someone onboard announced, "WITHHOLD! WITHHOLD! WITHHOLD!" and the radar navigator quickly disconnected the cannon plug.

The massive B-52 roared over the control tower as observers in the tower scrambled down the metal staircase, fearing for their lives.

Once back at Fairford, Nick debriefed the crew and started to investigate why they were dangerously off course. Nick and I were confused until he remembered that because we were using our U.S. charts instead of European charts, we had not applied a correction for the geodetic datum. The geodetic datum is a coordinate system (latitude and longitude), used to provide known locations and create maps.

During World War II, it was discovered that the mapping of Germany, the Netherlands, Belgium, and France had incompatible latitude and longitude positioning with the rest of the world, and after the war a correction was established in 1950. In a nutshell, it meant that the coordinates Nick and I pulled off an American navigation chart were not the same as if we had used a Dutch military chart. Conversely, if we were using data supplied by the Dutch, we needed to convert it to make our American bombing system accurate.

Nick applied the correct conversion factor and future live bombing missions scored a "shack," placing their bombs, not just within the plus sign, but inside the doors of the trucks.

As I finished telling this story at the bar, a Dutch major with a bushy handlebar mustache smiled at me and calmly said, "I was the range officer that day."

I couldn't believe it! "You almost got killed!" I told him.

He raised his beer and said, "I know." Grinning, he tapped my glass and took a sip.

And as for the JAMBO call sign that I had seen earlier on the radar screen, that also came into existence during that 1987 Busy Brewer exercise.

One of our B-52 crews took off for their mission with a young second lieutenant serving as their electronic warfare officer (EWO). Their mission included entering an electronic warfare range over northern France. Once within that airspace, the EWO was free to use the powerful electronic jamming equipment in a simulation of what they might encounter over Eastern Europe on a Cold War mission.

During this particular mission, the over-zealous EWO started his jamming too soon and was interfering with European air traffic controllers. The command of "Cease Buzzer! Cease Buzzer!" was quickly broadcast by ATC, telling any offending crew to stop their jamming of ATC radar.

The crew later reported that the EWO grumbled, "Fuck the French." and kept on jamming in the vicinity of Maastricht, a major civilian radar facility. Single-handedly, our young lieutenant unknowingly stopped all civilian aircraft departures from Paris, Brussels, and Amsterdam for almost 15 minutes!

Once back at RAF Fairford, another post-mission investigation ensued, this one conducted by the wing staff electronic warfare officer, who was my roommate on this deployment. It was an in-depth investigation, with reports going all the way to the Pentagon and apologies made by our Air Force to the European ATC facilities.

The young E-Dub had to go through retraining and an instructor ride with the staff EWO before being signed off to fly on his own with his crew. For the rest of our deployment, we nicknamed this lieutenant "JAMBO" (a combination of "jammer" and "Rambo"). This became his newly earned callsign.

Upon returning from England, SAC announced that squadrons could now adopt their own squadron callsign, instead of picking a revolving callsign out of a pamphlet for each training mission. The 62nd Bomb Squadron at Barksdale AFB, chose "JAMBO" as its callsign.

In a country the size of Indiana, I had just enjoyed two small world coincidences in one day. First, seeing a B-52 from my old squadron on the radar during a 30-minute facility tour. And second, meeting the Dutch range officer when an American crew almost bombed the observation tower near the North Sea. Small country. Small world.

CHAPTER 36
CULTURAL DIFFERENCES

(THE DAY OUR FLIGHT ENGINEER ALMOST DIED)

Bob, JT, Steve, and I found a dinner table at 6:00 and ordered drinks and appetizers while we waited for MSgt Mike Stinson to arrive. With no sign of Mike, we decided to order dinner. At 6:30, Mike hurried over to our table, wiping sweat from his forehead, sat down, leaned in, and quietly announced, "I almost died today!"

Months had passed as the conversion process to create two tankers slowly continued. The five American crewmembers spent our time behind computers, helping the Dutch write their Standard Operating Procedures (SOPs). During this time, we began to learn how life in the Netherlands differed from America. It began right at the front gate.

The Dutch were just phasing out their era of military conscription, requiring almost every able-bodied male to serve at least two years in the military. Serving in the military was not popular with everyone and the Dutch had a relaxed attitude toward "dress and appearance." Namely, there was no haircut standard or rules regarding body piercings and tattoos. The male gate guard at Eindhoven Air Base waved us through each morning as he stood with a ponytail extending twelve inches down his back and a large, silver metal ring piercing his right eyebrow. That was certainly different from a close-cropped American serviceman with a salute so crisp it could slice a tomato.

My Dutch counterparts noticed the excessive number of ribbons that Americans wore on their dress uniforms. Following all of the operations I took part in, I had four rows, consisting of thirteen multicolored ribbons, denoting various medals and awards. My awards at the 10-year point of my career included the Meritorious Service Medal, Air Medal, Aerial Achievement Medal, Commendation Medal, Humanitarian Service Medal, Expert Marksmanship ribbon, Outstanding Unit Award with Valor, and the National Defense Service Medal (which every military member is awarded). The typical Dutch uniform was adorned with just three ribbons, and I don't know what they signified. My Dutch friend once asked, "Why do you need to be rewarded or recognized for just doing your job?"

That was a very impactful question. Prior to arriving in the Netherlands, I had competed (unsuccessfully) for the coveted "Below the Zone" promotion to major. This was when the fast-burners in the military began to separate from the pack. Over the next two years, I transformed from a hard-charging "look at me" go-getter to an officer that simply did the best at the job I was given. I became less focused on recognition and adopted the attitude of whatever happened in my career happened. With this newfound perspective, I could not and would not be disappointed. I am very thankful for that realization.

Throughout 334 Squadron's various offices hung Heineken calendars, each month displaying a different beautiful, young, topless, Dutch lady. The female squadron members could have cared less about the photos. "It's no big deal," was their attitude. I respected and appreciated the Dutch (and European) attitude when it came to sex versus violence.

In the Netherlands, the portrayal of the naked body or sex was okay, but violence certainly was not. From the Dutch perspective, there was nothing wrong with the display of the human body, but violent criminal acts on television were abhorred. During their television shows a violent act was often alluded to with a scream and something happening off-screen, but never graphically depicted. This is the correct attitude. It is sadly ironic that our prudish American culture is afraid to display a woman's breast, but we can watch gratuitous, bloody mutilations on any evening crime show. The Dutch have the right sense of priorities: the body is beautiful, and violence is bad.

During the long KDC-10 conversion process, our five-man contract crew often visited Schiphol Airport to monitor the progress being made and talk to the McDonnell Douglas engineers. We stayed at a Residence Inn for days at a time and the long-term facility had everything we needed, including a nice restaurant, and a gym complete with a cedar-lined steam sauna. After a day at Schiphol, Bob Bruton asked, "Y'all want to meet for dinner at 6:00?" That sounded fine to the rest of us. That's when Mike finally rushed to the table thirty minutes late exclaiming that he had almost died. That certainly got our attention.

"What happened?" we asked.

"Well," Mike started in his Mississippi accent, "I went to the gym at 4:00 and worked out for an hour, then decided to use their sauna. That sucker is hot! And I'm in there for 20 minutes with nothing on but a towel and figure it's about time to leave. All of a sudden, the door opens from the Ladies side, and in walks this GORGEOUS Lufthansa flight attendant .... wearing nothing but a towel around her waist! Well, I can't stand up because Mr. Happy has risen to attention. So, I'm hunched over my pup-tent and figure I have to wait her out. After something like another 20 minutes goes by, I'm thinkin', I'm gonna die in here!" Welcome to Holland.

CHAPTER 37

REFUELING AROUND THE PERFECT STORM

The Royal Netherlands Air Force KDC-10 Fleet.
I'm flying the lead aircraft.
(RNLAF Photo)

The first Dutch KDC-10 finally arrived at Eindhoven in August 1995, after an eight-month delay. Having spent the previous months flying a DC-10 simulator in Brussels, Belgium, or "borrowing" a U.S. Air Force KC-10 to keep current, we finally had the first of two jets for the Royal Netherlands Air Force. By the end of the year, all of the Dutch pilots, flight engineers, and boom operators were fully trained and ready for missions.

The Dutch were happy to show off the capability of their new jumbo jets, flying the Queen's orchestra to concerts around the world, or refueling their RNLAF F-16s on flights over the Atlantic. On one such occasion I did both, taking a KDC-10, loaded with the Queen's orchestra while escorting a pair of F-16s from the Netherlands to Curaçao in the Caribbean to celebrate the Queen's birthday. The first leg of the journey flew over Iceland and the southern tip of Greenland before stopping for the night in Goose Bay, Canada. During the flight, the pair of F-16s refueled from the remotely controlled refueling boom, which was an advance in technology compared to what we used in the USAF.

The Dutch KDC-10s incorporated a modified way of aerial refueling. They used a three-dimensional (3-D) camera system and a boom operator station located just outside our cockpit door. Because the two Dutch KDC-10s were previously cargo versions of the DC-10 built in 1976, the McDonnell Douglas engineers decided it was structurally infeasible to cut a hole for the massive refueling window in the back of the large planes for a boom station.

Instead, five cameras mounted under the aircraft belly provided the necessary visibility. Three monovision cameras displayed a 180-degree aft-facing view of the aircraft, from wingtip to wingtip. This enabled our boom operators to see the approaching receiver aircraft prior to refueling. Two more 3-D cameras focused on the boom nozzle. Wearing a pair of polarized glasses, the boom operator now had the depth perception required to place the long, maneuverable, telescoping boom into the receptacle of the receiver.

After spending the night in Goose Bay, my Dutch copilot and good friend, Major Freek ("Frake") Vandervaart checked the weather for the next long flight down the eastern seaboard to the Caribbean. What we faced was "the perfect storm," because Hurricanes Edouard, a Category 4, and Fran, a Category 3, now blocked our southbound path.

From the weather shop in Goose Bay, we printed out the radar depiction of Hurricane Edouard, off the New England coast. I then called the weather shop at Roosevelt Roads Naval Station in Puerto Rico, and had them fax me a radar shot of Hurricane Fran, which was currently in their vicinity.

There are many wonderful lessons I've gleaned from aviation. Pilots learn to anticipate problems and become proactive, rather than reactive. We learn to "take the bull by the horns" and make good, safe decisions, rather than let controllers on the ground or Mother Nature determine our fate. Perhaps this is where pilots develop a reputation for being cocky or arrogant, but decisiveness can save our life and the life of those flying along with us in the metal tube.

Freek and I plotted a zig-zag course between the storms to Curacao. We planned to depart Canada to the southwest until well west of Edouard, then cut back to the southeast, splitting the two storms, until our path was clear to the little Dutch Caribbean islands. We entered the required navigation points on an international flight plan for our Altitude Reservation (ALTRAV). An ALTRAV was a special air traffic clearance used to block out the airspace required to refuel fighters over the ocean in what we called a "fighter drag." With our flight plan faxed to the Canadian controllers at Moncton Center, Freek and I headed out to the KDC-10 to begin our preflight and ensure enough fuel was loaded for the long flight.

During the middle of our predeparture cockpit preflight, a Dutch sergeant came on board holding a cell phone, which was a fairly new device in the mid-90s. He asked for Major Dale and I said that was me. Handing me the phone he said, "Moncton Center wants to talk to you."

This was certainly a first for me, and I suspect it never happened in the U.S., but the Canadian controller for our flight said he was looking at our flight plan and wanted to ensure we really wanted to fly a gigantic southbound backwards "Z." I explained that we would be refueling two F-16s in the vicinity of two hurricanes and needed to stay away from turbulent air. Understanding our logic, he filed our ALTRAV. The flight went off without a hitch and seven hours later we delivered the fighters and orchestra for the weekend air show event.

For the air show itself, we coordinated with the pair of fighters to fly around each of the "ABC Islands," consisting of Aruba to the north, Bonaire to the south, and Curaçao in the middle. Between the islands we flew at 4,000 feet, with one F-16 on each wing. Approaching each island, we descended to 1,000 feet, the boom operator lowered the boom, and one F-16 flew close to the refueling position, without actually making a contact. The islanders of this Dutch constituent country enjoyed seeing the RNLAF in action.

There are two well-known sayings in the military in general and the Air Force specifically. "Adapt and overcome" is one mantra popular in the Army. And "Flexibility is the key to air power" is frequently heard within the USAF. I thrive on problem-solving and enjoyed executing this plan to safely deliver two F-16s to the Caribbean, despite the two major hurricanes in our path.

CHAPTER 38
"HAVE YOU EVER BEEN SCARED?"

T he buzzards were everywhere! Dozens of them stood along the side of the runway. As we taxied by, a few took off and glided along beside my left cockpit window. These were the largest birds I had ever seen up close, with wingspans over six feet. They glided alongside our cockpit windows as I taxied toward the takeoff end of the runway. The massive African buzzards seem to be taunting me with a look that said, "I can take you out."

The Dutch government enthusiastically supported humanitarian causes. Countries in Africa, such as Rwanda and Uganda, needed their assistance when the 1994 genocide wars between the Hutus and the Tutsi minority faction created a humanitarian crisis. The Dutch didn't take sides in this conflict and delivered relief goods provided by the United Nations International Children's Emergency Fund (UNICEF) to both countries.

In mid-November 1996, my crew departed Eindhoven Air Base for Copenhagen to upload United Nations water purification equipment and 75,000 pounds of other goods bound for central Africa. We landed in Entebbe, Uganda, at the airport where 106 hijacked passengers of an Air France airliner had been detained by the dictator, Idi Amin in June 1976. The passengers being held were all Jewish Israeli citizens, and their lives were in grave danger. Their rescue by Israeli special forces was portrayed in the Richard Dreyfus movie, *Raid on Entebbe.*

In college I enjoyed reading *Self-Portrait of a Hero,* based on the letters and biography of an Israeli commando leader: Lieutenant Colonel Jonathan Netanyahu, older brother of former Israeli Prime Minister Benjamin Netanyahu. Lt Col Netanyahu was killed by

Ugandan gunfire while leading his commandos down the C-130 ramp as they crossed the Entebbe airfield. His 100-man team conducted a surprise raid to liberate more than 100 hostages, killing the four hijackers and 45 Ugandan troops. This book deeply impacted me with his sense of duty and leading from the front, and I looked forward to seeing the location of his heroic rescue operation.

After our cargo was off-loaded, our taxicab driver drove us around the runway to our hotel. He pointed to a small, dilapidated building near an unused runway and remarked, "That's where the Israelis kicked our ass."

Having read the biography and seen the movie, it was meaningful to see that location firsthand.

The next morning, we took off on a short 45-minute flight to Kigali, Rwanda to deliver the United Nations water purification equipment. The Kigali runway was deep in the jungles made famous by Sigourney Weaver's movie, *Gorillas in the Mist* about Dian Fossey's work with the mountain gorillas. During the approach to landing, we saw extremely large buzzards circling near our arrival corridor. Those birds could do some damage, even to a KDC-10.

There have been two crashes of E-3A AWACS, brought down after hitting flocks of large birds. One crashed in Alaska after hitting Canada geese, and the other AWACS was brought down in Greece by a flock of seagulls. There was no doubt that ingesting these large buzzards would take out one or more of our three engines.

It was a calm, blue-sky day and after landing safely I stood at the top of the mobile staircase, taking in the jungle landscape as the United Nations' humanitarian cargo was unloaded. With the water purification equipment safely delivered, we closed the cargo door and taxied to the runway to takeoff.

Taxiing toward the departure end, my Dutch copilot, Captain Bert Pijper, suggested that a firetruck run up and down the runway to scare the large birds away. He called the tower and our request was forwarded to the fire department, located alongside the midpoint of the runway.

I taxied into takeoff position and set the brakes as we watched the red fire truck pull out onto the runway. He drove toward us, made a U-turn and drove away from us, scattering the defiant birds, but only momentarily. With each pass, the birds took off, but only briefly before settling back down on and beside the runway. These really were determined bastards! We finally decided that perhaps they would be scared away as they saw our 400,000-pound airplane coming toward them, so we decided to take our chances and takeoff.

The runway was surrounded by dense jungle. The KDC-10, like all commercial aircraft, was built to fly with the loss of one engine and we calculated our maximum takeoff weight for this contingency. But if we hit any of those birds and lost two of the three engines, we would descend into the trees without any hope of surviving. I was so nervous I had to keep from shaking.

Ernest Gann, in his book, *Fate is the Hunter*, described the difference between fear and fright. Fright is the sudden reaction to an event, like the sound of a large bird smacking the cockpit window. Fear is the feeling of looming dread at a situation being faced. I was fearful.

We agreed to go and I pushed up the throttles to takeoff power. We gained speed, planning to lift off at 160 miles per hour. Approaching the birds and the midfield fire station, the fire truck driver decided to be helpful, at least in his mind. With our KDC-10 barreling down the runway, Mr. Fireman decided he'd clear our path of buzzards one last time and pulled out onto the runway in front of us. Bert and I couldn't believe our eyes!

I had not yet reached 90 mph and aborted the takeoff, pulling the throttles to idle and coasting toward the far end of the runway without overheating the brakes. Once again, the bastard buzzards took off as we came by, then settled back to the runway after we passed. I completed the 180-degree turn and taxied the full length of the runway for our second attempt.

Bert told the tower controller to relay to the fire crew that we no longer needed their assistance, if you could call it that. Perhaps our screaming jet noise finally did the trick because on our second takeoff attempt the flocks of birds did indeed get out of our way and we climbed up over the jungle canopy and headed for the Netherlands. I could finally stop shaking.

CHAPTER 39

MAJOR DALE, ARE YOU READY?

With the British Royal Air Force Tornados approaching from the west, Captain "Woody" Woodsma asked over the F-16's cockpit interphone, "Are you ready?"

I placed my hands on the hand grips just inside the Dutch F-16's canopy, tensed up to prepare for the G-load and responded "Yes."

From the backseat, I saw the same display as Woody's up front. Whatever he selected on his screen was repeated on mine in back. For the missile engagement, the fighter's 8-inch screen had a large circle, which Woody guided until over the adversary. Once he had a lock-on tone he pulled his trigger, simulating the launch of an air-to-air missile. Score one missile kill for Woody.

He checked his fuel and radioed Captain "Parky" Parkinson, the F-16 formation leader.

"We can stick around for the second engagement," Woody radioed the flight lead.

The four-ship fighter formation reset for a second mock battle against the two British Tornados. As briefed, Woody and I, flying in the fourth F-16, followed the #3 jet as we flew toward the oncoming Tornados. The two British fighters flew past us but didn't take the bait to turn on us.

Woody said, "We're through them! I'm going back for a gun kill."

He racked the F-16 into a tight turn and my vision closed to the size of a 50-cent piece as the blood rushed from my head. I grunted and strained against the high-G forces but didn't pass out or throw up. My two goals for the day!

Woody switched the display to the gun mode and the 8-inch screen displayed a smaller circle on the green screen. He pursued his Tornado target, placing it within the video-game circle and pulled the trigger. The tone and screen icon signaled a successful hit. Second "kill" of the day for Captain Woodsma!

Each year the NATO allies planned a live-fire realistic military exercise over Europe, called Central Enterprise; 1996 would be the first time the Dutch KDC-10 could participate, so in my role as an instructor and evaluator pilot, I needed to attend the coordination meeting at Brize Norton Air Base in England, west of London.

As I thought about transportation to England, it occurred to me that the Dutch F-16 units would send a representative, too, to coordinate their role with the other NATO fighter forces. I called the Dutch squadron in Leeuwarden, 80 miles north of Amsterdam and near the North Sea coast. I asked if their unit would be sending anyone to RAF Brize-Norton and was told it would be Captain "Woody" Woodsma, one of their top instructor pilots.

In a few moments, Woody was on the phone. He knew me from my earlier briefings to all Dutch F-16 squadrons about the capabilities of the KDC-10. I tried, initially, to deliver those presentations in Dutch, but everyone knew their English was far better than my Dutch, so my portion was delivered in English.

When Woody picked up the phone, he asked, "So, are you taking the KDC-10 to England?"

"No," I replied, "They won't give me the keys to the jet. How are you getting there?"

"I'm taking an F-16, but if you'd like, I can see if I can put a B-model on the schedule. Would you like to come with me?"

The Dutch had two versions of F-16s. Most were the single-seat F-16A, but they also had a handful of dual-seat F-16Bs for training purposes. This played out exactly as I had hoped. Woody arranged for a two-seater to fly us to England.

The following week, I boarded a yellow "fast train" bound for northern Holland, wearing casual civilian clothes and carrying a small duffle bag holding my green flight suit and black flight boots.

I also had my green nylon helmet bag with my lightweight, gray flight helmet with visor, and oxygen mask. This customized helmet had been molded to my head way back in Nav School in 1984, but still came in handy in 1996. After the two-hour train ride, I was met by a driver and taken to Leeuwarden Air Base.

I changed into my flight suit and boots and stuffed my civilian clothes into the duffle bag. My hosts asked me if I had flown in an F-16 before and I said no, but they knew I had flown the T-38 in pilot training. I was fitted with a G-suit, which look like chaps that cowboys wore in the Old West, but are in fact a series of air bladders that wrap around the pilot's thighs and calves. Once hooked into the aircraft, as the gravity forces increase, air is pumped into the bladders, constricting the leg muscles. This is meant to keep the blood from rushing from the top of our body to the legs and helps the pilot remain conscious throughout high-G maneuvers. The F-16 was known at the time for pulling the most G's of any fighter, up to 10 G's or ten times a normal body weight. The G-suit would be essential equipment for this flight.

After being properly outfitted, the Life Support personnel led me to a mockup of an F-16 ejection seat. I was shown how to strap into the seat and told what would happen if we needed to eject. In a matter of just a few minutes, I was deemed ready for flight.

This type of flight is called an off-station training sortie, so rather than just hopping into an F-16 and zipping across the North Sea to England, we needed to conduct training enroute to make the best use of the flying time. Woody and I would be #4 in a four-ship flight of F-16s launching out to meet two British Tornado fighters in a mock engagement over the North Sea. The leader of the formation was also an exchange officer, like me. He was a red-headed flight lieutenant named "Parky" Parker of the British Royal Air Force – the equivalent of a captain in the U.S. and Dutch Air Forces. As an exchange pilot with the RNLAF, he went by the title of "Captain" to align with his host nation's rank structure.

Anything spoken in a British accent is usually highly entertaining and Parky did not disappoint. In what could have been an old Benny

Hill comedy sketch, Parky briefed the other three pilots on the timing, formations, and tactics used in taking on the Tornados. To make matters more interesting, our adversaries that day came from Parky's old RAF squadron, so losing was not an option, according to him.

The briefed mission was for a simulated air-to-air missile attack on the first engagement. Once complete, Woody would check his fuel state and determine if he and I needed to depart the area for Brize Norton, or could remain with the formation for a second mock battle. For this second engagement, the #3 pilot and Woody and I in #4 would act as decoys and fly through the Tornado formation, in the hopes that they would turn on us, allowing Parky and his #2 wingman to roll in for a gun kill on our attackers. With the mission briefed, we jumped into the small vans for the short ride to our F-16 in a half-moon cement bunker, a hold-over from the Cold War.

The crew chief helped me stow my two small bags and strap into the back seat. I remember thinking how hard and stiff everything felt, built for purpose, not comfort. In very little time, Woody started the single jet engine and we taxied out of our bunker, joining the taxiway behind the other three F-16 Fighting Falcons.

The formation departed two by two, so Woody was slightly offset behind #3 as we matched his speed and chased him down the runway until airborne. The F-16's thrust was beyond intense, and I sank further and further back into the seat as it accelerated. Once airborne, the view from the bubble canopy was incredible, with the glass dome extending below my shoulder height.

After leveling off and heading out to sea, we flew in a loose echelon formation, not very close to the wingmen around us.

Woody then asked, "Would you like to fly?"

"Sure!" I said and placed my hand on the right-hand sidestick controller. "I have the aircraft."

"You have the aircraft." he repeated.

The F-16 is a fly-by-wire aircraft, revolutionary at its time back in the 1980s. Rather than a control stick placed between the pilot's legs, this plane had the usual set-up of the throttle on the left, but the control stick was just outside my right thigh. A conventional control stick was the size of a toilet bowl plunger and could swivel around in a two-foot radius circle. This sidestick controller barely moved at all. It was so responsive I practically just thought about the movement and the plane went that direction.

I was expecting a loose, slippery responsive feel on the control stick but it was actually very stiff and hard to move. I didn't go crazy and act like a born-again Thunderbird pilot. I just gently guided the jet left and right, keeping our distance from #3, who was ahead and to our right. After a few minutes, Woody took control of the fighter again and we prepared to meet the two British Tornados.

After our twenty-minutes of aerial battle between Holland and England, Woody checked his fuel gauge and announced that we were at our Bingo fuel, meaning it was time to depart for our destination. We separated from the F-16 formation and headed to RAF Brize Norton, in central England, 50 miles west of London. I regained my full vision and calmed my breathing. I was happy to still be conscious and not tasting vomit in my oxygen mask. Chalk those up as my own personal victories.

The coordination meetings were attended by representatives of each unit participating in Central Enterprise exercise, from the F-16s, flown by the Netherlands, Norway, and Belgium, to the older Jaguars flown by the Brits. Refueling tankers were represented by the U.S. KC-135s at RAF Mildenhall, north of London and the British VC-10s, an adapted 1960s British airliner. The timeline and airspace were briefed for all participants and I briefed the refueling capabilities of the KDC-10, stating that we could refuel fighters such as F-16s, F-15s and F-4s, using our boom, but we didn't have the hose and drogue capability to refuel the British Tornados or Jaguars. The evening wrapped up at the Officers Club with ham sandwiches and pints of ale. It was all very English.

The next morning, Woody and I attended a final session of coordination meetings and then prepared for our flight home. At 3:00 we headed back out to the F-16B for our return flight across the North Sea.

Woody took off from the British base, leveled off at just 3000 feet and pointed the nose east, toward the English Channel. We whistled along at 600 miles per hour when he suddenly spotted a small, red Piper civilian aircraft and quickly banked away from the slow-moving airplane. I'm sure the private pilot got an eyeful as our jet roared by and headed for the coastline.

Once over water, Woody dropped down to 100 feet above the water and we cruised smoothly along as I watched the whitecaps just below the canopy railing. Woody suddenly said, "Oops. Ship!" and quickly climbed and gently banked away from a cargo ship we rapidly overtook.

Once beyond the sea traffic Woody settled back down to the 100-foot altitude and asked, "Want to feel the power of this engine?"

"You bet!" I happily replied.

Woody ripped the throttle to idle and the jet glided along, gently losing speed. Woody raised the nose a bit to compensate for the lack of thrust and lift, but we never deviated from the 100-foot altitude. Once he was back to 150 miles per hour, he announced, "Ready? Here we go." And slammed the throttle full forward.

Just as in the earlier takeoff, I was pressed back into my seat, and still further I sank into the seat as the Fighting Falcon lowered its nose and accelerated towards 500 miles per hour over the ocean waves. That was an unforgettable thrill!

Next Woody asked, "Do you want to fly again?"

"Yes, but not at this altitude," I answered with a smile.

Since I didn't know how sensitive the pitch of the jet could be, the last thing I wanted to do was get into a "pilot-induced oscillation" (PIO) and splash our sleek fighter into the sea. Woody climbed up to 500 feet and I took control of the sidestick with my right hand. As I did the previous day, I gently guided the jet left and right, checking out the waves below. Had we been up higher and clear of other air traffic, I could have enjoyed a bit of acrobatics, but this was still an awesome experience, nonetheless. After a few minutes I gave the controls back to Woody as we saw the west coast of Holland ahead of us.

I checked my watch and saw that I wouldn't be able to catch the evening train back to Eindhoven. I told Woody I'd need to get a room at their Officer's Club, which was common at Dutch air bases. Woody radioed ahead to his squadron operations room that, "Major Dale won't be able to make his planned train trip back tonight, so can we make arrangements for him?"

Woody entered the overhead pattern of Leeuwarden Air Base, flying down the landing runway at 1000 feet above the ground, then aggressively rolled into a 90-degree bank, hard left-hand turn. I felt the G-suit activate and the air bladders squeezed my legs tightly, like a boa constrictor suffocating its prey. He rolled out after 180 degrees of turn and after a few seconds, lowered the landing gear and extended the plane's flaps, before making a gentle, descending left-hand turn toward the runway. With a "bump, bump" the wheels contacted the runway and we coasted down the runway, completing my second F-16 flight in two days.

Woody taxied back into the cement shelter and shut down the engine as the crew chief approached the left side of our canopy with a ladder. I gathered my two bags of gear and walked down the ladder as a van pulled in, just behind the aircraft's tail.

The driver asked, "Major Dale, are you ready to go?"

"Just about," I said. I shook Woody's hand, thanking him for two memorable flights.

I expected the van driver to take me to the Officer's Club, which had very spartan amenities for an overnight stay. But that was not what was planned for me.

The van driver continued down the flightline toward a small, glass-nosed helicopter. He stopped in front of the French-made Alouette training helicopter and with a smile, "We found you a ride home," he said.

I stepped out of the van as the young second lieutenant helicopter pilot extended his hand and asked, "Are you ready to go to Eindhoven, Sir?"

I couldn't believe my luck. I was being treated like a VIP, and this was totally unexpected. I certainly hoped I could luck into a Dutch

F-16 flight to England (all they can say is No, right?). But I never imagined a four-ship dogfight off the coast of Holland, or accelerating to 500 miles per hour just 100 feet above the North Sea. Now I was seated in the left seat of a helicopter with a glass nose, similar to but larger than the Army helicopters seen in *M*A*S*H*. The Dutch lieutenant started the rotor spinning, lifted us off the ground and headed south at 300 feet above the green fields of Holland.

After a half hour, the lieutenant asked, "Have you ever flown a helicopter before?"

"No, I haven't," I answered, hopefully.

"Would you like to fly?"

"You bet," I replied.

I gently placed my right hand on the control stick that was between my legs and placed my left hand on the collective, the control for pitch and power. My young instructor gave me some pointers, such as keeping the compass case in the windshield even with the horizon to maintain level flight. I didn't make any changes with my left hand, but used small inputs with my right hand to make a few turns as I kept the helicopter on course and level.

Years earlier, I did not start out as a smooth pilot, often over-controlling during pilot training formation flying, or during early attempts at air refueling as the receiver behind the tanker. In those years I was guilty of being a nervous student with a death grip on the controls. But ten years after joining our Air Force, I was a more confident pilot, and had learned the smooth techniques of a light touch on the controls and small inputs rather than large aggressive corrections.

I must have impressed the lieutenant, because he asked, "Are you sure you haven't done this before?"

I accepted his compliment and answered, "No, but it is a lot like air refueling behind another airplane."

We continued southbound, flying over green fields surrounded by dikes and channels of water, which kept the fields dry for planting. Each small Dutch town had church steeples poking above the flat horizon, it was all very picturesque. The sun was setting as we approached my home base thirty miles north of the Belgian border.

The lieutenant set the Alouette down on the tarmac near our squadron and wished me a good night. I gathered my two small bags and thanked him for the beautiful sightseeing tour of his country. That had to go down as two of my best days with the Royal Netherlands Air Force.

CHAPTER 40

EMERGENCY AIR REFUELING OVER THE ADRIATIC

Me, refueling an F-16 off the North Sea coast.
(Photo presented to me by Sgt Henk van Dijk, RNLAF)

By November 1996, the Dutch were ready to conduct their first combat operations since World War II. The genocide in Bosnia and Herzegovina had been brewing for years. After diplomacy failed, the United Nations began sending troops into the region. The Netherlands provided F-16s and the two KDC-10s for the air operations. Our KDC-10s were now certified to refuel

NATO F-15s, F-16s, German F-4s, and the NATO E-3 AWACS, all participating in this operation east of the Adriatic Sea.

While coalition F-16s flew missions from Aviano Air Base in northern Italy, the long-range KDC-10 flew its combat support refueling missions from our home base in Eindhoven. Each mission required a two-hour flight over the Swiss Alps and along the Italian east coast to arrive at our assigned air refueling orbit. Once in orbit, we checked in with the controlling AWACS, callsign "MAGIC," and remained in orbit for four hours before heading back home.

Prior to beginning our support operation, I, along with a Dutch pilot, flight engineer, and boom operator flew in a Fokker F-27 to Vicenza, Italy to receive the intelligence briefing and Special Instructions (SPINS) that would coordinate the air battle plan. The SPINS in this operation were similar to the tactics we used during both Desert Storm and Southern Watch.

At the conclusion of the briefing the U.S. Air Force officer asked if we had a callsign in mind. Normally, our callsign for peacetime missions was "Netherlands Air Force xxx" with a number associated with that day's mission. That was certainly a mouthful to say on every radio call, so we were happy to pick a shorter callsign.

Our boom operator, Bart, suggested, "How about "JUICE", since we are giving them the juice to fly?"

That sounded like a great idea, and the JUICE callsign was born.

It was a surreal feeling to fly the same combat support missions that I flew over the desert, but from "our own backyard." The Stars and Stripes U.S. military newspaper ran an article during that period, interviewing the American F-16 units permanently based at Aviano Air Base. With their families living alongside them, they flew daily combat sorties over a warzone. One pilot stated "It's very strange to be shot at one moment, then get home and your wife asks why you didn't remember to stop to buy milk. One minute you're mowing your grass and the next minute you're dodging missiles."

My experience was not nearly as dramatic, but I remember being invited to our friend's house for dinner with three other couples. I completed the eight-hour combat support mission and drove to the friend's house in my flightsuit and boots. Karin brought along a change of clothing for me, but I walked in to find everyone gathered around the dinner table, asking me about my "day at the office." They were quite happy to have me join them in my work clothes.

We planned our missions the day before each departure, running a computer flight plan that gave us our time enroute and fuel required. At 9:00 in the morning, I was leaning over a map with another pilot, Kees, when there was a large explosion that rattled the windows of our old 1950's wooden building. Kees looked up without much emotion and said, "Oh yes. They discovered an unexploded World War II bomb yesterday and they are detonating it this morning at 9:00 a.m." Thanks for the heads-up, Kees.

Holland was overrun by Germany at the outset of World War II, and Eindhoven had actually been a German bomber base throughout the war. In a strange bit of irony, any unexploded munitions discovered each year around Dutch construction sites were bombs dropped from Allied bombers.

Americans living in the U.S. during World War II were far removed from the daily dangers, but for the Dutch it was literally in their backyard. Our KDC-10 flight commander, Major Maarten Kuijpers, was born in November 1943. When I discovered this, he told me a family story. As an infant, he was placed in a bassinet outdoors on a sunny day for warmth and sunshine. A German V-2 rocket launcher sat in a neighboring field, aimed at England. One morning, a faulty V-2 exploded shortly after lifting off and Maarten's family ran outside to check on him. German V-2 shrapnel was embedded in baby Maarten's bassinet. He was lucky to be alive.

On December 17, 1996, our crew took off for the Adriatic and we rendezvoused with two American and two Dutch F-16s that were providing air cover over the region. We offloaded our required fuel load and remained in orbit until our allotted time was up, then called the controlling AWACS requesting permission to return to base, or RTB. With permission granted, we turned northwest and headed towards the Italian coastline.

We were still monitoring the Primary Air Refueling frequency when an excited voice called out, "Any Tanker! Any Tanker! Cobra 7-1."

I replied, "Cobra 7-1, this is Juice 2-0. Go ahead."

"We are a flight of two F-16s at Emergency fuel. Can you refuel us?" he asked.

"Yes." I answered. "We'll turn back toward you. Bring up your air-to-air TACAN."

Two military planes could dial in a reciprocal pair of channels on their Tactical Air Navigation (TACAN) aid and see the distance and bearing to each other. Additionally, the F-16 flight lead could also see our transponder code on his radar. Using those two methods, they completed the rendezvous within minutes.

As Cobra 71 pulled up behind us, his wingman, Cobra 72, took up his position off our left wingtip. Meanwhile, our boom operator, Dieter, lowered the refueling boom and prepared for contact.

Once Cobra 71 made contact with our refueling boom, his interphone system connected to ours, so we could talk to each other over "boom interphone" and not transmit outside the aircraft over the airwaves.

With contact made, we heard him exclaim, "Oh, man! That feels gooood! Brother, I was down to 600 pounds of gas and getting ready to punch out."

Six hundred pounds of fuel is about 90 gallons. This fighter jock only had about four minutes of fuel remaining before flaming out his engine and ejecting over the Adriatic Sea. That was definitely running on empty for a powerful single-engine fighter.

The two F-16s had been providing Close Air Support to our ground forces and had engaged an enemy unit attacking our allies on the ground. They were so engrossed in their life-saving mission that they had overflown their "bingo fuel" - the fuel necessary to get back to their air base. The lead F-16 on our boom said, "Just give me 1,000 pounds, then get my wingman on for 2,000, then I'll come back to top off."

Dieter obliged his request, making the contacts and the flight engineer activating the fuel pumps to give them their "juice." The entire emergency air refueling took just ten minutes to accomplish. With enough gas to safely fly back to Aviano, the two satisfied customers peeled off to our right and headed back to their base. We landed in Eindhoven that evening, logging seven hours of flying time and recording a "Save" of two American fighters. To quote our F-16 customer, "Oh, man! That felt good!"

CHAPTER 41
FLYING A DESK

O ne evening in early 1997 our phone rang in Waalre, a small
Dutch village just south of Eindhoven. A familiar voice
started the conversation: "Hey. What are ya' doin'?"

It was my KC-10 friend, Major Scott Mitchell, calling from the
Air Force Personnel Center (AFPC) in San Antonio, where he now
had a "career-enhancing" non-flying job.

"We just finished dinner over here. What's up?" I asked.

"We have to find you a job."

"Why's that?" I asked.

"'Cause you're not going to school," exclaimed Scott, delivering the
news that I wasn't selected for the next level of Professional Military
Education (PME), known as Intermediate Service School (ISS).
This course is designed for mid-level majors and I had completed it
by correspondence while in Holland, but attending in-person was a
stepping stone to becoming a squadron commander. I had not made
the latest round of school selections.

We extended our stay with the Dutch by six months so that a
summer time move would put us back in the States in time for a new
school year, both for our kids and myself. Now Scott was telling me
I had to scramble to get another job within the Air Force. At this
point in my career, it was time to step out of the cockpit and get a
staff job, something known to aviators as "flying a desk."

Through our KC-10 contacts, I emailed Major Jeff Mintzlaff, a
fellow Barksdale KC-10 pilot now serving as an executive officer to a
two-star general on the AMC headquarters staff in Bellevue, Illinois,
east of St. Louis. Jeff lined me up with a job in his Plans and Programs

(XP) Division as the KC-10 Program Element Monitor, or PEM, overseeing the fleet of 59 KC-10s for flying hours and modifications.

I received a bit of bad advice and good advice prior to our move. In a brief conversation, a colonel that I didn't know asked, "Are you an alternate for the service school that you missed out on?"

"No," I reluctantly replied.

"Well, then you probably aren't going at all." he advised. The colonel was telling me I likely would never attend ISS, so I should plan on staying at Scott AFB for a three-year tour. For this reason, we bought a house, intending to serve three years on the AMC staff.

Brigadier General Lichte had been our Barksdale Operations Group Commander colonel in 1994, and was with me during Southern Watch in Abu Dhabi. He was now based at Scott AFB and had a different, more hopeful perspective. He advised that we should return from overseas in early summer so that if school became a possibility for me the following year, I would have the minimum one-year time on station at Scott AFB to be released to attend ISS.

In June, 1997, my exchange tour with the Dutch came to an end after two and a half memorable years in Europe. During that time, our children attended the year-round Regional International School with teachers from England, Scotland, and Ireland. Shelby, now five, spoke with a beautiful English lilt, using phrases such as, "Can I have a go?" and "Will we do that straight away?" Daniel completed third grade with a strict Irish teacher named Ms. McNally, a no-nonsense lady who kept the eight-year-olds in line.

Within the military, service members were allotted 30 days of vacation or "leave" per year and could build up or carry over up to 60 days if they didn't use all their leave. I arrived in Holland in January, 1995, with a full bank of 60 days, having just completed Dutch language school. Over the next two and a half years, I continued to accrue another 75 days of leave, for a total of 135 days of leave.

The kids' year-round school schedule had one-week breaks every five weeks of the school year, so we set out for a different country at each opportunity: southern England, northern Scotland, Bavaria, Germany, Paris and nearby Euro-Disney, Nice, France, and Monaco,

Italy on the Mediterranean Sea. We even crossed the Austrian border to eat spaghetti in northern Italy. On Flag Day, June 14, 1997, we arrived back in the U.S., welcomed by the display of our country's flag everywhere we looked. I returned with a leave balance of just two days. We enjoyed 133 vacation days of touring Europe.

After buying a house in O'Fallon, Illinois, I started my desk job at Scott AFB in late June. Meeting my fellow officers in AMC Plans and Programs, was a gloomy experience. My predecessor, Major Mike Mendonca, introduced me to fellow captains and majors, pilots of the older KC-135, C-141, C-5, and the C-130, plus the newly built C-17 cargo plane. Each pilot was responsible for the upkeep of their particular aircraft type, and we all sat close to each other in side-by-side office cubicles.

As I met Major Ron Simmons, the C-17 Program Manager, sitting at the desk behind mine, he stuck out his hand and said, "Welcome to hell."

The faces of the other pilots truly looked downtrodden and beat, almost like prisoners in a POW camp. I had walked into an office where our boss, a well-meaning, eager-to-please colonel, worked from 6:00 a.m. to 6:00 p.m. Monday through Friday and many weekends, too. Ron told me later, "You know what Friday means, don't ya?"

"No, what?" I asked.

"Only two more workdays 'til Monday," he answered.

This was not going to be fun.

I settled into my office job, building Excel spreadsheets to track the millions of dollars necessary for the KC-10 flying hour training programs and upcoming fleet modifications. The other necessary evil was fielding phone calls from the Pentagon asking about the impact of forecasted budget cuts.

Just as Mike predicted when he trained me in our few days of overlap, often a "win" was NOT losing money. A typical workday started with a call from the KC-10 Program Manager at the Pentagon running a "drill" after receiving news of potential Congressionally-mandated budget cuts. The What-If scenario often asked the budget impact of cutting my KC-10 budget by 5 to 10 percent.

I plugged the numbers into Mike's Excel sheets and they showed that engine overhauls would be delayed or our aircrews would run out of flying hours in September, unable to complete their annual training requirements to maintain mission-ready status. This data was forwarded up the chain to the lieutenant colonel and colonel above me, then transmitted to the Pentagon. By the end of a 12-hour day the proposed budget cut was usually canceled, and I went home, with the same budget I started the day with. A whole day of effort just to maintain status quo.

On September 13, 1997, an American C-141 Starlifter cargo plane collided with a German Air Force transport off the coast of Namibia in southwest Africa at 35,000 feet. It was later determined the German crew was flying at the incorrect altitude for their direction of flight. If you've ever looked out of the window on an airliner and thought you saw another airplane uncomfortably close, rest assured they are separated by 1,000 feet from each other.

Airplanes flying any westerly heading will fly at an even altitude, such as 30,000 feet or 40,000 feet. Conversely, any eastbound plane will fly an odd-numbered altitude, like 29,000 feet up to 41,000 feet. I've always remembered this rule by thinking, "Easterners are odd."

This unfortunate mid-air collision could have been prevented had both airplanes been equipped with the new Traffic Collision Avoidance System, known as TCAS. With this technology, all airplanes emit a code with their transponder system, enabling other aircraft to see their position on a cockpit display and, if necessary, audible commands are given to climb or descend to avoid a collision. This technology was available in 1997, but it was not made mandatory for military airplanes until after this accident.

My contribution to the KC-10 fleet was the procurement and installation of TCAS, plus updated radios to comply with European airspace requirements. This laid the foundation for a modernized glass cockpit, enabling the KC-10 to fly in today's Global Air Traffic Management (GATM) modern airspace structure.

The modernized KC-10 cockpit with TCAS and glass screens installed.

By December, the new list of intermediate school attendees was released, and thankfully, I was chosen to attend the Army's Command and General Staff Course (CGSC) in Fort Leavenworth, Kansas. So, six months after purchasing a new spec-home in an Illinois cornfield, we learned the good news that I would be leaving the following summer. So much for that unknown colonel's prediction.

As the year on staff progressed, Scott Mitchell called again, telling me of his idea to interview at Andrews AFB, Maryland to fly as a VIP pilot, hopefully on the new Boeing 757 known as a C-32. Scott had also received a school assignment for the following summer to the Navy course in Newport, Rhode Island. His idea was to lock in an assignment at Andrews AFB before going to ISS so that he wouldn't have to compete with other school attendees the following year.

"C'mon Dave. You should go with me." he suggested.

We had nothing to lose. If we were turned down, we would simply return to fly the KC-10 after attending the major's course and prepare for a leadership job in our old airplane.

237

To apply for an Andrews interview, I had to submit a "Dream Sheet" which is the military's version of a job request. The higher my endorsement on the request, the better my chances of receiving the job. That meant making an appointment with the two-star general in charge of AMC/XP. If I gained his approval, then I had a much better shot of getting an interview at Andrews.

At 10:00 a.m. on a January morning I sat down with Major General Hogle in his office, asking for his support. General Hogle knew I had just been chosen for school in the upcoming summer. He was not a fan of the "career-ending" (his words) VIP squadrons at Andrews, regarding them as mere flying clubs with fancy civilian airplanes, but not truly supporting the Air Force mission.

The whole purpose of attending any intermediate service school (Air Force, Army, Navy, or Marines) was to prepare to become a squadron commander or a similar leadership position. In his mind, that was a wasted opportunity if all I was going to do was move to Andrews to fly their shiny airplanes. His words to me were, "If all you want to do is go to Andrews, then I don't see why we are wasting a school slot on you." I thought he was threatening to pull my school slot.

I told him it was my goal to become a squadron commander and if he was making me choose between ISS and Andrews then I would choose the school option. I left his office without his endorsement.

Fortunately for me, though, my immediate boss was Lieutenant Colonel Jim Wright, who previously served as the CT-43 (Boeing 737) squadron commander, flying VIP missions from Ramstein Air Base, Germany. He said I didn't need General Hogle's endorsement and suggested I forward my Dream Sheet with our colonel's approval and endorsement. Luckily, this turned out to be all that I needed to earn an interview at Andrews.

In March 1998, much to General Hogle's chagrin, Scott and I were selected to interview at Andrews, outside of Washington D.C. We prepared for the three-day event by going over potential interview questions in our Andrews AFB lodging rooms.

The first afternoon kicked off with a social event at the golf course, where the first person I bumped into was my old Vance AFB T-38 instructor pilot, Major Larry "Judas" Deist, now a Gulfstream instructor pilot at Andrews. I didn't know that Larry was part of the 99th Airlift Squadron but it was certainly good to see a familiar face.

They told us during the three-day interview event that this was a two-way street. Andrews personnel would see if we were the right fit for their unit and we would learn through the social times and squadron visits if the Andrews mission was right for us. Being assigned to Andrews could be very chaotic, with constant mission changes. The conventional wisdom was that if squadron members had a special event coming up, such as a child's play or a concert with our spouse, then we needed to take a day of leave. Otherwise, we were fair game for any missions that popped up on short-notice, and there would be many of those.

The afternoons were spent touring both the 99th and 1st Airlift Squadrons, informally known as the Little Airplane Squadron and the Big Airplane Squadron. The 99 AS flew two types of aircraft, the C-9 (a civilian 1960's DC-9) and three Gulfstream varieties, the G-III, G-IV, and newly built G-V. These were known by their Air Force designation C-20B, C-20H, and C-37A. The C-9 often supported the First Lady or flew stateside Congressional trips, while the Gulfstreams flew cabinet members, service secretaries, and congressmen on longer range international flights.

The 1 AS flew the 1950's-era VC-137 (a Boeing 707 formerly used as Air Force One) until it was retired and replaced by the new Boeing 757, known as the C-32. Scott's main goal was to fly the new C-32. That had been my desire initially, until I stepped foot on a Gulfstream. This sleek executive jet just oozed "cool" and "high class." All three variants of the Air Force Gulfstreams looked similar inside. Mahogany lined the entryway from the fold down door that created a small staircase for entry.

The cockpit was to the left of the entryway, while the Distinguished Visitor, or DV Cabin began to the right. Gleaming brown mahogany panels were complimented nicely by dark blue carpet and 12 blue leather first-class seats, six per side, extending to the aft galley, where the flight attendants prepared gourmet meals from scratch. Beyond the galley was a lavatory, also lined in mahogany, and finally the small baggage storage room was located near the tail. Once I heard about the Gulfstream's ability to fly long range while taking off and landing on just 5,000 feet of runway, I knew this versatile aircraft was the one for me.

The second evening was spent at another social event, where we not only exchanged information, but gave Andrews pilots a chance to see how the interviewees behaved away from work. Would we play well with others and be good representatives of our Air Force for this VIP mission? They wanted to observe the "whole person" and not just the formal interviewee.

The third day was the sit-down interview in front of a panel of representatives from both squadrons. Both squadron commanders and their deputies, called operations officers, sat in a U-shaped arrangement of tables, along with pilots from the training and evaluation divisions. Dressed in my Dress Blues of coat and tie, I sat in a lone chair, surrounded on three sides by the panel. The 99 AS commander was a KC-10 pilot friend of mine, Lieutenant Colonel Mike Zepf. Mike and I flew in separate squadrons at Barksdale AFB, Louisiana, but had played intramural softball together four years earlier. Mike would become Colonel Zepf of CVAM, who later told me to plan the clandestine C-37 mission to Amman, Jordan.

The panel members looked over my flying history from the manilla folders in front of them and asked questions about my previous experience as well as questions about how I would handle specific situations. Their purpose was to see how I balanced safety with mission accomplishment. Would I break flying rules to get the job done or keep the passengers safe? The Andrews' motto is "Safety, Comfort, and Reliability," so they hoped to determine from among the candidates who would accomplish their mission using those priorities.

The final question from Lt Col Zepf was, "Dave, although we can't guarantee what aircraft you would be hired to fly, if you had a choice, which plane would you choose?"

I replied, "Sir, I came to the interview fully hoping to fly the new C-32, but after visiting the 99th and seeing the capabilities and versatility of the Gulfstream, that's the plane I hope to fly."

The panel of officers thanked me for my time, and I was dismissed. I stood, saluted crisply, turned, and left the room, hoping for the best.

By April, Scott and I both learned we made the cut for an Andrews assignment, Scott to the 1 AS "Big Airplane" squadron and me to the 99 AS "Little Airplane" squadron, just as we had hoped. We could now set off for Intermediate Service School with our follow-on assignment already in hand.

The Army school runs during a normal school year, beginning each August. It is attended by 1,000 Army majors, plus 60 officers each from the other services, along with an equal number of international officers. Because we were not familiar with Army tactics, the Air Force, Navy and Marine officers reported in July to learn how to "speak Army."

Karin and I contracted a local property manager to rent out our one-year-old house and packed our belongings for a fifth household move in four years. During my Going-Away Party from Scott AFB, I was presented with a small wooden plaque on which was mounted a pewter replica of the St. Louis Arch and an engraved plaque that read:

To Major David Dale
June 1997 – June 1998
Not here long enough to break anything.

CHAPTER 42

AIR FORCE APPRECIATION TOUR

As one of the Air Force liaison officers for the war-gaming event, I was assigned four A-10 tank-killing close air support aircraft. Wargames are simulated computerized scenarios used to play out a battle or campaign. I was in the Florida panhandle with several other CGSC students for this culminating event. Another tanker pilot friend was assigned the role of providing refueling support. We quickly learned how the Army wanted to shape the wargame to suit their needs. Our request for KC-10 refueling support was denied and within the first hour my four A-10s were shot down.

I now sat on the sidelines, watching the scenario unfold. By the next hour my Army artillery buddy was cussing, "This is such bullshit!" as the wargamers eliminated his long-range artillery. He shouted, "They just wanted their classic heavy armor tank-on-tank battle and now they have it!" as he stormed out of the room. Apparently, the tip of the Army's spear didn't need our support.

In July 1998, Karin, Daniel, Shelby, and I settled into a 1970's-era row house on Ft Leavenworth to begin the one-year Command and General Staff Course. Our military had endured a high operations tempo, supporting continuous operations on the Arabian Peninsula since 1990, through the conflicts in Bosnia and Kosovo in southern Europe. Many military personnel felt burned-out from the non-stop deployments. For this reason, when we in-processed for this course, the Air Force colonel congratulated us on our selection and said, "Welcome to the Year of the Family." He meant we could now throttle back and enjoy our home life, attending Boy Scout and Girl Scout meetings, or T-ball and soccer games. It was a welcome relief.

The colonel also advised us that the Army teaches leadership very well and if we wanted to get in good with our Army brothers the following month, we should read Ken Shaara's *Killer Angels,* the historical novel that would become the Civil War movie, *Gettysburg.* I took his advice and read that paperback by the Army post swimming pool as the kids splashed and played. That book started my love of historical fiction that continues today.

I was truly inspired by the Union leader Joshua Chamberlain, who was merely a college professor when the Civil War began. Because he was highly educated, Chamberlain entered the Union Army as a captain, then rapidly progressed up the ranks to colonel and brigadier general. Without any previous military training, he learned Army tactics by reading books. Colonel Chamberlain yelled "Fix bayonets and charge!" as he bravely led a battle-changing counterattack during the Battle of Gettysburg. His audacious decision protected the Union's flank on Little Round Top from charging Confederate forces. For this, Joshua Chamberlain was awarded our country's Medal of Honor. I thought, *if he could become an effective military leader, then certainly I could, too.*

By August, I was attending class from 8:00 to 4:00 with my small group of 16 military officers: 12 U.S. Army majors, one Belgian Army major, one Thai Army captain, plus one Navy lieutenant commander (the equivalent of a major) and myself. The Naval officer and I were meant to represent our services during this year along with our Army, giving them an idea of what the sister services could provide. The Thai and Belgian officers provided an international perspective.

Within the Air Force, there are combat units, flying fighters and bombers, and support units, flying non-combat aircraft. There were also units performing other vital functions, such as Logistics or Finance. In our aviation pecking order, the combat pilot, at the "tip of the spear," thought the non-combat aircrews, such as my KC-10, were there to support their mission. And all of us in aviation squadrons thought that the non-flying units were there to support our flying mission.

Once we arrived at Ft. Leavenworth, the fighter egos were bruised when an Army major declared, "You are all Support! You are here to support the Army." To some degree, he was right. Even a hot-shot F-16 fighter jock or B-2 bomber pilot came to a combat theater to support Private Snuffy with his M-16 rifle in the infantry. I had never thought of that perspective.

Our year was spent studying past military conflicts from Gettysburg to the Battle of Midway to Vietnam. We dissected military tactics and strategy, along with effective or ineffective leadership. Classes were sometimes self-taught, as fellow students presented topics of military engagements, or papers were submitted covering a variety of military topics.

Throughout the year, we also hosted several guest speakers, from Vietnam fighter aces to Medal of Honor winners, all relating their stories of combat and leadership. I served as the escort officer for a World War II P-51 Mustang pilot credited with the first shoot-down of two German ME-262 jets, a revolutionary aircraft of that era. The white-haired man in his late-70's told the tale of completing his bomber escort mission over Germany, then turning for home and seeking "targets of opportunity." While we assumed this was going to be a tale of the powerful Mustang dogfighting with two new jets over the skies of Germany, the old pilot admitted that he destroyed the first one as it taxied toward the runway, then banked around and shot down the second jet as it lifted off the ground. Historic, but anticlimactic.

During the question-and-answer period that followed, a female Army major became very philosophical with her questions, asking him about his moral touchstones and motivations during this engagement. The old fighter pilot stood on stage confused. "My what?' he asked, perplexed.

She forged ahead, "What did you feel inside? What motivated you to carry out your mission?"

He brought the microphone to his lips and exclaimed, "Hell! I just didn't want to die!"

I've often thought about that straightforward reply when people ask me how I handle the pressure of landing a plane with passengers on board. How do I cope with the responsibility? Quite honestly, I'm just very selfish. I enjoy the challenge, the intense focus, and the rush of adrenaline that takes place during a gusty or stormy landing. However, I am solely focused on the runway in front of me and not the people behind me. Pilots concentrate on two things during a landing: aimpoint and airspeed. It was drilled into us during pilot training and many probably repeat over and over in their head, "Aimpoint. Airspeed. Aimpoint. Airspeed." When people say they are afraid to fly, I tell them their safety is a direct result of my selfishness. "Hell! I just don't want to die!"

The year at CGSC progressed like a college year, with a variety of classes offered, many with a large number of books to read. But this was, after all, "The Year of the Family," so several of us adopted the philosophy of, "It's only a lot of reading ... if you do it." The main goal was to pass and get on to our next military assignment, hopefully with a leadership opportunity.

Our on-post house consisted of four units in a row, each making up four sides of a rundown quadplex. These Army quarters were built in the early 1970s and were nearing the end of their 30-year life expectancy. The black and white speckled linoleum tiled floor was cracked throughout the house, as were the worn-out plastic window shades. After noticing a foul smell in the crawl space below the first floor of our unit, plumbers replaced a putrid broken sewage line.

The simple two-story townhouse had not been updated to include a dishwasher, so our kids enjoyed washing dishes after dinner, just as they had in Holland. Our neighbors were a friendly Army major and his very nice southern-belle wife from Mississippi. She remarked that this was the finest Army housing they had seen in their 12-year career. Karin and I kept silent as we thought that our Year of the Family was also our Air Force Appreciation tour.

While we may not have been impressed with the Army housing, I was certainly impressed with the officers we met throughout the year. When I began Air Force ROTC in 1980, the Army was hurting for manpower, having just weathered the unpopular Vietnam era. For this reason, the Army ROTC unit did not enforce a haircut standard during my years at the University of Texas and the Army cadets looked like slobs with their bushy hair resembling Hawkeye Pierce in *M*A*S*H*. I carried that opinion of Army personnel with me until I met these combat veterans at Ft. Leavenworth. Like me, these Army majors had been captains serving during Desert Storm and dangerous operations in Mogadishu and Bosnia-Herzegovina. They were hard-charging professional soldiers in top physical condition. I was amazed to see the base gym parking lot full at 0530 each weekday morning. Many arrived at 0430 … or so I heard, anyway.

Although it was not a requirement, I took part in their Army Physical Standards test, consisting of two minutes of push-ups and sit-ups, plus a 2-mile run. The Air Force had pretty lax physical standards in those days, leaving each person on their own to maintain physical fitness, which I gladly did. To test us, the Air Force for many years only held an annual 1.5-mile timed run. This unintentionally turned out to be pretty dangerous as couch potatoes tried to run 1.5 miles without any preparation. As a result, some airmen were either severely injured or worse, died of a heart attack.

The 1.5-mile run was replaced in 1997 with a cycle-ergometry test, using biometric data to assess our fitness level. Our body mass index (BMI) was also measured in this infallible test. Those who failed the cycle test or BMI measurement were placed in a fitness program to improve. But overall, the Air Force still used the "Big Boy Theory," placing the responsibility on the individual rather than mandating physical training (PT) sessions. When I arrived at Ft. Leavenworth, my Army classmates chided me, asking if I had ridden my stationary bike yet that day. Fortunately, I stayed in good shape and gladly tackled their PT test.

Of the three events, push-ups were my weakest link. It didn't help that my form was incorrect, head bent low and elbows not always breaking the 90-degree line. My Army PT buddy, the artillery officer, would not count my unqualified push-up, and instead double-counted until I corrected my form, counting 3,4,5,5,5,6 … In all, I probably accomplished 40 to 45 push-ups to meet their standard of 36 in two minutes. Knocking out 76 sit-ups in two minutes and my 2-mile run time of 14 minutes were not an issue, as I completed the test with a passing grade.

The culmination exercise was the springtime wargame simulating a major battle. We prepared our tactics and each person was assigned a role, either staying in Ft. Leavenworth, or "forward deploying" to Eglin AFB in the Florida panhandle to sit in the war room during the game. After learning that the Army really just wanted to focus on winning a major tank battle, we headed back to Ft. Leavenworth for the graduation ceremony. Although the wargame was a bust, the leadership I witnessed and the friendships that formed made the year memorable and valuable to my career ahead.

Karin, the kids, and I packed up from Fort Leavenworth in May 1998, and headed east to a townhouse in Springfield, Virginia. There I would begin a four-year "controlled tour," locking me in to one final assignment until I reached the twenty-year point of my military career – the first eligibility for retirement with full benefits. We looked forward to staying in one place for longer than just one or two years and sinking roots in Northern Virginia.

Chapter 43

FIRST ATP CHECKRIDE

C-20B, a military version of the Gulfstream III (Air Force photo)

Tater and I showed up at 7:40, coffee in hand, ready to go, 20 minutes early. We walked into our assigned pre-brief room, where a husky gray-haired man sat. He looked up and scowled, "You boys from the Air Force?"

"Yes sir!" I said, extending my hand. "I'm David Dale."

"And I'm Keith," Tater added, extending his hand.

Our evaluator glared at us and said, "You boys are 40-minutes late. I was just getting ready to pack up and go home."

Holy Crap! On the day of our first FAA evaluation, both Keith and I missed the fact that it was a THREE-hour pre-brief, and not the normal two-hour brief. We apologized profusely and told him neither of us caught the 7:00 a.m. show time.

Our gruff, old FAA evaluator (probably my age now) took pity on us and relented, "Well, we might as well get started."

All Gulfstream pilots at Andrews AFB start off in the G-III (C-20B). For many years, the pilots received simulator training from Flight Safety International (FSI) in Savannah, Georgia. The location was ideal because the beautiful business jets are expertly hand-built right across the parking lot from the FSI training center. After completing just five simulator training sessions, the Air Force pilots returned to Andrews for their flight training and an initial qualification checkride.

The VIP airlift community was rocked by the crash of a Ramstein AFB CT-43 in Dubrovnik, Croatia on April 3, 1996, carrying the U.S. Secretary of Commerce Ron Brown. The details of the crash investigation can be found elsewhere, but one of the outcomes of that was Air Force Distinguished Visitor (DV) airlift pilots now needed an FAA Airline Transport Pilot (ATP) rating to show that military pilots received the same level of training as their civilian counterparts. As a result, my FSI G-III training culminated with a checkride administered by an FAA evaluator.

My simulator partner was a great friend, Keith ("Tater") Tatum, with whom I served on the Air Mobility Command staff in 1998. Tater, a funny guy with a great sense of humor, was a Georgia-born comedian. He was Larry the Cable Guy, before Larry the Cable Guy. We studied our butts off for two weeks in Savannah, but enjoyed a lot of great laughs along the way. The training syllabus called for five four-hour training simulator flights followed by an FAA-administered simulator checkride on the sixth session. Tater and I worked and flew very well together. The fifth session was called the Recommend Ride, and if we performed up to standard, we would be recommended for the checkride.

Each day we arrived at 0800 for a two-hour prebrief, followed by a four-hour simulator session from 10:00 until 2:00. In my days in the KC-10, the instructor attended the evaluation session, running the computer panel, while an additional evaluator was brought along to observe our performance. This is what I expected to happen in Savannah.

At the end of the Recommend Ride, our Gulfstream simulator instructor said, "Great job, guys. You won't have any problems tomorrow," and signed us off as ready-to-go.

Relieved, we gathered up our flying gear and books. Leaving the debriefing room, I said, "See you at 8:00 tomorrow."

He smiled and replied, "See y'all."

The next morning, not wanting to be late, Tater and I arrived "20 minutes early" to a very angry FAA evaluator.

For the next two hours of our prebrief, Tater and I had diarrhea of the mouth, proceeding to verbally build a G-III, one system at a time: hydraulics, electrics, fuel, and pressurization. Luckily, we knew our stuff. Finally, our evaluator said, "That's enough. Let's go get some coffee."

We leaned against the railing overlooking the simulators, waiting for our sim to become available, because we had to wait for it to settle down on its motion-providing hydraulic lifts from the previous training session. With his anger now subsided, our evaluator asked, "Where you boys from?" with a distinct southern accent.

"I grew up in Houston." I answered.

Tater added, nonchalantly, "I grew up in a small town here in Georgia."

The old guy, now relaxed, asked, "Oh yeah? Where about?"

Tater replied, "It's a little town called St. Simons Island. Only about 10,000 people."

The old guy raised an eyebrow and said, "You're from St. Simons Island? I'm from St Simons Island."

All I could think was, *There is a God!!!*

Tater grinned and continued, "You know the Piggly-Wiggly on Third Street?"

"Sure, I do!" Mr. FAA replied.

"That's my uncle's store," Tater told him.

The next four hours went amazingly well! In fact, we knew our evaluation was going well when our evaluator started to offer advice, asking, "Have y'all ever tried this…?"

That meant he had seen enough of our evaluation and now just wanted to enjoy the training session for the allotted four hours. Tater and I earned our first FAA Airline Transport Pilot (ATP) Rating. The day ended on a much lighter note than it began.

CHAPTER 44
ANDREWS AFB GULFSTREAM TRAINING

With our ATP in hand, Tater and I headed back to Andrews to complete the flight training syllabus in the Air Force C-20B, built in the mid-1980s. The beautiful blue and white jets had the same interior as most other Air Force Gulfstreams: blue carpet, mahogany wood trim and pullout tables, and 12 blue leather, plush, swiveling and reclining chairs for our flying guests.

The Air Force crewed the plane with five crewmembers: two officers and three enlisted. The pilots were officers, from captains to lieutenant colonels, all highly experienced in worldwide airlift operations. Behind the two pilots sat a flight engineer, usually a technical sergeant, or senior non-commissioned officer, also with years of experience in cargo aircraft. Our C-20, or any Gulfstream for that matter, was not designed to require a flight engineer, but having one along certainly aided in our mission accomplishment.

The flight engineer was not very busy in flight but they ensured that our high-visibility VIP missions progressed smoothly. They preflighted the aircraft and were qualified to start the engines, then taxi the plane to the red carpet before each flight. This enabled the pilots to plan the flight at base operations, obtaining the latest weather information for our route and coordinating any changes to the trip with the VIP's liaison officer, known to us as "the contact." The flight engineer also acted as a third set of eyes when we flew into unfamiliar airfields or austere environments, such as Africa or the former Soviet Union. Finally, the flight engineer was also a certified FAA Airframe and Powerplant mechanic, capable of fixing our aircraft should minor maintenance issues crop up during these international missions.

Just aft of the cockpit, across the aisle from the entry door, sat the communications system operator, or CSO, in what amounted to a flying phone booth. He or she gained experience in the E-3 AWACS or C-130 Airborne Battlefield Command and Control Center mission before serving as the communications link for our VIPs. The CSO placed telephone calls inflight to the Pentagon, White House, or battlefield commanders "down range" and also received secure faxes and emails to pass to the dignitary.

The icing on the cake of these executive jets was the inflight kitchen galley, manned by an enlisted culinary-trained flight attendant (FA). The galley was the size of a recreational vehicle's kitchen and had a convection oven, plus small electrical appliances. These enabled the FA to make gourmet meals from scratch, served on porcelain china, with silverware and cloth napkins. One of the main perks of DV airlift was that the crew ate the same delicious meals as the customers. We all gained weight during that assignment.

Our flight attendants came to us from myriad assignments, such as forklift drivers, administrative specialists, or aircraft maintenance. Many just wanted the opportunity to fly. If an aircraft maintainer, or crew chief, was not selected to become a flight engineer, then they gladly settled for trading in greasy wrenches for a three-piece suit and apron. But they still retained their maintenance know-how.

Darrell, one of our flight attendants, used to be a C-20 crew chief based in Ramstein, Germany. During one mission, the crew was preflighting the aircraft while waiting for the customers, aka "the party," to arrive in their black Chevy Suburbans. The pilots noticed that one of the engine RPM gauges would not test properly and it was required for the flight to takeoff. As Darrell prepped his food in the galley, he saw the discussion up in the cockpit as two pilots and the flight engineer hovered over the inoperative gauge. Wiping his hands on his apron, Darrell went forward to ask what the matter was and was told about the dead gauge. Darrell offered, "I used to work on these at Ramstein. Want me to take a look?"

The aircraft commander said, "Sure!" and got out of the way.

Darrell pulled out his trusty Leatherman multipurpose tool, unscrewed the offending gauge, straightened a bent wire in the cannon-plug connection, and reassembled the gauge. It passed the self-test, and the crew was back in business. As he sheathed his Leatherman, Darrell said, "If you boys need me, I'll be in the kitchen."

Before I could enjoy any of these exciting international trips, I had to pass my systems oral evaluation and inflight checkride. Andrews was well-known for administering tough, stressful, thorough checkrides. Given the requirements of our mission, taking well-known government officials to unheard of places, passing a rigorous checkride was essential. Our aircraft systems knowledge was far beyond that of corporate pilots. We fully understood how the AC and DC system worked, from the start of a darkened power off aircraft, all the way through engine start and placing the generators online. Similarly, we could illustrate the fuel system by following a drop of gas from the fuel truck, through the fuel tanks, the engines and out the exhaust pipe. The same could be done with our pressurization system, following an air molecule from the atmosphere, through the engines and all the way through our air conditioning system. I was not technologically oriented, but I certainly learned a lot about aircraft systems in those three months of intense training.

On the flying side, each three-hour training mission consisted of multiple practice instrument approaches flown at other airports in our vicinity, from northern Virginia, to Maryland, to southern Pennsylvania. In previous flight training courses, crews only needed to deal with one issue at a time, such as degraded navigation equipment or an aircraft system malfunction, but typically not both at the same time. That gentleman's rule did not apply at Andrews. "Compound Emergencies" were fair game, so as I flew a single-engine approach (the "dead" engine was operating at idle power, not shut off, so it could be regained for thrust when required) the evaluator could also take away the instrument landing system (ILS), requiring a back-up approach to be flown at the last minute. Tater and I each received our five required training flights before being recommended for our initial qualification checkride.

My evaluator was a well-respected pilot named Major Greg Cayon, who also served as a Presidential Pilot on Air Force One, the mammoth Boeing 747. Greg was an easy-going, fun-loving, but very hard-working pilot. He knew any inflight evaluation could be a nerve-racking experience.

I'll never forget his ice-breaking words of wisdom, "Just remember. Every checkride is a learning experience. But if you're still learning too much, you fail."

I walked him through all of the aircraft systems, chasing electrons, drops of gas, and air molecules on system diagrams, then we headed out to fly the G-III along with a squadron flight engineer. For the next three hours, I concentrated heavily, handling simulated emergencies and degraded navigation equipment. Greg challenged me as I flew numerous approaches to several Delaware airports, including the small New Castle airport near Wilmington, and the huge Dover Air Force Base. By the end of September 14, 1999, I was proudly an ATP-rated, USAF-qualified, C-20B pilot.

CHAPTER 45

MOSCOW AND THE HOLY LAND IN FIVE DAYS

A Personal Journey

I stood in awe on Moscow's Red Square, posing for a picture in front of the brilliantly colored onion domes of Saint Basil's Cathedral. Fifteen years earlier, I "sat alert" on week-long tours, trained and ready to drop a nuclear bomb from our B-52 on this very spot. This was both surreal and mind-boggling.

Standing in front of St Basil's Cathedral on Moscow's Red Square.

By mid-May 2000, I was crewed as the copilot for Major Matt Newman on a five-day operational mission evaluation (OME) culminating in Matt's upgrade to aircraft commander. Our evaluator, Major Mike Grenke, later served as an Air Force One pilot during President George W. Bush's secret mission into Iraq on Thanksgiving Day, 2002. Our three enlisted flight crewmembers were Master Sergeant Mike Della Valle, Sergeant Andre Florence, and Sergeant Dawn Roberts. The primary passenger for the delegation was President Clinton's National Security Advisor Sandy Berger, accompanied by ten of his support staff members.

Moscow was a seven-hour flight from Andrews, which was plenty of time for Major Grenke to quiz Major Newman and observe how he led his crew on an international VIP mission. I was able to sit quietly, listen, and observe, knowing that my OME was just months away. We landed at Vnukovo Airport, on the outskirts of Moscow, in the evening of May 17. The old airport was lined with dozens of Aeroflot Russian airliners, each with a glass nose. We were told this was so they could film and gather intelligence as they flew their commercial flights to various countries.

While Sandy Berger conducted his business the day after our arrival, we were free to tour Moscow. Matt hired a tour guide with a minivan and the six of us set out to see the sights of our former adversary. The most memorable were Gorky Park and Red Square outside of the Kremlin. I remember the Soviet Space Shuttle, a failed attempt at copying our own, sat unceremoniously in Gorky Park. Their version of our Enterprise was now a park attraction that children crawled around on. Nice try, Ivan.

Following my remarkable photo op in front of St. Basil's Cathedral, we drove to a Russian open-air market on a gloomy, overcast, "this must be Russia" day. Like all good tourists, I bought the famous brightly painted nesting wooden dolls for our daughter and a Russian bear-fur hat for my dad, which he wore proudly during Colorado winters.

With the delegation's work wrapped up in Moscow in two days, Matt flew all of us to Ben Gurion Airport in Tel Aviv on May 19, landing just before evening. There was so much to see and do, we hardly knew where to start. By the next morning, Matt, Mike, and I were floating in the Dead Sea, and caking ourselves with its therapeutic mud. From there, we toured the location of the Dead Sea Scrolls, taking in the sight of the ancient scrolls lying under Plexiglas. We were near the Jordan River, so I scooped up a small jar of water from the location of Jesus' baptism. My younger cousin, Tina, had recently had a baby and this Holy Water would be used in her daughter Kylie's baptism. We headed back to the hotel, cleaned up, and prepared for the big event -- a tour of both Bethlehem and Jerusalem.

Major Mike Grenke and me, caked in Dead Sea mud.

Just by happenstance, of our six crewmembers, the three pilots all still attended church regularly, while the three enlisted personnel had not gone to church since childhood. Major Grenke, a large, rough and tumble hunter on his days off, surprised everyone, telling us that he still taught Sunday School. Our planned Holy City tour with a guide would cost each person more than $200.

Grenke matter-of-factly advised us, "Look guys. I know people who spend $2,000 to come on a tour of the Holy Land. I'm telling you; we won't pocket any per diem on this trip. There's too much history to see." He was right.

Our driver, a very nice short, squat Jewish man in his early 40s, picked us up at our hotel in his white van and we set off for Jerusalem. We went straight to a market to buy souvenirs, where I bought small crosses and tiny creches (nativity scenes) carved from local olive wood. Space was very limited in our plane, so large items were out of the question.

Pope John Paul had visited Israel at Easter, a month earlier. Signs of unrest were already beginning, with the newspaper reports detailing small riots and tires burning in the streets. The town of Jericho and the West Bank were off-limits to us. I will never forget the tense, quiet seriousness of crossing two heavily armed military checkpoints during our tour. These Israeli soldiers, most likely combat-hardened, were alert and not kidding around.

With our white plastic bags of trinkets and souvenirs, we set out for Bethlehem. What surprised me the most was that 1,000-year-old churches now stood as shrines over sites where 2,000-year-old Biblical events took place. A church stood over the birthplace of Jesus and we all joined the long line of pilgrims, shuffling along, silently looking up and around the reverently still cathedral. We finally funneled down a circular, stone stairwell and into the cramped area of the manger scene. Whether it was truly the location of Christ's birth, I do not know, but I stood quietly in awe. As suggested earlier by our guide, we each took turns placing our plastic bags of gifts on the location of Christ's birth, allowing them to be blessed.

Placing our gifts on the site of Christ's birth.

From Bethlehem, we headed toward the Mount of Olives and read quotes of Jesus' Sermon on the Mount from the Gospel of Matthew. These included three-foot by five-foot, blue and white ceramic tile depictions of the Lord's Prayer written in every language imaginable. This took me back to my many days of Sunday School and Bible studies. Suddenly, everything around me was familiar and coming alive.

The next stop was the Garden of Gethsemane, where Jesus was betrayed by Judas. Exiting the garden, we could see in the distance Jerusalem's massive protective stone wall and the gate where Jesus entered the city on what we now call Palm Sunday. So much Biblical history! I soaked it all in my head on a swivel.

Our group returned to the white van and drove toward the huge, gold Dome of the Rock in the center of Old Jerusalem. After parking, our Jewish guide advised us to place our gifts under the back seat, and he locked the van. The seven of us walked toward the Western

Wall under the shadows of the gold dome. There, our guide told us that this was the holiest place for Jews to pray because it was close to their previously destroyed temple. Jews would write a prayer on a small scrap of paper and, praying fervently, place it within the cracks of what is also known as the Wailing Wall. We silently took part in that ritual, placing our small scribbled prayer in the limestone wall.

Thirty minutes later we arrived back at the van to find the side windows broken out. Our driver's day planner was stolen, and the van had been rummaged through, but all of our "blessed gifts" remained under the rear seat. What a relief! We were thankful to still have our families' gifts intact.

Our tour van after it was broken into.

Our informative Jewish guide then led us on a spiritual pilgrimage, walking a portion of the Stations of the Cross. These were the twelve locations identified during the cross-laden procession of "your Jesus" (his words) to Calvary, the site of His execution. Arriving at Calvary, outside the city wall, we once again filed into a 1,000-year-old church erected over the site where three crosses once stood.

Not far away was the final stop of our meaningful day and tour: Jesus' tomb. Sadly, the line was extremely long, wrapping around the massive rectangular stone shrine of the tomb. And our time was short. I was struck by the physical proximity between the cross and the tomb. I wasn't certain if these were the actual locations or approximations for the Christian pilgrims. Regardless, our eager-to-please guide led us to a nearby collection of other tombs. One by one, we each took turns getting down on all fours, peeking inside to understand what Jesus' tomb could have looked like. What an ending to this impactful day.

I believe religion is an individual choice, and it is not for me to pick or choose which religion is right or wrong. I was raised (somewhat unwillingly) attending the Presbyterian Church and fidgeted through many sermons. I am not one to evangelize or proselytize. I can only tell those wanting to know what I've seen and heard.

In a remarkable personal journey, just four days earlier, I stood on Moscow's Red Square, a target I was willing to wipe out with a nuclear bomb. Now, standing in Jerusalem, everywhere I looked I was surrounded by many of the events detailed in the Gospel. In a single whirlwind day, we soaked in the sites of Jesus's life: His birth! Teaching the Lord's Prayer! His palm branch-strewn route into Jerusalem! His betrayal! His suffering! His crucifixion! His death! And the tomb from which He rose! This was the monumental trip of a lifetime.

"For we cannot stop speaking about what we have seen and heard." Acts 4:20

Air Force C-37A parked at Ben Gurion Airport, Tel Aviv, Israel.

Chapter 46

SYDNEY 2000 OLYMPICS

January 1, 2000. Y2K. How will the world's computers respond? Will our aircraft navigation systems work? Will our country's air traffic control (ATC) system function properly? We were about to find out.

The day before, on December 31, 1999, Major Rob Crone and I flew the Chief of Staff of the Air Force, four-star General Mike Ryan, to Burbank, California. Five years later, Rob would be the Lajes command post officer in the Azores for the clandestine 310 AS mission, picking up Special Envoy John Bremer in Amman, Jordan.

But on New Year's Day, 2000, General Ryan was honored to serve as the Grand Marshal of the Rose Bowl Parade as the nation hoped their laptops and banking websites still worked. Just before departure time, Rob and I powered up our C-20B. No Y2K bugs! We took off from California that evening with a content general on board. Four hours later, we touched down at Andrews at 1:00 a.m. Sunday, January 2. What a relief!

By January 2000, I had six months of Gulfstream C-20B flying under my belt and was ready for my second Gulfstream qualification. Andrews had a diverse fleet of Gulfstream aircraft: the C-20Bs (G-III), C-20Hs (G-IV) and C-37s (G-V). To assist in scheduling the missions using the entire fleet, pilots could be qualified to fly two of these three variants. For safety's sake, the Air Force decided that trying to keep the specifications of two airplanes in our head was okay but did not want to overload us with a third set of numbers and procedures.

This diverse fleet and separate crew qualifications created a scheduling nightmare. While all pilots could fly the 1980s C-20B, the crew force was split evenly between those who were qualified in the C-20Hs and C-37s, which had different engines and other systems. If, due to a maintenance issue, a mission was switched from a C-20H to a C-37, the scheduler had to find different pilots to fly that Gulfstream.

How were 99 AS crews picked to fly the early 1990s C-20H or the brand-new C-37? It wasn't by merit, but merely by Flight Safety International's training calendar. Which course did the Savannah training center have coming up next month? G-IV or G-V? Four of us in the squadron were ready for our next Gulfstream type when Savannah said they had four G-V training slots available. I was paired with our squadron commander, Lt Col Scott Hanson, a good friend from our days as captains flying the KC-10 at Barksdale. Scott and I worked great together during seven simulator training sessions. Because of our KC-10 background, we knew about advanced cockpit avionics and enjoyed our time in Savannah, learning to fly the beautiful, new G-V. Following a week of G-V academics, we were fortunate to be assigned a respected veteran flight instructor. Homer Bentley, sporting white hair and a white mustache, spent the second week instructing us as we flew simulated flights into various major airports around the world -- Aspen, Memphis, Paris, San Francisco, and Frankfurt. Together, Scott and I learned the intricacies of our new toy.

Our FAA ATP evaluation day was planned for and lasted 10 hours. Kicking off with a four-hour pre-brief (we showed up on time!), our morning included walking around a newly built G-V. Scott and I took turns describing all the systems to our evaluator, pointing to various parts of the right-off-the-assembly line aircraft.

After a short break, the four-hour simulator session began, which was very similar to the grueling G-III evaluation I took with Tater during the summer. The main difference between the G-III and G-V were the modern avionics and displays, more powerful engines and a very cool and useful Heads-Up Display (HUD).

The G-V HUD was a round-edge 6-inch by 7-inch piece of glass that flipped down in front of the left seat pilot's face. On the glass, projected in green, was all the vital flight information shown on the instruments in front of our chest – airspeed, altitude, heading, and the wind speed and direction. In the distance, beyond this green formation, the pilot could also see the sky or runway, depending on the phase of flight.

The HUD turned flying into a video game. A small circle, called the guidance cue, depicted where I needed to guide the airplane. My actual position was represented by a smaller circle, about the size of a BB. All I needed to do was place my small circle inside the larger floating guidance cue circle and the plane would fly the headings and pitch necessary to find the runway on a foggy day. The HUD enabled very precise flying and came in handy during landings in low visibility, such as when the clouds were a mere 100 feet above the runway. In not-so-technical terms, this was called "PFM," which stood for "pure fucking magic." It's just the way some things in aviation work.

An hour-long debrief session wrapped up our very long day, and our evaluator complimented both our aviation knowledge and teamwork. Scott and I happily accepted our second ATP rating, now in a G-V. After hearty handshakes around the debriefing room, we packed up our gear and headed back north to Andrews.

The Air Force C-37 was pure joy to fly. Think of any favorite finely-tuned sportscar – Porsche, Ferrari, Lamborghini. That's what flying a G-V was like. The state-of-the-art cockpit itself was ultra-modern, professional-looking with soft gray instrument panels, rather than stark black metal panels. It was the consummate quiet professional. The overhead panel above the pilot seats contained push-button one-inch black square capsules, instead of the chunky knobs, switches, and dials of older aircraft. It was designed as a "blacked-out" cockpit, which meant that when everything worked properly all the capsules were black. If a problem occurred, a capsule would turn blue, amber, or red, depending on the severity of the issue.

The audible tones were gentle to our ears, such as a soft "bing-bong" when the autopilot or auto-throttles were disconnected. Think of HAL in *2001, A Space Odyssey*, calmly giving the pilot information. This was so much more pleasing than the blaring horns and "quacking duck" audible alarms of other aircraft, loudly declaring a change in status or configuration. Our luxury jet also boasted two Rolls Royce engines, each providing 14,000 pounds of thrust to take us anywhere we wanted to go for up to eleven hours. Squadron pilots often remarked, "Can you believe we actually get to fly this plane?!" Pure joy.

The C-37A (G-V) cockpit

By September 2000, I was eligible for upgrade to aircraft commander. This required an international VIP mission with a full five-person crew, plus an evaluator, similar to Matt's mission to the Holy Land three months earlier. The mission taskings came to us from the Pentagon's Assistant Vice Chief of Staff Special Air Missions Division (CVAM), in charge of scheduling VIP airlift. CVAM served as the arbitrator for all of the dignitaries vying for any 89th Airlift

Wing aircraft. Our 99 AS crews never knew where they might be 48 hours in the future.

On one particular "day-in-the-life" at the 99 AS, I was paged by the squadron scheduler, or seen by him as I walked by his desk (this was known as Line-Of-Sight scheduling). During this eight-hour duty day at the squadron I was on and off five different missions: China, Africa, Israel, Russia, Japan! "You're going here. No, wait! You're going there!" By the end of the day, I went home and wasn't assigned to any of them. Life at Andrews AFB was truly organized chaos.

My upgrade evaluation mission was no different. For three days I planned to take a delegation eastbound to Moscow in an old C-20B. Then, just five days before departure, I was switched to flying the White House delegation, consisting of Secretary of Health and Human Resources Donna Shalala and First Daughter Chelsea Clinton, westward to the Sydney 2000 Olympics in a new C-37. This was a much better deal, without a doubt, but in a different Gulfstream model to an entirely different region of the world. I was very thankful, however, for the change!

My crew consisted of Major Dave Schermer, a qualified AC serving as my copilot; Senior Master Sergeant Dave Rossner (FE), Master Sergeant Kevin McQuay (CSO), Technical Sergeant Marcy Wright as our flight attendant (FA), and Major Trent Bigler as my evaluator.

Trent, my evaluator, was a senior member of the Andrews Gulfstream community and worked in the highly respected 89th Operations Group Standardization/Evaluation division. He had a reputation for changing his mood from happy to ticked-off rather quickly. This variability became known as Good Trent and Bad Trent. I was hoping for Good Trent. Fortunately, he was ecstatic to be going to the Olympics for the week.

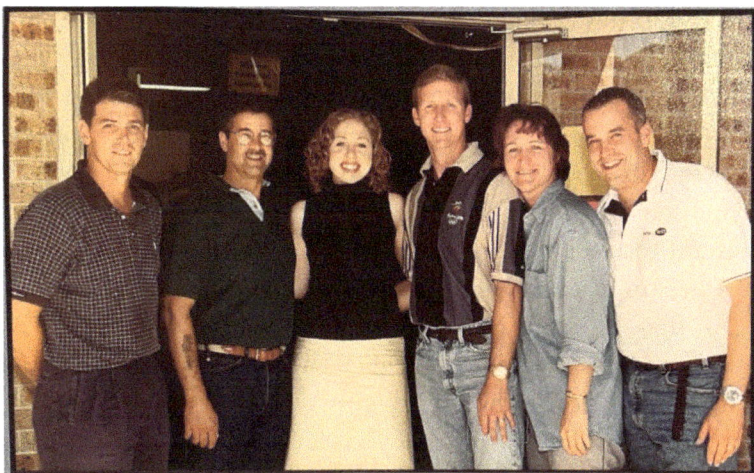

Major Trent Bigler (Evaluator), SMSgt Dave Rossner (FE),
First Daughter Chelsea Clinton, me,
Sgt Marcy Wright (FA), and Major Dave Schermer (Pilot)
(White House Photo)

I sat in the left seat of the Gulfstream C-37 on September 12, ready to start both engines, as President Bill Clinton's black limousine pulled up alongside our fold-out staircase. The President hugged his college-age daughter, seeing her off on this week-long international adventure. The President and First Lady stayed home at this time as Mrs. Clinton continued her campaign for a U.S. Senate seat from New York.

On a side note, during the summer and fall of 2000, I flew the First Lady twelve times as she campaigned for the Senate, attended Democratic fund-raisers, or carried out her First Lady duties. I only had one brief personal encounter with her and it was very nice. Normally, she would board our aircraft and immediately turn right, taking her seat in the VIP compartment. On a trip throughout California, she returned to our waiting jet in Sacramento, carrying a large green basket of huge strawberries. After climbing our short staircase, Mrs. Clinton turned left and came into our cockpit. With a big smile she said, "You have got to try one of these strawberries!"

Each red berry was bigger than a golf ball, and my fellow pilot, Lieutenant Colonel Art Smith, and I each enjoyed her tasty treat.

Chelsea Clinton, sporting long, red, curly hair, joined Donna Shalala (all 5' 0" of her) to form the White House delegation to the Olympics. The two were joined by a social secretary for the delegation (known to me as "the contact"), and by Huma Abedin, who served as an assistant to the First Daughter. Security guards and Ms. Shalala's support personnel rounded out the eleven-passenger manifest for this trip. Our first leg was a 10.5-hour flight to Hickam Air Force Base, Hawaii, for an overnight stop. Our C-37 whistled along westward at 44,000 feet, chasing the setting sun.

After a good night's rest, the next day I performed the preflight walk-around, knowing that I was about to step inside and strap into the left seat for a second 10.5-hour flight to Sydney. That second pre-flight has always stuck in my mind as a reminder for why I don't want to fly long-range international flights anymore. Two back-to-back 10.5-hour flights were certainly enough. The long flights also gave Major Bigler ample time to quiz me about how to plan and carry out our high-visibility mission. With a set of Gulfstream flight manuals and Air Force regulations at his fingertips, Trent played "Stump the Dummy" with me for hours as we cruised over the Pacific Ocean. I held my own, correctly answering or quickly looking up the answers to his probing questions.

We landed in Sydney on September 13, and I taxied up to the red carpet for our delegation's VIP arrival. Ms. Shalala and Miss Clinton deplaned and spoke to reporters from a podium as we sat quietly in our seats on a silent aircraft. Our engines and auxiliary power unit remained off so as not to interfere with the arrival ceremony and press conference.

In a crazy "small world" coincidence, my original C-20B mission to Moscow was given to my friend, Major Steve "Action" Jackson, for his aircraft commander upgrade evaluation. Steve told me later that he walked into his Moscow hotel room, turned on the television to CNN International, and watched my C-37 taxi to a stop on the red carpet in Australia. It's a funny little world.

We stayed in Sydney for the first week of the Olympics, but with so little advance warning, my six-person crew did not have tickets for any of the events. We managed to buy scalped tickets to men's gymnastics preliminaries, men's tennis, and of all things, judo. We attended judo only because the venue was right across the street from our hotel. There, I learned that some of those international competitors' Olympic Moments could last just four seconds!

On September 18, our crew was watching the Olympics in Kevin's room when my cell phone rang. The phone was an international cell phone provided by the U.S. Embassy so we could maintain contact with our delegation while in Australia. Our party's contact, a very nice older lady, offered, "We are meeting the Basketball Dream Team tomorrow at their practice. Would your crew like to go?"

Without polling my crew, I replied, "Certainly!"

"Okay," she continued. "You'll need to work your own transportation but meet us at our hotel and we'll caravan to their gym."

I told my crew, "We're going to see the Dream Team tomorrow!"

Amazingly enough, there were no objections. Imagine that.

I then immediately called our embassy contact, Rodney, and asked, "Hey Rodney! How would you like to meet the Basketball Dream Team?"

"That'd be great, sir!" he replied.

"Good!" I said, "You're in charge of transportation."

"I'm on it, sir!" he replied and hung up.

The next morning, a caravan of four cars headed out of Sydney to the suburbs and pulled up to a high school gymnasium. Our crew mingled around, but as a rule of etiquette, we did not approach our VIP party. Finally, a large tour bus pulled into the parking lot and off stepped the tallest men I had ever seen up close: Alonzo Mourning, Kevin Garnett, Steve Smith, Vince Carter, Jason Kidd, and coaches Rudy Tomjanovich and Tubby Smith, the University of Kentucky coach. Okay, Tubby was round, not tall.

We followed them into the basketball court and stood courtside, chatting with Tubby Smith and the renowned Houston player and coach, Rudy T. I told Rudy I was from Houston, where he had played until 1981. In December 1977, while playing against the Lakers, Rudy received a bone-crushing punch to his face. It was a life-threatening, season-ending injury that viewers would not soon forget. Fortunately, Rudy fully recovered and went on to coach the Rockets and now our country's basketball team.

Many of my crewmembers grabbed Olympic programs and pens that morning for autographs, but Rodney had the best plan. The night before, he bought a commemorative Sydney 2000 basketball and a black permanent marker. Somewhere in a glass case sits this prize basketball signed by a gold-medal-winning U.S. Dream Team.

SMSgt Dave Rossner, Major Trent Bigler,
our Embassy contact Rodney, me, Major Dave Schermer, and
MSgt Kevin McQuay (kneeling), holding Sydney 2000
basketballs on the U.S. Dream Team's practice court.

We sat among the NBA all-stars on the school's bleachers as they started lacing up their shoes and pulling on their practice jerseys. My copilot, Dave, looked at his watch and realized it was dinner time back home in Washington D.C. He asked me for the Embassy's international cell phone so he could call his 12-year-old son.

Dave sat to my left, telling his son about all the NBA players sitting just a few feet from us when suddenly a hand appeared between us and tapped him on his right shoulder. We both turned back to see Jason Kidd, asking for the phone. Jason had been listening to Dave's conversation and wanted to surprise his boy.

Dave handed over the phone and Jason started chatting with a young Air Force son sitting at his dinner table outside of Washington D.C. From there, Jason started handing the phone around to other players and we just laughed at what this kid must've thought. Finally, Jason reached toward Kevin Garnett, a total badass, who with a very serious face said, "Man ... I ain't talkin' on no phone."

Jason punched Kevin Garnett in the shoulder and said, "Hey! It's that man's son. Talk to the boy!"

Kevin took the phone and in his very deep voice said, "Hello? Yeah. Your dad's kicking my ass in one-on-one." and handed back the phone.

We died laughing. What a memorable Olympic Moment for us all.

SMSgt Dave Rossner laughing as Jason Kidd talks to
Dave Schermer's son back home.
(The photo date is incorrect because of the International Date Line)

The following morning, I flew the long flight back to Hickam AFB, near Honolulu, where Major Bigler finally announced that I had passed my evaluation. As a newly minted Gulfstream aircraft commander, I gladly treated my crew to Mai Tai rum cocktails in a beachside celebration. Good Trent happily took the C-37's left seat for the final ten-hour leg home to Andrews from Hawaii.

CHAPTER 47
DON'T GET COCKY

Aviation has influenced my life in so many positive ways. As I mentioned at the beginning, I grew up shy and lacked self-confidence. It wasn't until I started taking flying lessons at age 16 that I ventured out on my own to pursue my own dream. Through aviation, I learned to make decisions, some of which could have life or death consequences.

I scared myself a few times, but truly think that from when I started flying in 1978 until I joined the 89th Airlift Wing in 1999 I embodied the slogan, "What doesn't kill you, makes you stronger." Completing a challenging instrument approach in bad weather or leading a crew on international missions to austere locations bolstered my self-confidence and decisiveness to the point of now wanting to be a squadron commander. I came out of my shell to become a "people-person," happily talking to anyone, anywhere. Karin even remarked that I was now the "social butterfly" of our marriage. I felt ready for greater responsibility and a bigger challenge.

According to Maslow's well-known Hierarchy of Needs, humans are motivated by five needs: Physiological (food and clothing), Safety (job security), Love and Belonging (friendship), Esteem (respect, status, recognition), and Self-actualization (the desire to become the most one can be). My Air Force flying career fulfilled these needs. I moved beyond my childhood friends and set out on a career my uncle had enjoyed. I persevered from my days as a bomber navigator to realizing my dream of becoming an Air Force pilot. I now belonged to a fraternity of aviators, providing both friendship, recognition, and respect. Once selected to be an Andrews AFB Gulfstream pilot,

I was surrounded by like-minded, highly professional pilots, whose main goal was the perfect execution of a smooth flight in support of our very important passengers. We wanted to be the best we could possibly be.

The history of the Andrews VIP air mission dates back to the Truman and Eisenhower administrations. The early overseas diplomatic missions flown from Washington D.C. were designated "Special Air Missions - Foreign", which was abbreviated SAM-F. In the military phonetic alphabet, the letter F is Foxtrot, so the Andrews missions were eventually dubbed SAMFOX, and everything we did was to the SAMFOX standard of excellence. This instilled a great source of pride.

I never think of myself as "the best pilot," or God's Gift to Aviation. My aim, however, is to be one of the most conscientious pilots, striving to give my passengers an enjoyable flight experience. But beware. With this newfound confidence, cockiness and over-confidence can rise up and humble a person. Sometimes I've been put back in my place.

Each year, every pilot goes through a flight evaluation. These aren't enjoyable, but a necessary, stressful part of our job. According to aviation conventional wisdom, pilots hope the ride before our checkride goes poorly, so we'll peak at the right moment under the watchful eye of the evaluator. As the aviation saying goes, "Anyone can have a bad day. You just don't want it to be on checkride day."

One year after I upgraded to aircraft commander, I was due for my annual evaluation, conducted by a long-time Andrews pilot named Lt Col Herb Finch. Herb was a great guy and we had flown several fun Gulfstream trips together, so I was quite at ease as we prepared for this training sortie.

During the two-hour oral examination, called a "ground eval", I answered all of Herb's questions about airplane systems and how I would handle various aircraft malfunctions. Once I had finished verbally "building the airplane" for Herb, we set out for the flightline to begin a three-hour flight.

From Andrews AFB, we flew 30 minutes south to Patrick Henry Airport, in Newport News, Virginia. Herb told me which approach to plan for and I briefed the required items: radio frequency, inbound course heading to the runway, how low we could descend (known as the Decision Altitude) before committing to land or executing a go-around, and any obstructions in the vicinity. Throughout the approaches, Herb added distractions or restrictions, and I had to factor those into my approach.

One such challenge occurred during a go-around. Once safely above the runway, Herb slowly pulled one of the two throttles back and said, "Okay, you've just lost that engine." In actuality, the engine was still running, but only at idle power. Herb told me to fly an antiquated radio beacon (VOR) approach. I flew the procedures for an engine-out approach, followed by Herb's directed single-engine go-around, climbing out on just one engine's power. This required a lot of concentration, but the powerful C-37 performed masterfully.

Satisfied with my single-engine work, Herb said I could use the "dead" engine throttle again and from Newport News, we flew to Richmond, Virginia. There, I continued my approach work, flying all sorts of instrument approaches that the C-37 was capable of performing. These ranged from 1950's-era radio beacon approaches, to the low-visibility instrument approaches using the glass HUD just inches from my face, to the brand-new GPS navigation approaches. Each task that Herb gave me I accomplished flawlessly that day. I remember thinking to myself as we departed Richmond for the last leg to Andrews, "This is going great today!" I had flown each approach perfectly and I was riding high.

I could tell by Herb's light-hearted voice that he thought things were going well, too. We were enjoying a beautiful day of flying. As we set up for the final approach to complete the checkride at our home station, Herb said, "Okay, I want this to be a Min Run landing. You need to get off the runway by the second taxiway."

One of the capabilities I loved about the C-37 was its versatility. This sleek executive jet could takeoff at a maximum gross weight of 90,000 and climb straight up to 43,000 feet, cruising above all of the airliners, which were capped at 41,000 feet. It could do this while taking off and landing on runways as short as 5,000 feet. Most airport runways range from 8,000 to 11,000 feet, so a runway less than one mile long is considered short. We had to demonstrate we could land on a short runway during each evaluation.

The Gulfstream was built with a big, beautiful wing, capable of holding a lot of fuel and generating a lot of lift. When coming into land on a short runway, the last thing I wanted to do was float down the runway, with the far end quickly approaching. To avoid this, we trained to point the nose short of the intended landing zone, pull the power to idle at 100 feet above the ground, glide in, and touchdown in the first 500 feet of the runway. We wanted to use the minimum amount of runway, so the landings were nicknamed "Min Run." The second taxiway Herb was challenging me to use was only 4,000 down the runway. I was up for that challenge.

Swelling with pride from the previous three hours of flying, I distinctly remember thinking to myself, "*I am going to water his eyes,*" and impress the heck out of Herb. I picked my aimpoint, short of the touchdown zone and headed for the runway. There was a strong crosswind blowing from our left to right. I pulled the power to idle, glided over the approach end of the runway and the wheels touched as planned in the first 500 feet of the runway. I aggressively applied the brakes to slow the airplane to make the taxiway but didn't fully take Mother Nature into account.

By slowing so quickly, the rudder became far less effective in controlling the aircraft. As a result, my rudder pedals alone could not keep the plane from turning into the wind. The nose now started pointing left and we were headed for the left edge of the runway as I applied brakes to slow us down. The C-37 has electronic nosewheel steering, which is extremely sensitive. The nosewheel is controlled by a small V-shaped steering wheel called the tiller. If used at too high of a speed there is a risk of over correcting and going on Mr. Toad's Wild Ride, swerving down the runway. For that reason, we could not use the tiller until reaching a slow speed. Due to my rapid deceleration, that time was now.

There is another saying regarding checkrides: "Never scare your evaluator." As Herb started yelling, "Tiller! Tiller! Tiller!" it was obvious that I had just violated this principle. I moved my left hand from the yoke to the small tiller, straightening the nose to parallel the runway edge, about 50 feet to our left. The cockpit became very quiet as I slowed to 10 miles per hour for the turn off the runway. I taxied in silence to our parking spot. In my effort to water Herb's eyes, I almost soiled his pants. I hung my head, knowing I had just busted a near-perfect checkride.

Days later, I flew my "recheck" with Major Rob Crone. The prebrief for this re-evaluation consisted of me describing the nose-wheel steering system of a Gulfstream and how to properly execute a Min Run landing with a crosswind. Rob and I then headed back out to a C-37 where I demonstrated the proper Min Run landing and successfully completed the recheck within an hour.

There is no doubt that my ego and cockiness got the better of me that day. It was certainly a "teachable moment." To this day, as I fly instrument approaches in bad weather as an airline pilot, I interrupt my intense concentration with this recurring thought: Don't get cocky.

CHAPTER 48

TIMING IS EVERYTHING

B y the winter of 1999 I had been promoted to lieutenant colonel and was serving as the Assistant Director of Operations, or ADO, of the 99 AS. Our squadron commander, Lt Col Scott Hanson, was out pheasant hunting in his home state of Iowa. Meanwhile, the squadron director of operations, Lt Col Nancy Vetere, was home on convalescent leave following major knee surgery. That left me "minding the store" on a Friday morning, sitting at Nancy's desk and answering official squadron emails, coming from the echelons above.

One email caught my attention. The wing commander of MacDill AFB in south Tampa, Florida, asked our Andrews wing commander if he had any C-37 instructor pilots who would like to help start up a new squadron, supporting the seven 4-star combatant commanders around the United States. MacDill would receive three new C-37s the following summer and needed a cadre of instructors and evaluators to train the new crews. The email made its way down to the Group Commander, Colonel Dave Fadok, and finally to me at the 99 AS, where I read it with interest. Could this really happen? I had only been at Andrews for one and a half years of a four-year tour. I wasn't an instructor yet but was due to upgrade at any point.

I called Nancy at her house and asked what she thought of this job opportunity. We knew that the long-range plan was for me to move up to operations officer and eventually become the 99 AS squadron commander. With Scott Hanson out of town on leave, I asked Nancy if I could talk to Colonel Fadok about the assignment and she said yes. I called the group commander's secretary that afternoon and made an appointment with Col Fadok for 10:00 a.m. on Monday morning. I then headed home to tell Karin about this opportunity in Tampa.

When assignments need to be filled, the Personnel Center ran a matrix of qualified individuals, which included factors like current qualifications, how long candidates had been at the base, known as time on station, and how long they had left to serve in the Air Force. I was coming up on 17 years in the Air Force, so I had three years to go until my projected retirement. I had been at Andrews almost two years and would be an instructor in a matter of months. According to the matrix, all of the candidates younger than I were not instructors or lieutenant colonels yet, and those that were already instructors were too close to their possible retirement to move to MacDill. I was the only willing candidate that met the criteria.

Monday morning, I sat down with Colonel Fadok and asked him what he thought of me putting in for the assignment. His reply was memorable, but not exactly confidence-boosting. "To tell you the truth, Dave, we hadn't really thought about you," he said.

Although this sounded like a put-down, what he meant was that I was not being considered for MacDill because I was already in the plan to move up within the Andrews AFB hierarchy. Col Fadok asked me what Scott thought of the idea and I said I hadn't talked to him because he was out on vacation. Col Fadok closed with, "Let me track down Scott and run it by him. Then I'll let you know."

Within a few days the emails reversed course and my name was forwarded up to the Andrews wing commander then over to the MacDill wing commander for consideration to start up their 310th Airlift Squadron (310 AS).

Once approved by the chain of command, the Air Force Personnel Center, AFPC, in San Antonio had to grant me a waiver to move after only 22 months at Andrews. This was quickly approved because I was now heading to a leadership position.

My next task was to build a cadre of instructors from each crew position who would build up the C-37 crew force at MacDill. Each crewmember had an assignment officer in San Antonio, and that person had the overall say as to who would receive the MacDill assignment. For this special, short-notice assignment, this depended upon their aircraft qualifications and the desire to move. The selected cadre consisted of two additional pilots; Major Bob Giddings, as Chief of Training, and Major Lee "Ice" Icenhour, as Chief of Standards and Evaluations. Master Sergeant Kevin McQuay was our Communications Systems Operator instructor. Staff Sergeant Allison Miller was selected as the Flight Attendant instructor, and Technical Sergeant Tony Radcliffe rounded out the crew as our instructor Flight Engineer.

Bob had flown KC-10s and was extremely professional and competent. Working with him was the first time in my 17-year career I could delegate a task and the result exceeded my abilities and expectations. Ice was with me in the KC-10 during the Southern Watch deployment when Ken Reed died in a T-37 crash. Kevin was my CSO during the high-visibility Sydney Olympic mission in 2000. Allison was an extremely sharp flight attendant and, although lower in rank than her colleagues, performed her job with 110% effort. In my mind, she set the bar for excellent service. Tony was everybody's favorite person in the 99 AS. He was so proactive in finding answers and seeking information that he made everyone's life easier. We were extremely lucky to have this hard-working, life-loving flight engineer on our team. Four years later, as Tony prepared for retirement, he was diagnosed with Stage 4 cancer. With a wife and young son, Tony fought valiantly for 18 months before succumbing -- a heart-breaking moment for everyone who knew and loved this great American.

Although Ice would join us from his C-20 assignment in Ramstein, Germany, the others were at Andrews with me. We gathered in my ADO's office to begin our plans for the move to MacDill AFB and the stand-up of the C-37 operation there. Other members of the 99 AS jokingly referred to us as the "MacDale Crew." As the birds migrated north in March of 2001, we headed south to Florida.

CHAPTER 49

CREATING A SQUADRON

310 AS patch and nametag in new squadron colors.

The pinnacle of my career began in March, 2001, with our move to Valrico, Florida, 30 minutes east of Tampa. Moving after only 22 months at Andrews didn't go over very well with Daniel and Shelby. Our family thought I would finish the last five years of my career at Andrews but instead, I now moved them a sixth time in eight years. I will never forget Daniel telling me, "Why should I bother to make friends. You're just going to move me again anyway." Ouch. This was vastly different from me growing up across the street from Larry Leonard. Ten years later, Daniel commissioned as an Air Force second lieutenant and began serving as a logistics officer. He has now moved five times in eleven years. The sting of moving the kids to Florida was lessened when we bought a home, complete with swimming pool, and only 80 miles from Disney World.

By late spring 2001, many of the initial core of instructors for the new 310th Airlift Squadron had settled into the Tampa Bay Area. Several of the squadron's crewmembers were already in place, having been assigned to the EC-135 (Boeing 707) and CT-43 (Boeing 737) as part of D Flight of the 91st Air Refueling Squadron, the KC-135 squadron at MacDill. These two aircraft flew VIP missions supporting Central Command (CENTCOM) and Southern Command (SOUTHCOM). CENTCOM's General Tommy Franks, an Army four-star general, flew in the large four-engine EC-135. The SOUTHCOM commander, Marine four-star General Peter Pace flew on the smaller two-engine CT-43. Those two planes now belonged to the new 310 AS while we awaited the three new C-37s.

General Frank's missions departed from MacDill AFB, heading eastward towards Qatar, Bahrain, and what we called the "Stan-lands": Kyrgyzstan, Kazakhstan, and Turkmenistan. General Pace boarded his CT-43 in Miami before continuing south toward Central and South America. SOUTHCOM missions included regular trips to Bogota, Colombia for the ongoing War on Drugs.

In the past, all military four-star commanders were entitled to fly on Andrews AFB's Gulfstream fleet. Due to competing demands from higher-ranking civilian leaders, these commanders often were trumped by congressmen and service secretaries in their need for airlift. To solve this, Congress decided to adopt a civilian practice and create a corporate flight department like NetJets. They authorized the procurement of three MacDill AFB C-37s to be shared by seven U.S.-based combatant commanders. CENTCOM, SOUTHCOM, and Special Operations Command (SOCOM), also headquartered at MacDill, were based in Florida. They were joined by Transportation Command (TRANSCOM) in southern Illinois, Strategic Command (STRATCOM) in Omaha, Northern Command (NORTHCOM) in Colorado Springs, and finally Joint Forces Command (JFCOM), who we nicknamed "JIFFYCOM," in Norfolk, Virginia. There's a musical called *Seven Brides for Seven Brothers*. In our newly formed squadron, we had "Three Jets for Seven Generals (or Admirals)" - and they had to learn to share.

Many of the crewmembers flying the EC-135 and CT-43 eventually trained to fly the C-37 or moved on to other assignments. New crewmembers transferred in to build up our manning to 20 pilots, 10 flight engineers, 10 communication system operators and 10 flight attendants. With administrative support included, the new 310th Airlift Squadron boasted 65 members. In a novel arrangement, our three C-37s were leased instead of purchased and maintenance was provided by contracted Gulfstream civilian personnel.

On a sunny January afternoon in Tampa, the 310 AS was activated under the command of Lieutenant Colonel Eden Murrie in a ceremony inside of Hangar 3. I flew down from Andrews to attend the event and soon became her Operations Officer (310 AS/DO). We immediately began working to establish our new squadron.

Eden, a KC-135 and EC-135 navigator, had been the Operations Officer for the 91st Air Refueling Squadron and maintained her office in that building until our squadron building was renovated. Next door to Eden's office was a storage room, converted to a narrow office for three desks and chairs. How narrow was it? My desk was the furthest from the door and when I needed to leave, the other two guys had to get up, push their chairs in and leave the room so I could get out. That's narrow.

Throughout the spring, Major Bob Giddings, our lead C-37 instructor pilot, TSgt Tony Radcliff, MSgt Kevin McQuay, and SSgt Allison Miller, helped Eden and me compile a budget request to fund our new flight operation for the remainder of the fiscal year. Fortunately, from my time at Air Mobility Command Headquarters, I learned about Excel spreadsheets and budget requests. Taking the inputs from our pool of instructors and squadron leaders already at MacDill, we tabulated a request for $214,680. This would fund the remaining four months of the fiscal year for training flights for the incoming crew members and procured everything from luggage to clothing to accessories for the airplane.

On a May morning, we walked our request over to the finance squadron commander, Major Randy White, who had worked across the cubicle from me at AMC headquarters three years earlier. Randy reviewed our request, gave it his stamp of approval and emailed it to the AMC Comptroller, our money friend, Mr. Chuck Mavrogeorge, at Scott AFB. We fully expected that we'd have to answer questions, justifying our budget request or fight for more dollars when less was eventually allocated. Returning to the air refueling squadron, I resumed work in my storage room office.

At 4:00 that afternoon, Eden yelled out from her office, "Dave, come look!" Her voice was her own PA system.

Bob, Tony, and I shuffled out of our office, and came in to look over Eden's shoulder at her computer screen. She had been copied on an email from Chuck to the AMC Finance office, stating, "Please fund the 310th Airlift Squadron with an attached request for $214,600." We joked that he stiffed us $80, but we were now fully funded and ready to fly! Now we just needed our first C-37 to arrive on time in July 2001.

Starting up a squadron gave Eden and me the leeway to pick squadron colors for our squadron scarf and nametags, plus a squadron patch. Or so we thought. The 310 AS was originally created during WWII as the 310th Troop Carrier Squadron and its patch was a yellow spread-wing eagle on a blue background, circled with a white ring. The eagle, drawn in the 1940s, was a very poor rendition and often referred to as the Dead or Rubber Chicken. One of the EC-135 crewmembers, Major Keith Peloquin, redrew the yellow bird with crisp angles more resembling a Rising Phoenix.

Since the patch already had a white circle around a blue background, Eden suggested we add an additional outer red circle, with the words Combatant Commander Support across the top and four stars at the bottom. This signified that our mission was transporting the four-star commanders of our U.S.-based combatant commands, and gave our patch a patriotic red, white and blue look.

Our customers came from the Army, Navy, Air Force, and Marines. Military operations involving multiple services are called Joint Operations and are typically represented by the color purple. Eden and I discussed replacing the red ring with purple to signify joint/multi-service transportation. The purple just didn't look right, so Eden suggested burgundy as a color that could pass for either red or purple. Our new burgundy, white and blue squadron patch looked great with Keith's crisp yellow eagle in the middle. Hundreds were ordered for our incoming crews to wear proudly on their flightsuits.

Unapproved, beautiful 310 AS coin (left) and
Rubber Chicken coin (Right)

Now we needed two-tone colored nametags and scarves to add to our Air Force flightsuit attire. Squadron scarves are a tradition dating back to the first aviation units in WWI. Eden selected yellow lettering and trim for the burgundy nametags and yellow lightning bolts for our burgundy scarves. Tampa, home of the NHL's *Lightning* hockey team, declared itself the "Lightning Capital of the World" with its numerous thunderstorms, so lightning bolts were appropriate.

Our operations group commander, Colonel AJ Stewart, was a KC-135 Strategic Air Command "SAC Warrior" through and through. During our updates on squadron progress, he chided Eden and I about our beautiful Gulfstream executive jet, and our renovated building with brand new furniture, claiming we weren't real warfighters. We gladly accepted his ribbing, knowing anyone would love to be in our squadron.

Once he saw our new patch with burgundy and yellow colors, Colonel Stewart declared, "Y'all are the Wine and Cheese Squadron. Why, even your squadron colors are Merlot and Cheddar!"

He probably didn't expect it, but we quickly adopted the moniker of MacDill's Wine and Cheese squadron. In future Newcomer Orientation briefings, the 310 AS was introduced as the Wine and Cheese squadron, while the 91 ARS was introduced as the Beer and Bologna Squadron – a very fitting description for both flying squadrons.

Eight years later, long after I departed, a new 310 AS commander learned that all squadron patches and colors are governed by the Air Force Heritage Office and could not be changed without approval. Our 310 AS tri-colored patch and "wine and cheese" colored nametags and scarves were disapproved. The squadron sadly reverted to its original blue and white colors and the ugly Rubber Chicken patch.

After numerous trips to the Gulfstream plant in Savannah, Georgia, we accepted our first C-37, tail number 10028. The plane touched down at MacDill AFB on July 18, 2001, flown by AMC's four-star commander, General Tony Robertson, with Bob Giddings serving as his instructor pilot in the right seat. The arrival ceremony was a big event, attended by Tampa's Mayor Dick Greco, in front of our new home in Hangar 3. Our second plane was scheduled to arrive on September 13, 2001.

CHAPTER 50

FIRST TRIP TO BOGOTA, COLOMBIA

The CT-43 flight crew and I climbed into the U.S. Embassy's old Chevy van for the drive back to the airport. We were taking some backroads, but I didn't know where we were to begin with. I noticed Captain Joe Brewster and Major Dave Knight looking at each other and eventually Joe whispered to Dave, "I've never gone this way before. Have you?" Dave shook his head no.

Now my mind started to spin. Was this an arranged kidnapping? We drove along a route lined by dense jungle trees and after 40 minutes, arrived at a rusted back gate of the Bogota commercial airport. We took a side road around the runway, finally arriving at our aircraft parked near Natalie's office. Natalie coordinated the servicing of military aircraft and took care of our transportation needs. As Dave and Joe began their preflight inspections, Natalie came aboard the plane via its small staircase. Knowing that the longer drive put the crew behind schedule, she quickly explained, "I'm sorry about the longer drive but two car bombs exploded downtown this morning, so your driver had to take an alternate route."

In May, as we waited for the first C-37 delivery, I accompanied a CT-43 crew to Bogota, the capital of Colombia, to learn the ins and outs of the operation down there. We flew into an airfield surrounded by rugged mountains and in a country that was currently battling rebel forces called the Revolutionary Armed Forces of Colombia, otherwise known by their Spanish initials, FARC. The guerilla group funded their operation through kidnapping ransom and extortion payments, as well as the sale of illegal drugs. Although not directly cultivating illegal drugs, such as cocaine, the FARC raised $60-100 million annually through the taxation of drugs and extortion of the drug growers and landowners. Over the past 30 years, they had conducted approximately 25,000 kidnappings. Our SOUTHCOM general visited Colombia monthly to coordinate U.S. military assistance to their government.

Our CT-43, piloted by Captain Joe Brewster and Major Dave Knight, landed in Bogota and taxied to the corporate jet parking ramp. Upon arrival, Natalie warned us of recent intelligence -- the FARC would charge a $1,000,000 ransom for any American crewmember caught in a flightsuit. So now we had a million-dollar bounty on our heads. Great.

The U.S. embassy provided a van with bulletproof windows, as their driver transported us to a hotel on the outskirts of the city. As my pilot friend, Lieutenant Colonel Kevin Oatley, later informed me, our van wasn't a nice, sleek black Suburban like those in Tom Clancy's movie *Clear and Present Danger*. Ours was an old Chevy beater, with three-quarter-inch bulletproof glass bolted on as an afterthought. Homemade brackets on the inside of each window held the additional glass, individually screwed over each window. It wasn't very reassuring.

The flight crews were very familiar with Bogota and had usually enjoyed the overnight stay, with the ability to walk down the sidewalk and have dinner in the city. With the new threat of kidnappings and a ransom, this was no longer possible. We were cautioned to stay in the hotel and only dine inside.

At first, I thought I'd miss one of the prime benefits of visiting Colombia: their beautiful selection of green emeralds. Fortunately, one of our two flight attendants, Crystal, contacted a jeweler, Ligia. Arriving with a small briefcase of sparkling green and gold jewelry, Ligia showed me her beautiful selection. I picked out a gold ring, a set of earrings, and a heart-shaped pendant, each adorned with small, bright green stones. I planned to hold on to them until Karin's October birthday.

Natalie's news of the ransom threat and the morning's car-bombing certainly alerted me to the security situation our Gulfstream crews faced. As a result of the ongoing security threats we faced, 310 AS flight crews never again overnighted in Bogota. They dropped the SOUTHCOM commander off and either waited on the ramp inside the aircraft, or flew to a different location, returning the next day to pick up the general. Bogota became a monthly high-threat mission faced by our aircrews.

CHAPTER 51

9/11

A t 9:42 a.m. Eastern Time on September 11 the emergency broadcast came over our aircraft radio.

"Attention all aircraft. Due to security reasons, the United States is implementing the National Airspace Closure program. By order of the Federal Aviation Command Center, all air traffic are directed to land immediately."

That Tuesday morning, I took off at 8:00 a.m. for a planned two-hour flight with Major Barry Beavers in the left seat, receiving his initial checkride in our gleaming, blue and white C-37, complete with its "new-car-smell". Onboard were flight engineer Master Sergeant Ken Griffith, and a third pilot, Major "Ice" Icenhour. The four of us departed on a routine training flight so I could give Barry his qualification flight. Ice, an evaluator pilot like myself, came along to watch me conduct the checkride so that he could take over our evaluation division in the squadron as we certified more new pilots.

We set out first for Fort Myers airport about a 30-minute flight south of MacDill AFB. I sat in the right seat as Barry flew a series of approaches that either ended with a touch and go landing or a go around, and went back into the pattern for more approaches with simulated emergencies.

At around 9:00 a.m., as we flew a practice approach to the Fort Myers runway, the tower controller asked if we had heard about a plane hitting some buildings in New York City (which happened at 8:46 a.m.). Not wanting to be distracted, I quickly replied that we had not heard about it and I resumed giving the checkride. My first inclination was that perhaps two airliners had collided over the city and one of them fell into downtown.

We finished our approach work at Fort Myers and headed north toward Lakeland airport, about 30 miles east of MacDill. Barry continued flying his required instrument approaches while Ice went back to the passenger cabin and tuned in a local radio station. As we were completing the checkride, Ice came running up into the cockpit, leaned over Ken's shoulder, and exclaimed, "The radio just announced there's a terrorist attack underway on the United States!"

I thought Ice was purposely trying to be a distraction to see how Barry could operate under pressure and I replied, "That's not funny, Ice."

Ice said, "No, Dave. I'm serious!"

Barry was one of our strongest pilots in the squadron and had flown very well that morning. I looked over at him and said, "You passed. Qual 1 (the highest grade). Now take us to a holding pattern."

While Barry set up a holding pattern over Lakeland airport, I contacted the MacDill Command Post on a second radio. MacDill had already broadcast over the military UHF radio that the base was now closed. I didn't want to land this military airplane at a civilian airport, especially since we could see MacDill from our holding pattern at 4,000 feet. The command post relayed our request for permission to land to the wing commander, Brigadier General Wayne Hodges. Within minutes, he granted our request to land.

Our cockpit was very silent as Barry exited the holding pattern over Lakeland and we returned to MacDill, landing at just past 10:00 a.m. As we taxied toward our parking spot, we could see the President's back-up aircraft, the blue and white C-32 on our ramp. At that same moment, President George W. Bush was just down the road from us in Sarasota. In a now-famous video clip, he was reading a book to young school children when the message was passed to him that America was under attack. We watched as the Andrews' aircrew quickly headed out to their plane.

Barry parked near Hangar 3 and shut down the engines. Normally, a checkride ended with smiles and handshakes as the tension of a stressful flight subsided. That didn't happen on September 11. We quietly packed up our flight gear and began walking across the tarmac toward our squadron.

One of our Gulfstream contract crew chiefs had previously been a C-37 flight engineer while on active duty at Andrews AFB with Tony, Bob, and me. His last name was Bacca, so naturally, we called him Chewy (as in *Star Wars* Chewbacca). Chewy had grown out his hair and now had a thick, bushy mop of wavy gray hair. With America under attack and knowing that we would pick up our second aircraft in just two more days, Chewy looked stunned and asked, "What do I need to do?"

"Get a haircut. We might need you soon," I said as I headed back into the squadron. (In actuality, he remained a Gulfstream contract employee until I retired.)

Once inside our second-floor squadron operation center, the large flat-screen TV hanging in the corner broadcasted images of the smoking towers of the World Trade Center. At 10:28 a.m., everyone stood stunned, watching as the North tower crumbled to the ground. There were about thirty of us packed in the room that day, all staring in disbelief. We knew our lives had changed forever, and we were about to become very busy.

The squadron's manpower divided into small groups that very day as we transitioned to an around-the-clock duty schedule. One of my assistants, Lieutenant Colonel Keith Kreeger, along with a handful of others, volunteered to take the first night shift. This began week-long 24-hour operations throughout all military bases. Our military, like everyone else in America, was still trying to understand if future attacks would occur.

Like many Americans, I got home late in the evening on 9/11 and relived the horrible news with my family. We found out much later through friends at Daniel's junior high that when our 12-year-old son heard of the terrorist attacks he started sobbing. He told his teacher, "Now my dad will be leaving." I'm certain many young military dependents had the same realization. It's not only the active-duty members that serve our nation, but our spouses and children serve as well.

I will never forget my drive to work on September 12. I listened to my usual classic rock station as the DJs tried to comprehend what happened the day before. They announced a blood-drive taking place at the Tampa Bay Buccaneers' Raymond James Stadium. When I got off the freeway and onto south Tampa's MacDill Avenue leading into the back gate of the base, traffic came to a stand-still. All U.S. military bases had implemented 100% vehicle searches, and MacDill was a base with 5,000 employees.

I inched along for more than 2 hours through a tree-lined neighborhood. In a heartwarming patriotic gesture, the people living along that avenue opened their houses for emergency bathroom breaks. They also graciously offered drinks, pastries, and cookies to the standstill line of military commuters. I witnessed kind-hearted Americans coming together during this catastrophic event. Due to the horrendous driving conditions leading to the base, I decided that day to stay on MacDill AFB for the next few nights.

As if the terrorist attacks were not enough, Mother Nature decided to join the events of that week. Tropical Storm Gabrielle was churning in the Gulf of Mexico and made its way up the west coast of Florida, presumably heading for the Florida panhandle. On Thursday afternoon, September 13, I was still in the squadron with Lt Col Eden Murrie. She had returned with General Tommy Franks on the EC-135 from Greece, flying across the eerily quiet Atlantic Ocean on September 12.

Karin called me and asked, "Are going to evacuate your planes for the hurricane?"

I replied, "No, it's heading for Pensacola."

She informed me, "No, the news just came on with an update. Gabrielle is now a Category 1 hurricane and made a right turn. It's coming right towards Tampa Bay."

That was certainly timely information to get from my wife!

Eden and I immediately went down the stairs from our squadron, crossed the large, cement hangar floor and entered the weather shop nearby. A technical sergeant was looking down at his weather charts as we approached his desk. I asked, "Do we need to start thinking about evacuating our aircraft?"

He looked up and stuttered, "Y-, y-, yes."

Eden chimed in, "And when do we need to do that?'

He replied, "Now would be good!"

"When were you going to tell us?!" I asked, amazed.

"I was just about to pick up the phone to call you," he stammered.

So, thanks to Karin's warning, we quickly assembled our crews to evacuate the EC-135, the CT-43, and our one Gulfstream C-37 before gale force winds exceeded their takeoff limits. Our commander, Lt Col Murrie, flew out on the EC-135 and I remained behind to watch over the squadron.

A light-hearted moment during these stressful days was provided by a British tanker crew. They had landed their Royal Air Force VC-10 refueling tanker at MacDill on September 10. The call went out September 13, directing that the Brits fly their tanker to a safer location. The VC-10 aircraft commander, in his distinct British accent and a bit of a slur, replied, "Right, Mate. That's goin' ta be a bit o' a problem. Me and me mates have been drinking quite a bit. Do you have a hangar you can put our airplane in?"

This was passed along to Brigadier General Hodges, and he directed that their tanker be placed inside one of our American hangars to ride out the storm. It was a bit of levity during those heavy days.

Our squadron was on the second floor and the forecast called for major flooding of our low-lying airbase, just 13 feet above sea level. I remained in the squadron for three nights, sleeping on a blue cloth sofa I pulled into the squadron operations center. From my second-floor perch, I'd stay well above any potential flooding as the parking lots below took on water.

On Friday evening, September 14, I sat alone watching a rebroadcast of our nation's memorial service led by President Bush and Reverend Billy Graham from the National Cathedral in Washington D.C. That was a very somber but meaningful ceremony. Sitting alone in the silent, dark squadron, I soaked it all in quietly.

That evening, Karin finally broke down in tears, telling me over the phone, "I can handle a terrorist attack and a hurricane, but not both in the same week!"

Sympathizing with her, I said, "Go into our bedroom and look under my nightstand."

As I waited on the line, Karin retrieved the box of jewelry from Bogota. As she opened it, I told her, "I was saving those for your birthday, but I think you need them right now."

She opened the box to find the gold ring with four green emeralds, matching earrings, and a heart-shaped pendant of sparkling green emeralds. My gift was much appreciated and provided a loving moment between us, which was just what she needed at that moment.

CHAPTER 52

COIN TOSS

On Sunday morning, September 30, I flew General Tommy Franks to Jacksonville, Florida, where he would perform the coin toss at a Jacksonville *Jaguar's* football game against the Cleveland *Browns*. After the coin toss, we were scheduled to fly him up to Washington D.C., where he routinely met with Secretary of Defense Donald Rumsfeld and President Bush.

After I parked the aircraft at Jacksonville Airport, the general's aide, a major, came up and asked, "Will you be staying here with the aircraft?"

I answered, "Yes. We'll always have someone onboard."

The twelve members of the general's party deplaned and headed for the waiting black Suburbans. The major returned before leaving and asked once again if I was certain the plane would always be occupied or locked up while they were away. I told him, "We keep power on in the aircraft and will stay inside the plane while y'all are gone." His questioning was curious, but I didn't think anything more of it.

Within a couple of hours, General Franks returned from his coin-toss duties, and everyone boarded the plane. We closed the door, taxied away, and took off for the two-hour flight up to Andrews AFB. Our crew stayed in Maryland for the night and the next afternoon we brought General Franks back home to MacDill AFB.

Tuesday evening, the national news reported that General Franks briefed our President on the options he could take against the Taliban. I now understood why the major wanted to know if our C-37 would always be occupied. Unknown to us at the time, our plane might have been carrying the war plan for our future attack on Afghanistan.

CHAPTER 53
BISHKEK, KYRGYZSTAN

By October 2001 we had our full fleet of three C-37s and the majority of our crew force was qualified and ready for missions. The first international mission was flown by Major Barry Beavers and me. We flew the Transportation Command (TRANSCOM) commander, General John Handy, to the Middle East to begin setting up military basing agreements with Qatar and Kyrgyzstan.

Our first stop was an overnight stay in Incirlik, Turkey before proceeding to Doha, Qatar. After staying at the Intercontinental Hotel in Doha our crew departed for a relatively new air base out in the desert named Al Udeid. We had a bit of an embarrassing security issue on that flight.

The morning of departure a sergeant working for General Handy rolled a baggage trolley down the hotel hallway, collecting the luggage of the military party to be transported on our Gulfstream. With our passengers and their baggage on board, we departed for the austere desert location. The brown, drab air base was so hard to spot in the dull, flat desert that Barry and I built our own approach using GPS coordinates to guide us to the runway.

After landing at Al Udeid Air Base, we proceeded to download our party's luggage from the cramped baggage compartment in the back of our jet. Everyone had nearly identical black suitcases and they were all piled in a circle. Among the luggage sat two large, blue suitcases. The general departed for his meeting with the base leadership and everyone else reached into the circle of luggage to claim their bags. After all of the black bags were claimed the two powder blue suitcases still remained in the center untouched. We looked around and asked if anybody knew whose luggage this was? Nobody stepped forward to claim them.

A sergeant on the general's staff took the luggage aside and checked the luggage tags. He discovered that they actually belonged to two Brits from the Intercontinental Hotel. We later determined that when the vacationing couple opened their hotel door that morning, they saw the baggage trolley and thought that a nice doorman was providing excellent service. They happily placed their two blue suitcases on the trolley of military luggage when the sergeant wasn't looking. While this would have been funny under other circumstances, this certainly violated our strict security protocol. Happening only one month after 9/11, we were lucky there was nothing sinister inside their luggage. After the couple was contacted, their luggage was placed on the next transport flight returning to Doha.

After departing Al Udeid, we flew General Handy further east to Bishkek, Kyrgyzstan. We landed in this Central Asian former Soviet republic using a challenging approach flown at night, surrounded by mountains. Kyrgyzstan flew by Russian aviation rules, using meters instead of feet on their altimeters. Fortunately, our advanced aircraft could switch the altimeter from feet to meters with the push of a button. We also had to be on our guard as we flew an unfamiliar nighttime approach over the mountains, using procedures we rarely saw other than during our simulator training.

The language barrier made it very difficult to understand the air traffic controllers in their broken English, as they also used non-standard terminology. Deciphering the controller's instructions took intense concentration from Barry, me, and our flight engineer, Technical Sergeant Jake Piascik. Barry completed a safe nighttime landing and taxied our business jet to the enormous ramp, dimly lit by sparsely spaced light poles.

What I remember most about Bishkek was how dry, gray, and dusty the area was. We stayed at a nice international hotel, but as we drove through the city everything looked colorless and drab. When we checked into the hotel, the clerk requested to see our passports and then left the room, carrying a stack of them. I'm certain that they were being copied in their back office and we now had the beginnings of our very own Russian dossier.

We stayed in this location for two nights while General Handy completed the coalition basing agreements, giving the U.S. the rights to use this airfield in any upcoming conflict. Air operations supporting Operation Enduring Freedom would begin a few months later in December 2001.

The night before our departure I was sound asleep when I heard a rustling at my door. I got out of bed and walked in the dark toward my hotel door when I saw a large manila envelope being pushed underneath. Nobody ever knocked on the door and no words were exchanged. I turned on the lamp in my room and saw a thick manila envelope, completely taped around the entire package. On a sticky note, attached to the package was scrawled, "Lt Col Dale, Please deliver this package to Andrews AFB Intel."

I thought I had been dropped into a scene from *Mission Impossible*. One of my main concerns about this envelope was it arrived during the same few weeks that America was being terrorized by anthrax-laced envelopes circulating around Washington D.C. In my movie-fed imagination, I wondered if I was about to deliver an anthrax-laden package to the intelligence office at Andrews AFB. The Happy Pessimist now had a supporting role in his own spy movie.

Our flight departed Kyrgyzstan and headed west, stopping briefly in Incirlik, Turkey for a refueling stop and then proceeded to Ramstein Air Base, Germany for a rainy, overnight stay. The next morning, we flew across the Atlantic to Andrews AFB, where I left the airplane to deliver the thick, sealed package to the intelligence office. I explained my midnight courier assignment to the captain accepting the package. I have no idea what the envelope contained, but I imagine it was an intelligence assessment of the air base and its surrounding area. Our coalition's large air operation soon began. Eventually, the air campaign included tankers, cargo aircraft, and B-1 bombers flying from Kyrgyzstan's Manas Air Base. All of this was in support of Operation Enduring Freedom, the war in Afghanistan against the Taliban and Al-Qaeda.

CHAPTER 54

PROVIDING FIVE-STAR SERVICE
TO THE FOUR-STARS

T he ceremony narrator read the order relinquishing Lt Col
Eden Murrie of her command and passing that command to
me. The sergeant handed the guidon to Lt Col Murrie, who
passed it forward to Colonel Rob Kane, stating, "Sir, I relinquish
command." She then stepped to her right and two steps backwards as
I stepped forward. Colonel Kane passed the guidon to me, holding it
out for me to take. After I accepted this symbol of taking command, I
then passed it back to the sergeant on my right. I turned and saluted
Colonel Kane sharply, stating, "Sir, I assume command."

At 3:00 p.m. on July 22, 2002, Lt Col Eden Murrie passed the
command of our 310th Airlift Squadron to me in a ceremony based
on an age-old military tradition, dating back to Frederick the Great
of Prussia in the 18th Century. At that time, organizational flags
were developed with color arrangements and symbols unique to
each unit. The soldiers of the unit would proclaim their loyalty and
trust to the commander and the unit, as represented by this flag.
When a change of command took place, the flag was passed from
the outgoing commander to the individual assuming command. This
ceremony took place in front of the unit so that each soldier could
witness their new leader assuming command.

Colonel Kane, the commander of our 6th Operation Group
presided over the event and thanked Eden for her excellent work
over the previous one and half years -- she built a cohesive team and
molded the 310 AS into the Air Force's newest squadron. From what
had once been a two-airplane flight of the 91 ARS, Eden established

a 65-member DV Airlift squadron on par with any flying squadron at Andrews AFB.

Eden gave her parting remarks, thanking the squadron members she led and the chain of command above her. She wished us all the best of luck as she departed to attend Senior Service School (the "Colonel's Course"). Lt Col Murrie eventually rose beyond colonel to one-star brigadier general and commanded the 100th Air Refueling Wing in Mildenhall, England.

Following Eden's remarks, the two of us stood at the front of the stage, with Colonel Kane standing to her left and me to her right, as viewed from the audience. When Colonel Kane gave the order, Eden and I made a right-face 90-degree turn to face our commander. The squadron guidon was brought forward by our ranking enlisted member, Senior Master Sergeant Ray Ikone. The guidon was a small dark blue flag on a wooden pole, with bright yellow letters depicting "310 AS" above a yellow eagle with outstretched wings.

After assuming command, I thanked the base leadership for placing their faith in me. I assured the 310 AS members in attendance that we would continue to excel at our DV airlift mission. Knowing that we were continuing a high-visibility, no-fail mission, I challenged the squadron to "earn their PhD in Air Mobility."

Our squadron endured some growing pains throughout the previous year as we merged the established crews dedicated to serving just the CENTCOM and SOUTHCOM commanders crews with the large number of inbound personnel. All of our crews were highly capable, but not all stayed at MacDill to transition to the C-37s. For some, it was the right time in their career development to move to another assignment for advancement.

One major stressor for our squadron was that General Franks, the CENTCOM commander, did not want to lose his large EC-135. Thanks to its inflight refueling capability, the EC-135 could transport 34 people (16 aircrew members and 18 passengers) non-stop to Doha, Qatar, or Bishkek, Kyrgyzstan. As the commanding wartime general in the Middle East region, he was in no mood to fly in a 12-passenger executive jet that required a refueling stop in Germany or Italy before proceeding to the desert. The CT-43 retired as scheduled to the Arizona desert on September 30, 2001, but the EC-135 was extended after General Franks appealed directly to Secretary of Defense Rumsfeld. The EC-135 crews needed to stay with us for the time being.

Every three months for the next year, the Air Force extended the operation of the EC-135 for another quarter. These quarterly extensions cancelled assignments for outbound EC-135 crew members who thought they had another Air Force job lined up. It threw into turmoil families trying to make decisions to sell a current home, buy another, and decide what school their children would attend the next year. My heart went out to these families but it was our mission to continue supporting the CENTCOM commander in his EC-135.

Six months before the change of command, I wanted to ensure everyone focused on our squadron's mission. As the 310 AS/DO, I wrote and then read a memo to the available aircrews at a gathering in our squadron. I distributed a copy (found in Appendix 3) to those who were out flying missions.

The portion below reflects the message I repeated at my assumption of command on July 22, 2002:

What does it mean to be a part of the 310th Airlift Squadron? To me, it means being a part of THE BEST C-37/CT-43/EC-135 Combatant Commander Support unit in the Air Force. It means working with people that want to study every bit of useful information about the aircraft, want to showcase their talents in every meal served, and want to provide the commanders with the finest communications platform this Air Force has to offer. In short, we will provide Five-Star Service to the Four-Stars.

We can also have fun performing our mission. For me, the Harlem Globetrotters have always been an inspiration. They master their talent first, and then go out and have great fun doing their job. That's how I approach my job in the Air Force and that's how I hope you approach your job in the 310th as well.

Being a lieutenant colonel is as far as I want to go in the Air Force. Building the 310th is the pinnacle of my career. We are going to be the premier C-37 flying unit in the Air Force.

The 310th Airlift Squadron: Providing Five-Star Service to the Four-Stars.

That motto remained the squadron's motto until it closed September 30, 2019.

Once the 310 AS was deactivated, the three MacDill C-37s were dispersed to Hawaii, Belgium, and Andrews AFB to continue supporting warfighting commanders from those bases.

310 AS C-37A, "Wine & Cheese" scarf, both sides of the squadron coin, and the seven coins from our Combatant Commander customers.

CHAPTER 55
"THANKS FOR KEEPING ME SAFE."

On a snowy December morning our C-37, callsign SPAR 29, was more than 30 minutes late as I began the approach to Runway 19L, the left of two parallel southbound runways at Andrews AFB. In the cabin not far from our cockpit sat CENTCOM's commander, General Tommy Franks, and a Marine Corps major, an F-18 fighter pilot, who served as the general's aide. The right-side runway at Andrews was closed, perhaps for snow removal, so we could not fly a Category II Instrument Landing System precision approach down to 100 feet above the ground. Because of the less precise instrumentation on the left-side runway, we were instead restricted to using the approach to Runway 19L, which could only be flown to 200 feet above the ground. That 100-foot difference was important on this white winter morning.

According to our C-37 policies, I flew the approach using the Heads-Up Display (HUD) while my copilot peered through the clouds, hoping to spot the runway lights by the time we reached the 200-foot Decision Altitude. My copilot, Don Axlund, an excellent officer and pilot, had just completed his check out in the C-37 the day before. This was his first operational VIP mission, which he got to fly with me, his squadron commander. No pressure, Don.

I briefed the ILS approach and lined up for the approach. I emphasized to Don, "If you don't see the runway, it's okay. Just call the 'Go Around' and we'll try it again."

As we approached 300 feet AGL, Don announced, "Approaching Minimums." At 200 feet, with nothing but white in front of us, Don commanded, "Go Around." I applied full power and our C-37 rose quickly through the dense white clouds.

Two hours earlier, Captain Don Axlund and I had departed Tampa International Airport with General Tommy Franks onboard, bound for Andrews AFB. It was time for him to present another Operation Enduring Freedom update to the President and the Secretary of Defense.

During this timeframe, our MacDill AFB runway had been closed for repair. We were forced to operate out of Tampa International Airport, which was a 30-minute drive north of our air base. This mission got off to a poor start with a delayed takeoff after the general and his party arrived at our C-37 well past the planned takeoff time. The flight north to Washington, D.C. took two hours but we knew we were flying into a major snowstorm. There is a tendency in Distinguished Visitor Airlift to do anything to please the customer. This led to some crews pressing the corners of the safety envelope to accomplish their mission on-time.

On April 3, 1996, US Secretary of Commerce Ron Brown, and 34 other passengers had died in an Air Force CT-43 crash into a mountainside near Dubrovnik, Croatia. The crew had departed five minutes early but due to the wartime routing into Croatia, they were assigned a route that took fifteen minutes longer than planned. In their attempt to provide an on-time arrival, the crew flew faster than normal on their approach to the airfield. Additionally, they were flying a primitive Non-Directional Beacon instrument approach into a cloud deck that was only 400 feet above the ground. The combination of a non-precision approach flown in bad weather while trying to make up time resulted in a tragic accident. The crew strayed off course in low visibility and impacted the side of a hill, killing all onboard.

At the time of the accident, I was flying NATO troops into Split, Croatia in the Netherlands Air Force KDC-10. Now, as a commander of a DV Airlift squadron, I was constantly aware of the pressures our crews faced to press the limits of safety in an effort to please our customers. As I had learned during my two years at Andrews AFB, it's okay to say no.

Two important safety lessons I brought with me to this new Florida squadron were 1) If the VIP gets mad because you didn't think it was safe to land, just let it flow like water off a duck's back. They'll get over it, but you will all still be alive. 2) Don't bend over backwards to set a precedent that your fellow squadron pilots can't meet. In other words, don't be the reason that the general or his staff could say, "Well, the last guy did it."

Unable to see the Andrews runway, I applied Go-Around thrust and the powerful C-37 pitched up and climbed quickly to 2,000 feet. Just seconds before the go around, we could see snow covered trees directly below us, so the vertical visibility was almost 200 feet, but the forward visibility in front of us was still low. That restricted forward visibility kept us from seeing the runway or even the bright white approach lights once we reached the Decision Altitude.

Knowing we were so close to breaking out, Don requested vectors for a second approach attempt. Ten minutes later, we were on final approach and descending again into the blowing snow. Nothing improved on this second attempt, so rather than "ducking under" the clouds in the hope of seeing the runway, Don again correctly called for the go around, which I performed.

Part of the thrill of instrument flying is intense concentration while flying an approach. Pilots are not concerned with the people riding along in back. We are focused solely on our instruments, the runway, and Mother Nature. Whenever I jockey the throttles to remain airspeed during gusty winds, I am constantly reminded of my teenage days with Mr. Lovell barking, "Stay on speed!" Or during buffeting crosswinds, he commanded "Fight for centerline!" then commented if I was one or two feet off centerline after I touched down.

Pilots take on Mother Nature's challenges but strive to keep everything within safe limits. If it's not safe to land, we can always go into a holding pattern and wait, or divert to a better location. Safety, then Comfort, then Reliability. Keeping those priorities in that order is a life-saver.

The winds were very light that particular day, only blowing five miles per hour out of the south. Most airplanes can handle landing with a 10-knot tailwind, so I asked Don to request an opposite direction approach from the south to the north. There were no other planes in the area to create a conflict, so permission was granted, and we lined up for the northbound right-side runway. Fortunately, the weather south of Andrews was clearing. As I approached 300 feet, the bright white approach lights and the runway came into view through the low clouds. At 200 feet, Don announced, "Runway in sight." Staring through the HUD, I transitioned my focus from the green instruments on the glass to a visual aimpoint 1,000 feet down the runway.

On this gloomy winter day, Don and I safely delivered General Franks to Washington D.C. … but 45 minutes behind schedule. President Bush and Secretary of Defense Rumsfeld were kept waiting for their warfighting general.

How would General Franks react? Some uppity VIPs are known to not give a hoot about excuses and only want to remain on schedule at all costs. Several of those ranting celebrities or businessmen have paid for that attitude with their lives.

We parked the jet on the red-painted cement "carpet" near Base Operations and our flight engineer opened the door, allowing the brisk winter breeze to blow through the cabin. General Franks and his aide, the Marine F-18 pilot, prepared to exit. Having a fellow aviator onboard turned out to be a Godsend. Although he and his fellow passengers could see the white snow-covered pine trees directly below us on approach, the Marine pilot explained to the other passengers that forward "slant-range" vision is often restricted and considerably less than looking straight down.

People that knew I flew General Tommy Franks often asked me, "What is he like?"

My reply: "Loud! He can be really happy or really pissed off, but he's always loud!"

As General Franks departed our Gulfstream on that white winter day in Washington D.C., he stepped into our cockpit, popped me on my right shoulder with his large fist and in his deep baritone Texan voice boomed, "Thanks for keeping me safe!"

I could not have asked for a better aviation lesson than that for my new copilot.

Chapter 56

Highs and Lows

My Last Overseas Mission

On April 14, 2004, I set out for my final overseas trip in the C-37 and of my Air Force career. I had interviewed with Southwest Airlines one month earlier and was hoping to hear some results any day. Our eight-day trip retraced a lot of the same cities and bases I had flown to in October of 2001, two and a half years earlier. This time our customer was the new Special Operations (SOCOM) commander, Army General Doug Brown.

We made stops in Doha, Qatar, and Bishkek, Kyrgyzstan, before flying over the mountain range into Bagram Air Base, 45 miles north of Kabul, Afghanistan. Employing a combat arrival technique, we overflew the air base at 20,000 feet, then spiraled down, staying within the confines of the airfield in order to limit our potential exposure to shoulder-fired missiles or anti-aircraft gunfire. The base was a major installation for our Air Force and numerous coalition forces, with American F-16s and A-10s flying daily combat missions. After spending the night at Bagram Air Base, we departed the next day heading south towards Pakistan, before turning west towards Muscat, Oman, where I had flown KC-10 missions during Operation Desert Storm in 1991.

As we flew over Pakistan, a datalink message arrived from our squadron telling me that someone from Southwest Airlines had called looking for me. I knew that had to be a good sign! With our satellite air phone on the aircraft, I called the squadron and spoke with Lt

Col Steve Kowalski, who was manning our Squadron Operations Center that day.

"Hey Dave. I thought you'd like to know that a lady named Mary called for you and asked you to call her back," he said, passing along her Dallas office phone number. I thanked Kowalski for the message and told him that I'd return the call as soon as possible.

After hanging up, I told my copilot, Lt Col Steve McAllister, the news. Steve grinned and goaded me, "You should call her back right now."

"You really think so?" I asked.

"Sure!" he replied.

I picked up the satellite-phone and dialed the 214-area code number. A lady from the Southwest People Department answered the phone and I told her who I was. She said it was time for me to schedule a drug test. She couldn't commit to the fact that I was hired, but this was the next step and meant that I had passed the interview process. Southwest was now wrapping up the final details before they could offer me a job.

I told her, "I'm currently out of the country, but I'll take care of that as soon as I get back home."

She asked, "Where are you right now?"

"Well, I'm currently flying over Pakistan," I told her. Yes, I was showing off.

"Oh, that's so cool!" she replied.

That was the end of a very happy but short conversation.

I hung up and Steve grinned at me, chuckling, "Congratulations!"

This was fulfilling the second part of my teenage dream. I told myself as a high school senior that I wanted to serve 20 years as an Air Force pilot and then fly for Southwest, my home-state airline. This was the same airline that launched when I was in junior high, famous for its flight attendants in hot pants and go-go boots.

An hour later, we landed at Seeb Airport, Muscat, Oman, for a night's stay. The base had come a long way since the tent city of 1990 to 1991. The desert military installation now had hard-sided buildings, a vast collection of tan, rectangular single-story portable shelters, each with window air conditioners and generators humming away.

Our communications system operator for this mission was a young, 23-year-old enlisted crewmember named Abbey. The next day, as we strolled around the crunchy gray gravel paths of the small base, I told her that when she was 11 I lived for three months in one of fifty canvas tents alongside the runway. We made our way over to the new chow hall where we saw General Brown's aide, an Army major.

We joined him at a table and he exclaimed, "This has been the greatest trip ever!"

"Oh, yeah? Why's that?" I asked.

He told us he now was able to see the camps that had come into existence after his clandestine efforts back in the fall of 2001. This major had a very mild-mannered appearance, looking like any big-city accountant walking down a sidewalk. In actuality, he had been a Special Operations captain after the 9/11 attacks and had parachuted into the mountainous regions of Afghanistan with CIA agents carrying suitcases full of hundreds of thousands of dollars. Their mission, detailed in a lengthy *New York Times* article, was to buy the allegiance of the warlords within the area so we could have safe passage in our upcoming fight with Al Qaeda and the Taliban in Afghanistan. The groundwork of Army outposts that he helped create back in 2001, riding horseback and carrying suitcases of money through the mountains, had now come to fruition.

That afternoon, on April 22, we departed for the westbound trip back to Florida. A few hours into the trip, in the dark skies over the Atlantic the Army major came back up into the cockpit, yelling, "Son of a bitch!"

I turned around, asking, "What's wrong?"

"Pat Tillman has just been killed." he answered.

This was the night a firefight took the life of Pat Tillman, the Arizona *Cardinal's* National Football League player who walked away from millions of dollars to become an Army Ranger immediately after the 9/11 attack. The unfortunate deadly shooting later turned out to be from our own troops, but on this still night over the ocean nobody knew the details of his death. Everyone thought it was an enemy ambush on our forces.

This was a somber, low point of a roller-coaster two-day period. What had started with the excitement of my potential hiring with Southwest Airlines now concluded with the death of a true American hero. Our cockpit was very quiet as we flew westward over the dark ocean.

Chapter 57

COMING FULL CIRCLE

"Would you like to see our jet?" I asked.

"I suppose so," Mr. Lovell answered quietly with a smile, and we walked slowly out to the beautiful blue and white C-37 with *United States of America* painted above the line of six oval windows. We climbed the short fold-out staircase and turned left so he could see the modern glass cockpit of six screens in front of the pilot seats and the panels overhead consisting of only black push-button squares. It was a very smooth, clean cockpit.

I then guided Mr. and Mrs. Lovell down the blue carpeted, cramped hallway and into the VIP cabin adorned with mahogany wood and 12 blue leather First Class-sized chairs, each with its own spacious window. The Lovells each took a seat and looked around the cabin.

"What do you think?" I asked my old mentor.

Mr. Lovell sat with his cane between his legs and replied, "Well, they all fly the same. Keep the shiny side up and wheels on the bottom." He was trying not to sound impressed.

One of the final trips of my 20-year career was to take Air Force General Ed Eberhart, commander of Northern Command (NORTHCOM) on visits to the Air National Guard and Air Force Reserve bases in the southeast and south-central United States. Our first stop was Homestead AFB, near Miami to see the Jacksonville Air National Guard F-15s, maintaining their alert rotation. We then headed north to Jacksonville Airport, where the former F-15 fighter pilot took a flight in one of the National Guard F-15s.

The next morning, we set off for New Orleans, visiting yet another F-15 fighter unit. Our planned final stop would be Ellington Field, just south of my hometown of Houston, Texas. As we flew toward New Orleans, I told the other pilot, my good friend Major "Ice" Icenhour, that I learned to fly at LaPorte Municipal Airport, not far from Ellington. He said, "That's cool! You should call up your old flight instructor!"

I told him my instructor, Richard Lovell, was a Korean War Navy veteran, and I wasn't sure if he was even still alive. I had last seen Richard and Sylvia in 1990, when we took our baby boy, Daniel, to visit them in Pasadena, Texas. Ice told me I had to call him and tell him we'd be at Ellington tomorrow. I really dreaded making that phone call, fearing Sylvia might answer and sadly tell me that Mr. Lovell had passed away. With Ice's continued prompting, I got up my courage and dialed his number. On the second ring Mr. Lovell answered the phone. What a relief!

I told Mr. Lovell we would be flying a new Gulfstream V into Ellington the next day with a four-star general onboard. Without me prompting, Mr. Lovell asked, "Can we get together for dinner?"

I smiled and told him, "That would be great! And I'd like to show you the aircraft after we land."

Ellington Field is a joint civilian and military air base open to the public, allowing visitors to park near Base Operations. We taxied our C-37 up to the painted cement "red carpet", where an entourage of colonels waited to greet their visiting four-star general. The group whisked General Eberhart away to visit the F-16 squadron that had escorted President Bush's Air Force One 747 on 9/11.

Once the passengers left, I walked along the red carpet to find Mr. and Mrs. Lovell sitting on an outdoor wooden bench, looking like Ma and Pa Kettle. Mr. Lovell's once curly hair was now thin and he leaned forward on the bench, supported by his wooden cane.

I owe my flying career to Mr. Lovell. I never called him or knew him as Richard, only Mr. Lovell. It had been 26 years since he took over as the leader of our Aviation Explorer Post in south Houston. Twenty-four years had passed since I last flew with the 5' 6" former

Navy boxing champion with a permanently crooked nose. The tough old cuss no longer dipped and swallowed Copenhagen chewing tobacco, but he sucked on the inside of his lower lip out of habit.

As was the case with a lot of teenagers, my training stagnated in the late '70s. Sometimes it was due to family vacations and other times it was because I had to put my restaurant paycheck into car repairs instead of flying lessons. The result of my poor consistency led to retaking lessons to regain flying proficiency, a common occurrence in private flying.

The FAA requires students to have 20 hours of flight instruction and 20 hours of solo time, including cross-countries, to take their Private License flight evaluation. By the summer of 1980, after my high school graduation, I was approaching 60 hours of flying time and would be leaving for college by mid-August. Mr. Lovell was the one who kicked me in the pants to complete the rating, telling me, "If you don't finish it before starting college then you'll never finish it."

I am a pilot today because of that caring, no-nonsense pilot. In the days leading up to my wedding he sent me a heart-felt congratulatory letter, found in Appendix 5.

After a quick tour of our jet, I changed clothes and the three of us went out for seafood along the Kemah Boardwalk, between Houston and Galveston. We spent the evening catching up over a fish dinner. I told them all about Karin, Daniel, and Shelby, and my international flying since September 11.

I gladly treated the Lovells to dinner that night as a very small repayment for his patience and graciousness during my teenage years. After dinner, Mr. Lovell brought their large four-door Ford sedan up near the restaurant door as I waited with Sylvia. I held the passenger door open for Sylvia and as she started to climb in, she squeezed my elbow, leaned in close to me, and whispered, "You'll never know how much this means to him."

My flying career had come full circle. As I prepared to retire from the Air Force and join the ranks of airline pilots, I happily thanked the gruff old guy who taught me to fly.

Relinquishing command of the 310 AS

On July 27, 2004, I handed over command of the 310 AS to the next squadron commander, Lt Col Monty Perry, and retired from the Air Force on that same day. Five days later, on August 2, I realized my second dream and became a Boeing 737 pilot for Southwest Airlines.

My Shadow Box, expertly crafted by SSgt Keith O'Steen,
310 AS flight engineer.

Awards: Five Meritorious Service medals, Air Medal, Aerial
Achievement, Commendation, Combat Readiness, National Defense
Service, Armed Forces Expeditionary, Southwest Asia Service,
Humanitarian Service, Kuwaiti Liberation medal.
Other awards: Outstanding Unit with Valor, Expert Marksmanship

Now a Southwest Airlines Boeing 737 Captain

APPENDIX 1
THANKS MOM AND DAD

MY 2006 ARTICLE IN THE BRANDON, FLORIDA NEWSPAPER

"I'd like to introduce you to my mom and dad," I said to my Southwest Airlines crew. Mom AND Dad. This may not seem like an unusual thing to say, but if you are a child of divorced parents, it is a statement many long to say and I relished that for three days in November, 2006. Like many marriages in the 1970s, my parent's marriage dissolved when I was in grade school. I am not exactly sure when, since it was a long-drawn-out process, but I believe I was about 10 or 11 years old. I cannot speak for my brother or sisters, but I think we were fortunate in some aspects because I do not remember our parents fighting or squabbling in our presence. Many marriages end with bitter feelings, but from my perspective, theirs fizzled out instead of exploded. Nonetheless, my siblings and I joined the ranks of the many children of divorced parents and moved on with life.

My parents both went through the marriage/divorce cycle one more time before my dad married a great lady willing to put up with him (no offense, Dad) and my mom remains close with life-long friends but single. The best part of their relationship is that they have remained cordial and friendly over the years. Many children may not be able to say this of their married or divorced parents. My mom lived in the Houston house I was raised in until the mid-90s. By that time, my sisters were raising families in the Denver area and my dad, stepmom, and stepsister lived south of Denver. Mom's house was too big for her and was a lonely, empty nest. My dad suggested, "Why don't you move out here to Denver, since this is where most of the grandkids are?" So, Mom sold the house and moved to Denver to prepare for her retirement years.

When some marriages crumble, the couples cannot bear to be in the same room together, and my heart goes out to them and their children. We have been fortunate that when our family gathers for holidays or birthdays, Mom and Dad are both there, usually at one or the other's house. Still, there are struggles for any child of divorce. At a young age it is, do I *want* to go to Dad's house this weekend just because it is "his turn?" Then, in the teenage years it might be, "Which house do I want to live in?" As an adult, young or old, there is always the question of which parent's house do I visit first when I come into town, or where should I stay? Maybe it is a self-imposed guilt-trip, but the thoughts are there, year after year. Although I admire my stepmom and am very grateful to have her and my stepsister in our lives, many kids would wish that their parents were together again. I got to enjoy that feeling this past weekend and am forever thankful.

For the past two years I have thoroughly enjoyed flying as a first officer for Southwest Airlines. I was extremely excited when my November 2006 schedule came out to see a three-day trip with overnights in Denver and Washington D.C. The wheels started spinning. My stepsister and my cousin, Tina, (Mom's niece) both live in the D.C. area. I first ran my proposal by my stepmom, Karen, because Dad refuses to use e-mail. Dad and Karen could fly with me on Day 2 from Denver, through Chicago to D.C. and visit their daughter and son-in-law. Then on Day 3, I would fly them from D.C. to Florida and see my family before the Thanksgiving holidays. Karen had a conflict and couldn't go, but she wanted Dad to go. That presented some challenges. Dad has not traveled much in this post-9/11 world and not at all as a standby passenger on our airline. Mom on the other hand has spread her wings in retirement and cruises through airports like a pro. Well, a slow pro.

I wrote back to Karen to ask if it would be okay if I offered the trip to my mom as well so that she could visit her niece and help Dad through the travel wickets. Karen replied, "Are you asking if it is proper? Hell, I don't care! We're all one big happy family, aren't we?" We have discovered that Karen has mastered the art of yelling through email, but at least I had her blessing.

The weekend adventure got off to a gratifying yet stressful start. The gratifying part was introducing the flight crew (captain and flight attendants) to Mom AND Dad. It has been more than 32 years since I have stood solely with my parents and said, "I'd like you to meet my mom AND dad." It was a pleasure I hoped to repeat over the next three days. First, however, we had to get out of Denver. Let me just say that when trying to get your 70 and 72-year-old parents through Denver International security and terminal, it is anything but The Amazing Race! Mom breezed through security, while Dad struggled to get out his ID, set off the screener with his cell phone and was sent back again to take off his Velcro shoes. Sorry Dad. I could have forewarned you, but like the lessons of my youth, some things you just have to figure out for yourself! Try telling that to the eye-rolling, rat-racing fellow passengers.

We strolled to the gate only to find that 136 of the 137 seats had sold. Hmmm. Dilemma time. Which parent goes, which parent stays behind. That self-imposed guilt trip started to surface again. I was not about to pick, so since they had worked out their divorce amicably, I figured they could work this out, too. They each insisted the other go-- talk about selfless and considerate! In the end, their kindness was rewarded when only 134 passengers checked in. The 'Mom AND Dad Adventure' was underway.

The skies over the Midwest and Appalachian Mountains were clear and the air smooth throughout the whole trip, which added to the sense that all was right. I landed in D.C. and we began the mile-long trek to the curb where my cousin would pick us up. AARP Magazine would not rank Dulles Airport highly as my dad struggled with the long walk, stopping to rest along the way, my mom offering what assistance she could. Cousin Tina had to "go-around" at the curb and went back out to the "holding pattern" in the cell-phone lot until we got closer.

That evening we split up for dinner, Dad dining with his daughter and son-in-law, and Mom and I visiting Tina and her family. I rejoined Dad at the crew hotel later that night and Mom spent the night with her niece.

The next morning, I started my typical airline morning at 5:30 a.m. and flew two legs before returning to Washington for the final trip to Florida. That allowed my parents time to sleep in, and Tina to swing by the hotel with Mom and take Dad back to the airport. Tina had the forethought to arrange two wheelchairs to help them traverse the airport. When I found them at the top of the Jetway, Mom told me about their "wheelchair race" to the gate. I piloted them down the East Coast, making sure to point out the sights via the P.A. system -- Charleston, Savannah, and St. Augustine and Cape Canaveral in Florida. The flight attendants doted over them and told me how nice they were. On final approach for my landing, the captain told me, "Buddy, you can land as long as you want, but it better be smooth. Your parents are onboard." I treated them to a smooth landing.

Once home in Florida my kids enjoyed the rare treat of having my parents visit without other family members present. Large family gatherings can be fun, but this was special, at least for me. Sunday was Thanksgiving and Christmas morning rolled into one, regarding my relationship with my parents. After church the three of us sat on our sunny lanai enjoying ham and cheese sandwiches by the pool. We took advantage of the "Chamber of Commerce" weather and drove over the Sunshine Skyway Bridge to Fort DeSoto Beach. What followed was a memory of a lifetime. Under the blue 70-degree sky we slowly walked along the beach as my mom searched for seashells and they told stories of their lives, together and apart, over the past 50 years.

That evening my wife joined us for a Mostly Pops Pre-Holiday Concert at our Brandon church. It was a perfect way to cap a memorable visit and begin the Thanksgiving and Christmas season. The orchestra played everything from classical Mozart, to Louis Armstrong's perfectly appropriate *What a Wonderful World*, to holiday medleys, and sing-along Christmas hymns. Life does not get any better than to hold your wife's hand, listening to Mom's soprano voice sing *O Come All Ye Faithful* as Dad taps his foot. As we left the performance, I took the opportunity to say to friends, "I'd like you to meet my mom AND dad." Thanks Mom and Dad.

APPENDIX 2
"THE LOSS OF OUR FRIEND, KEN REED"

Lt Col William "Dub" Splawn's Letter Regarding Captain Ken Reed's Death

FROM: 1700 ARW, DET 1/CC   1 9 SEP 1992

SUBJECT: The Loss of Our Friend, Ken Reed

TO: All KC-10 Crew Members deployed

    On the 18th of Sep, Friday afternoon, (Barksdale time) Captain Ken Reed died in a T-37 accident. At times we are brought uncomfortably close to death and I am very much grieved by this tragic loss of a close friend. In truth, each one of us are but one heart beat, one breath away from death ourselves. Life is precious, but very fragile and death is certain. However, there is hope even in the face of death. Please allow me to share some very personal thoughts with you.

    I find comfort in the words of Jesus Christ. He said, "I am the resurrection and the life; he who believes in Me shall live even if he dies, and everyone who lives and believes in Me shall never die." (ref John 11:25-26) Corrie Ten Boom who faced much death in a German concentration camp during World War II told of a story her father told her that goes something like this:

    "A man and his son went over a long narrow bridge. It was over a broad river, and the boy said, 'Daddy, I am afraid. Do you see all that water down there?' 'Give me your hand boy,' The father said. The moment the boy felt his father's hand, he was not afraid. In the evening they had to go back again, and this time it was pitch dark. 'Now I am more afraid than this morning!' The boy cried. The father took the little fellow in his arms. Immediately, the boy fell asleep to wake the next morning in his own bed. This is what death is like for the Christian; he falls asleep and wakes up at home."

    Lieutenant General "Stonewall" Jackson, a devout Christian man, also looked death in the face. He stated in his dying words, "Let us pass over the river, and rest under the shade of the trees."

    It was about 2:00am Saturday (UAE time) when I received the sad news of Ken's death. I grieved but I was also comforted by the following scriptures. I include them for your consideration and trust you will also be benefited.

    "Just as a father has compassion on his children, so the Lord has compassion on those who fear Him. For He Himself knows our frame; He is mindful that we are but dust. As for man, his days are like grass; as a flower of the field, so he flourishes. When the wind has passed over it, it is no more...But the loving kindness of the Lord is from everlasting to everlasting on those who fear Him." (Psalm 103:13-17)

    "Lord, make me to know my end, and what is the extent of my days. Let me know how transient I am." (Psalm 39:4)

    "Precious in the sight of the Lord is the death of His godly ones." (Psalm 116:15)

    "My times are in Thy hand..." (Psalm 31:15)

    Ken, we'll miss you.

William J. Splawn

WILLIAM J. "DUB" SPLAWN, Lt Col, USAF
Commander

APPENDIX 3
310 AS/DO MEMO TO ALL AIRCREW PERSONNEL

MY 2001 MEMO TO ALL 310 AS FLIGHT CREWMEMBERS GIVING MY LEADERSHIP PHILOSOPHY

There has been a lot of discussion lately about the 310th Airlift Squadron. Who are we? How do we do business? What is our unit's style? When I came here, I'm sure many of you thought I would try to create an "Andrews South." I admit that a lot of what I have brought down here, I learned at the 89th Airlift Wing at Andrews AFB. But I did not and do not agree with everything Andrews does. Instead, I also brought down lessons I've learned from standing up a new unit with the Dutch Air Force, and items I've picked up from 18 years and 16 assignments in the Air Force.

So, what does it mean to be a part of the 310th? To me, it means being a part of THE BEST C-37/CT-43/EC-135 Combatant Commander Support unit in the Air Force. It means working with people that want to study every bit of useful information about the aircraft, want to showcase their talents in every meal served, and want to provide the commanders with the finest communications platform this Air Force has to offer. In short, we will provide Five-Star Service to the Four-Stars.

Let me tell you what was good about the 89th Airlift Wing: Positive Peer Pressure! You did not want to be a slug. You studied Gulfstream information as a hobby so you wouldn't be a weak link in the squadron. You anticipated communication needs and proactively coordinated details with the next destination without being asked. You cleaned up the aircraft because you were part of a 5-person team that didn't get to the hotel until everything was done. And you strived to look sharp each and every day.

We can also have fun performing our mission. For me, the Harlem Globetrotters have always been an inspiration. They master their talent first, and then go out and have great fun doing their job. That's how I approach my job in the Air Force and that's how I hope you approach your job in the 310th as well.

Being a lieutenant colonel is as far as I want to go in the Air Force. Building the 310th is the pinnacle of my career. We are going to be the premier C-37 flying unit in the Air Force.

The 310th Airlift Squadron: Providing Five-Star Service to the Four-Stars.

APPENDIX 4
CHANGE OF COMMAND AND RETIREMENT SPEECH

MY SPEECH GIVEN THE DAY I RELINQUISHED
COMMAND OF THE 310TH AIRLIFT
SQUADRON AT MACDILL AFB

JULY 27, 2004

I would like to thank all of you for attending today, especially my family; my sister, Lucy; and my minister, Rebekah Maul, and her husband, Derek Maul. Two years ago tomorrow I took command of the 310th. Many of you in this room were not here that day, so I'm just going to reuse that speech.

I sincerely thank my wife, Karin, and children, Daniel and Shelby, for their patience and understanding as I put in a few long hours – not only at MacDill, but for the past 20 years as well. I think my family has been proud to have been associated with the 310th, especially when the airshow VIP passes and Tampa Bay *Lightning* hockey tickets came out! But I don't think they will miss the cell phone calls and e-mails.

As for those I worked for, I thank the Wing and Operations Group leadership for the opportunity to lead this VIP Airlift squadron. Your support and trust in me have been tremendous and I thank Colonel Brian Kelly, Lieutenant Colonel Jim Fowler, and "Uncle Mac," Steve McAllister, for their leadership, trust, and guidance during these past years.

I must also thank those at the very heart of our 310th mission – those I have worked with day in and day out. You cannot believe the honor it has been to work with people such as Bob Giddings, Lee Icenhour, Tony Radcliffe, and all of the other proud 310th members. From the bottom of my heart, I thank those that have led this squadron – Jon Banks, Keith Kreeger, Dan Perez, the section chiefs and assistants, and Mary Shoemaker, our wonderful secretary.

I am incredibly proud of what the whole squadron has accomplished since becoming operational two years ago. For those that believe we are just the "Wine and Cheese squadron," let me tell you a little of the behind-the-scenes accomplishments of this unit. We, with the help of Current Operations and Gulfstream Maintenance, are completely self-sufficient from flight planning through mission execution with our missions tasked directly from the Pentagon, not Headquarters AMC. When a problem arises, the whole squadron jumps into action to solve it. Those are the moments I have been most proud about – the way the unit tackles problems to keep our nation's military leaders on time.

Without a doubt you have succeeded in providing a critical transportation service for our nation -- from the Secretary of Defense, to the Chairman and Vice Chairman of the Joint Chiefs of Staff, the seven Four-Star Combatant Commanders and most recently a White House Special Envoy. I have swelled with pride to hear personally from three different four-star generals that they prefer to fly with MacDill's 310th crews. We could not have pulled this off without folks that are masters of their job – from each crewmember to the personnel manning our Operations Center, Flight Records, our awesome Gulfstream maintenance team, the Security Forces men and women, and the problem-solvers in Current Operations. Your work does not go unnoticed and is truly appreciated.

Concerning the bright future of the 310th, I will say that I have had the privilege of getting to know Lieutenant Colonel Monty Perry and his wife, Arlis, for the past year. I am proud to say that he is a caring leader, a great aviator, and good friend. I know he will lead the 310th to new heights and uphold its tradition and reputation for providing a 5-star service for the leaders of the United States.

And now it is time to close out my 20-year career. I can honestly say I have never had a bad assignment, from B-52s, to KC-10s, to the Gulfstreams, each aircraft was newer than the last. My first aircraft was older than I was, and the last one was right off the assembly line!

The Air Force has been awesome for our whole family. I hope you enjoy your time in it, too. I will leave you with these words from the book *FISH*:

"*As you enter this place of work you choose to make today a great day. Your colleagues, customers, team members, and you yourself will be thankful. Find ways to <u>play</u>! We can be serious about our work without being serious about ourselves. Stay focused in order to be <u>present</u> when your customers and team members most need you. And, should you feel your energy lapsing, try this sure-fire remedy: find someone who needs a helping hand, a word of support, or a good ear - and <u>make their day</u>!*"

APPENDIX 5
LETTER BEFORE MY WEDDING
FROM MR. LOVELL

11-28-84

Dear David, (aka Lt. Dale)

Young man you are something else. For as long as
I have had the pleasure of knowing you. You have
left me in complete awe. You have set your goals
and have steadily attained every one of them.

You never took the time to realize that you had
a steep hill to climb. That life could have dealt
you a little better hand. You just took what you
had and went with it. You have gone a long way.

Sylvia and I, both, wish to congratulate you, and,
to wish you always the very best. We will not be
able to attend your wedding. We will be there in
spirit and with our prayers. Praying that this
union will truly be blessed, with eternal love and
happiness.

Karin, such a pretty name. Since we saw you last
we have gained a new grand-daughter whose name
is Carin. They , for some reason decided to spell
it with a C instead of a K.

Please; at your earliest convenience. Come and
bring your wife for us to meet. We will be looking
forward to that day.

My friend, I think of you often and pray that you
will be safe and under Gods care. You are special
to Sylvia and I. Only you among all the explorers
has kept in touch and allowed us to share your
life. We are very grateful for this.

May God bless you and keep you and yours.
Until we meet again. Hopefuly soon.

Your Friend,

Richard

Richard Lovell

APPENDIX 6
MILITARY RANKS

Rank	Abbreviation	Years of Service	Comments
Second Lieutenant	2nd Lt (O-1)	0-2	100% selection
First Lieutenant	1st Lt (O-2)	2-4	100% selection
Captain	Capt (O-3)	4-10	90% selection
Major	Maj (O-4)	10-24 (max)	80% selection (50% of 2nd Lts still in)
Lieutenant Colonel	Lt Col (O-5)	15-28 (max)	75% selection (33% of 2nd Lts still in)
Colonel	Col (O-6)	20-30 (max)	33% selection (10% of 2nd Lts still in)
Brigadier General Major General Lieutenant General General	Brig Gen 1-star Maj Gen 2-star Lt Gen 3-star General 4-star	22-35 (max)	0.5% of the original 2nd Lts still in

	O-1	O-2	O-3	O-4	O-5	O-6	O-7	O-8	O-9	O-10	SPECIAL
ARMY	Second Lieutenant (2LT)	First Lieutenant (1LT)	Captain (CPT)	Major (MAJ)	Lieutenant Colonel (LTC)	Colonel (COL)	Brigadier General (BG)	Major General (MG)	Lieutenant General (LTG)	General (GEN)	General of the Army (GA)
MARINES	Second Lieutenant (2ndLt)	First Lieutenant (1stLt)	Captain (Capt)	Major (Maj)	Lieutenant Colonel (LtCol)	Colonel (Col)	Brigadier General (BGen)	Major General (MajGen)	Lieutenant General (LtGen)	General (Gen)	
NAVY	Ensign (ENS)	Lieutenant Junior Grade (LTJG)	Lieutenant (LT)	Lieutenant Commander (LCDR)	Commander (CDR)	Captain (CAPT)	Rear Admiral Lower Half (RADM)(L)	Rear Admiral Upper Half (RADM)(U)	Vice Admiral (VADM)	Admiral (ADM)	Fleet Admiral (FADM)
AIR FORCE	Second Lieutenant (2d Lt)	First Lieutenant (1st Lt)	Captain (Capt)	Major (Maj)	Lieutenant Colonel (Lt Col)	Colonel (Col)	Brigadier General (Brig Gen)	Major General (Maj Gen)	Lieutenant General (Lt Gen)	General (Gen)	
COAST GUARD	Ensign (ENS)	Lieutenant Junior Grade (LTJG)	Lieutenant (LT)	Lieutenant Commander (LCDR)	Commander (CDR)	Captain (CAPT)	Rear Admiral Lower Half (RADM)(L)	Rear Admiral Upper Half (RADM)(U)	Vice Admiral (VADM)	Admiral (ADM)	

Source: aviationexplorer.com/US_Military_Rank_Abbreviations_
Air_Force_Navy_Marines_Army.html

APPENDIX 7
B-52G FACT SHEET

Contractor: Boeing

First B-52G Flight: Feb 13, 1959

Last Flight: 1994, to comply with the START II treaty

Production: 744 (Total B-52s, including 193 B-52G, the most of any variant)

Aircraft Location: Barksdale AFB, La.; Edwards AFB, Calif.; Minot AFB, N.D.

Active Variants: B-52H. Longer-range variant with more efficient turbofan engines.

Dimensions: Span 185 ft, length 160 ft, height 40.7 ft.

Weight: Max T-O 488,000 lb.

Power Plant: Eight Pratt & Whitney J75, each 14,000 lb. thrust

Performance: Speed 634 mph, range 7,100 miles (without air refueling).

Ceiling: 46,000 ft.

Armament: Nuclear: 12 AGM-86B ALCMs externally, and eight ALCMs or gravity weapons internally. Conventional: Mk 62 sea mines, Mk 82/84 bombs, CBU-87/89 cluster bombs.

Accommodation: Pilot, copilot, radar navigator, navigator, electronic warfare officer, and gunner (until 1992) on upward and downward ejection seats.

Source: Air Force Magazine. https://www.airforcemag.com/weapons-platforms/b-52/

APPENDIX 8
KC-10 FACT SHEET

Contractors: McDonnell Douglas (now Boeing); Collins Aerospace (CNS/ATM)

First Flight: April 1980

Delivered: March 1981-April 1990

Production: 60

Inventory: Approx. 50 - Declining monthly as KC-10s are retiring to the Arizona desert.

Operator: AMC, AFRC (Reserve Associate)

Aircraft Location: Travis AFB, California; Joint Base McGuire-Dix-Lakehurst, N.J.

Active Variant: KC-10A. Modified McDonnell Douglas DC-10 designed as a multirole cargo-tanker

Dimensions: Span 165.4 ft, length 181.6 ft, height 58 ft.

Weight: Max Takeoff 590,000 pounds

Power Plant: Three GE Aviation CF6-50C2 turbofans, each 52,500 pounds thrust

Performance: Speed 620 mph, range 11,500 miles, or 4,400 miles with max cargo (air refuelable)

Ceiling: 42,000 ft.

Fuel Capacity: 356,000 pounds, or 53,000 gallons (1 gallon = 6.7 pounds)

Fuel Offload: 1,100 gal per min by boom, 470 gal per min by hose and drogue

Accommodation: Pilot, copilot, flight engineer, boom operator

Load: 27 pallets up to 170,000 lb. Or up to 75 people and 17 pallets of cargo

Source: Air Force Magazine. https://www.airforcemag.com/weapons-platforms/kc-10/

APPENDIX 9
C-37A FACT SHEET

Contractor: Gulfstream Aerospace
First Flight: October 1998 (C-37A)
Delivered: Oct. 14, 1998-present
IOC: Dec. 9, 1998
Production: 16 (planned)
Inventory: 10 (C-37A)
Operator: AMC, PACAF, USAFE
Aircraft Location: MacDill AFB, FL (until Sept 2019); Joint Base Andrews, Md.; Joint Base Pearl Harbor Hickam, Hawaii; Ramstein AB, Germany, Chièvres AB, Belgium
Active Variants: C-37A and C-37B. Military version of the Gulfstream V and G-550
Dimensions: Span 93.5 ft, length 96.4 ft, height 25.8 ft.
Weight: Max Takeoff 90,500 pounds
Power Plant: Two BMW/Rolls-Royce BR710A1-10 turbofans, each 14,750 lb. thrust
Performance: Speed 600 mph, range 6,300 miles
Ceiling: 51,000 ft.
Accommodation: Pilot, copilot, flight engineer, communication system operator, flight attendant
Load: Up to 12 passengers
Source: Air Force Magazine. https://www.airforcemag.com/weapons-platforms/c-37/

ABOUT THE AUTHOR

David Dale, a native of Houston, Texas, graduated as a fourth-generation Longhorn from the University of Texas at Austin with a Business Administration degree and was commissioned in 1984 as a second lieutenant in the United States Air Force. His flying assignments during a 20-year military career included navigating the B-52G, piloting both the U.S. KC-10 and Dutch KDC-10 air refueling tankers, and finally the Gulfstream C-20B and C-37 for high-level dignitary missions. He is married to the former Karin Smith of Corpus Christi, Texas and they have two grown children, Daniel and Shelby. David is currently a Boeing 737 captain for Southwest Airlines. He and Karin reside in the Texas Hill Country west of Austin.

ReadyForTakeoff310@gmail.com
Facebook: David S. Dale

Lightning Source UK Ltd.
Milton Keynes UK
UKHW020656150223
417035UK00025B/292/J